R0061887949

05/2012

First to the Pole

D1546261

PALM BEACH COUNTY
LIBRARY SYSTEM
3650 Summit Boulevard
West Palm Beach, FL 33406-4198

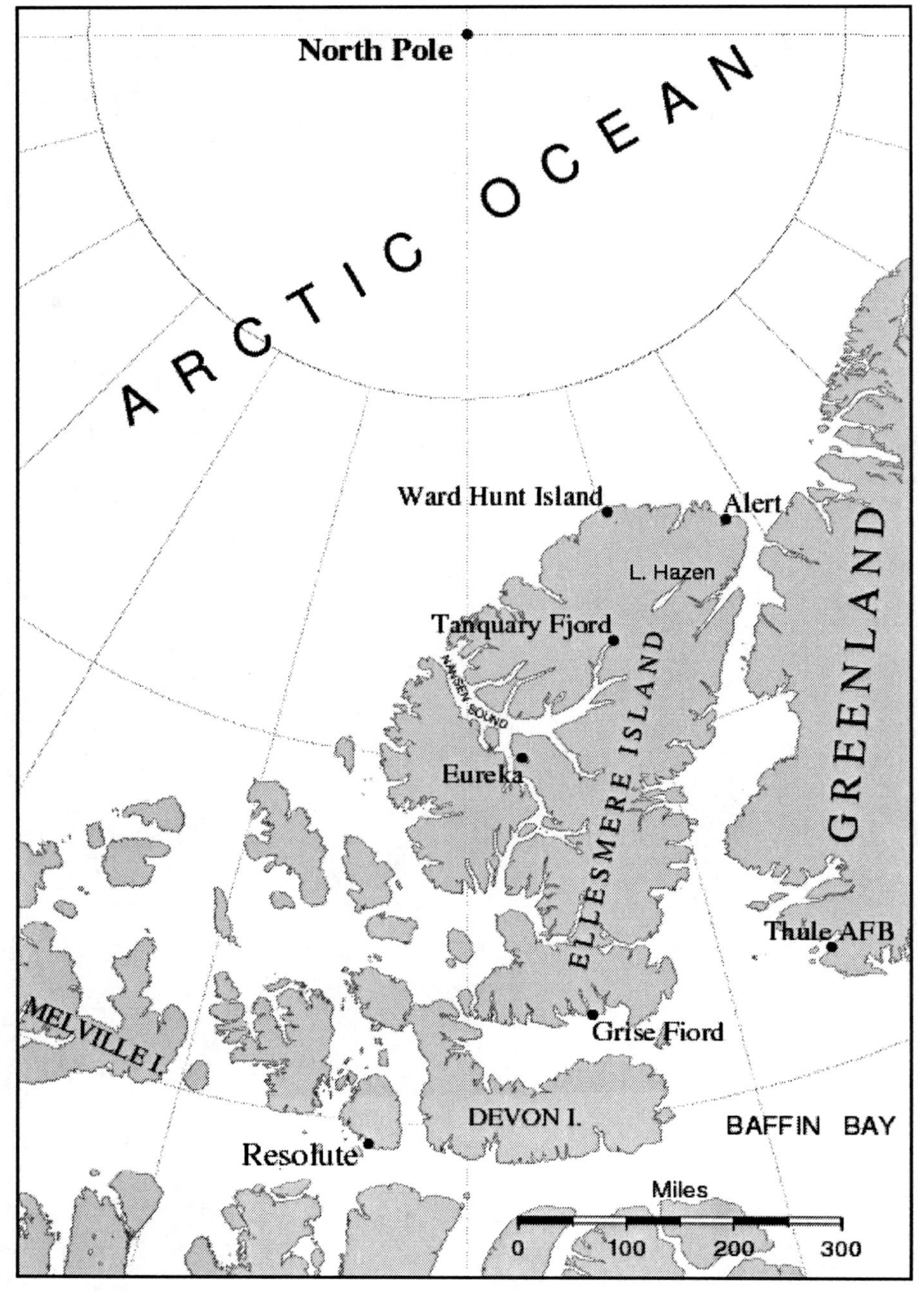
North Pole
ARCTIC OCEAN
Ward Hunt Island
Alert
L. Hazen
Tanquary Fjord
NANSEN SOUND
Eureka
ELLESMERE ISLAND
GREENLAND
Thule AFB
MELVILLE I.
Grise Fiord
DEVON I.
BAFFIN BAY
Resolute
Miles
0
100
200
300

First to the Pole

The exciting true story of a salesman from Minnesota and his friends who became the first to reach the North Pole over the ice

C.J. Ramstad

and

Keith Pickering

North Star Press of St. Cloud, Inc.

Saint Cloud, Minnesota

Copyright © 2011 Keith Pickering

ISBN-13: 978-0-87839-446-3

All rights reserved.

This is a work of fiction. Names, characters, places, and incidents are the products of the author's imagination or are used fictitiously. Any resemblance to actual events or persons, living or dead, is entirely coincidental.

First Edition, September 2011

Printed in the United States of America

Published by
North Star Press of St. Cloud, Inc.
P.O. Box 451
St. Cloud, Minnesota 56302

www.northstarpress.com

Foreword

THIS IS A TRUE STORY ABOUT REAL PEOPLE, some of whom are still alive. The incidents described here really happened, and in spite of its dramatic style, the facts have not been exaggerated for effect. Although the conversations presented here are the authors' own storytelling devices, the ideas behind the words are accurate, as near as we can determine from the diaries by, and interviews with, those who actually took part.

This book has had a long and torturous road to publication. At various times Art Aufderheide, Gordon Mikkelson, Charles Kuralt, and Don Shelby picked up the reins of research before demands of time and health turned them away. Much of what you read here was written by C.J. Ramstad, who would have finished it had he not lost his life in a tragic accident in 2007. When I picked up the book project in the spring of 2008, I was astonished by what had already been accomplished, although it was scattered in dozens of odd files and formats, both paper and electronic. But I knew right away that this book could only be finished in the same style in which it had been started: exciting, intimate, conversational, and eminently readable. If I have succeeded, you won't be able to tell where his writing ends and mine begins. If I have failed, the responsibility is mine alone.

One of the most important things historians do is to set the record straight. Sometimes that involves reducing or even eliminating credit previously given to others. When Ralph Plaisted set off in 1968, like everyone else he was convinced that Robert Peary had been the first person to reach the North Pole. As time went on he learned more of Peary's story and began to have doubts. Today, those doubts are ubiquitous among historians. Nowadays, the views of Peary's North Pole story range from skepticism to outright disbelief. Too much of Peary's story fails too many tests, of both common sense and the limits of possibility. Peary certainly got a long way out on the ice, but he also certainly did not reach the North Pole.

Who, then, deserves the credit that Peary stole for himself? The list is a long one. The first people to reach the Pole by any means were Roald Amundsen of Norway, Umberto Nobile of Italy, Lincoln Ellsworth of the United States, and thirteen other crewmembers of the dirigible *Norge*, who flew over the pole without landing in 1926.

Surprisingly to some, their claim holds up only because yet another fraudulent claim, by Richard E. Byrd, is now also known to be false. Byrd's diary, discovered by Raimund Goerler in 1996, shows erased but legible sextant readings that refute the account in his official report and confirm the doubt long held by serious scholars.

Following the *Norge*, many reached the Pole by air or submarine; but the first to arrive at the pole entirely over the surface were Ralph Plaisted and his companions in 1968, Jean-Luc Bombardier and Walt Pederson. Jerry Pitzl, who was with them at the end, had been flown to the ice partway out; while Art Aufderheide and Don Powellek, both of whom started the trip, each nobly sacrificed his own chance to stand on the pole in order to deal with problems at base camp that would have doomed the expedition to failure otherwise.

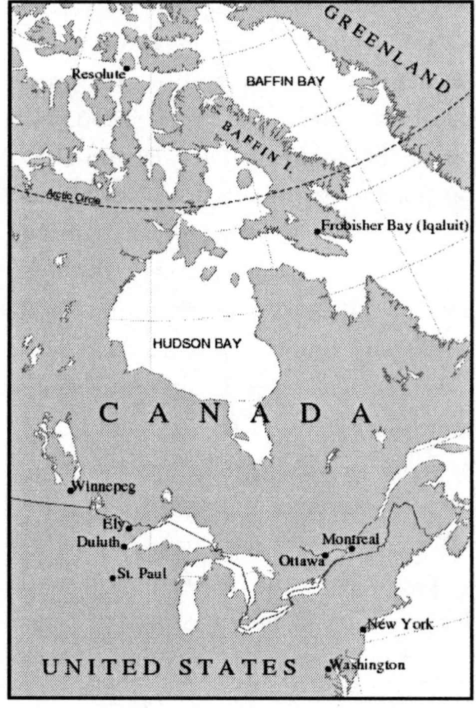

The first to reach the pole by dogsled was the doughty Englishman Wally Herbert in 1969. Like so many others, including Plaisted, Herbert eventually came to feel cheated of his due by the bogus claim of Peary. And while Herbert's 1989 biography of Peary, *The Noose of Laurels*, still stands as one of the best biographies (and most damning indictments) of that complex man, the book did not achieve Herbert's goal of assuring his own rightful place in history. It is, therefore, more than a little sad that, at the end of his accomplished life, Herbert sought to increase his own fame by casting aspersions not just on the fraudulent claims of Peary, but also on the legitimate achievements of Ralph Plaisted. In private interviews beginning in the early 1990s, Herbert repeated a rumor that the Plaisted expedition had been airlifted over leads of open water, and, thereby, had not traveled entirely by surface. Of course, if the rumor were true, that would make Herbert himself the first to arrive at the Pole by surface. But the toxic residue of the frauds of Peary and Byrd is this: *even the bare existence of this rumor by itself, unsupported by the tiniest shred of evidence*, was enough to allow Herbert's obituary to claim that his party was the first to reach the Pole "unquestionably" by surface travel.

Having done the research, having read the diaries of all members of the 1968 expedition and talked with all members who are still alive and loved ones of those who have since died, I can say this unequivocally: that rumor is totally false. Not one inch of the distance between Ward Hunt Island and the North Pole was covered by air in 1968. Among the many records of the expedition are affidavits signed by both expedition pilots testifying to that fact. Those affidavits appear in this book. Peary and Byrd were legitimate explorers with legitimate accomplishments to their credit. But in the final analysis, each stole fame, headlines, or honor to which they were not entitled. It's time to put that right.

K.A.P.
Watertown, Minnesota

Ralph Plaisted

1

Better Than Dogs

"I'm telling you, Art," said Ralph Plaisted earnestly, "forget about those dogs. The snowmobile is the future of winter travel."

Dr. Arthur Aufderheide looked at his affable companion over the top of a frosty glass of beer. Art had not known Ralph long, but he recognized the ebullient, I-can-do-anything attitude that sometimes overcame his hard-headed common sense. It was the same attitude that just the previous year had inspired Plaisted to ride his new Ski-Doo snowmobile from Ely, Minnesota, hard on the Canadian border, all the way to St. Paul—a distance of 250 miles in one long day. In 1965 the snowmobile was still a fairly new invention, a winter novelty, and Plaisted's feat had attracted attention from the local press and television, briefly turning Ralph into minor celebrity.

Now in March of 1966, as Aufderheide planned a dogsled excursion to remote Bathurst Inlet in northern Canada, a mutual friend had suggested that Ralph Plaisted was a logical choice to seek out for advice. The two Minnesotans hit it off quickly, as they shared a love for the outdoors, and both were fond of the special opportunities that only winter presented. Aufderheide shifted his gaze out the window of the Pickwick bar and restaurant, across Duluth harbor, to the Lift Bridge and the vast expanse of Lake Superior beyond.

"Someday, maybe, when there are gas stations all over the Canadian wilderness, the snowmobile will replace the dog," replied Art, "but that day's not here yet. In winter up there you need reliability. And that means dogs. Trust the Inuit, Ralph; they've lived there for centuries."

The two friends could hardly have been more different. Quiet and thoughtful, Aufderheide was a cautious and meticulous planner, always taking extra care to foresee the unexpected and prepare for even remote contingencies—skills that had served him well on his trip the previous year to the MacKenzie River in northern Canada. Not just highly educated but highly intelligent as well, his medical training had taught him to be a keen observer of human nature and to be acutely aware of the feelings of others around him.

Plaisted was as gregarious as Aufderheide was reserved. Art was an M.D., while Ralph was a high-school dropout who had worked a dozen jobs before finding his niche as an insurance salesman. The insurance business is built on trust, and Plaisted had an outgoing sociability that turned strangers into friends in short order. But he also knew that trust was built on following through with his promises. Plaisted was nothing if not reliable.

"A snowmobile doesn't really use that much gas," persisted Ralph. "If you tow enough spare gas cans behind you on a sled, you could go a hundred miles between towns, and you could do it a hell of a lot faster than a dog can run. I know you have experience with dogs, but snowmobiles today are a lot more reliable than you imagine. Think about it, Art. You could be the first person to make a long-distance traverse by snowmobile in the Canadian arctic!"

"I'm not after glory, Ralph," replied Art. "And there's something to be said for the quiet of the far north without engine noise to disturb you. Besides, it's not just the gasoline, it's the breakdowns. One breakdown up there could kill you. If you really want to convince the Inuit to switch to snowmobiles, you'd have to do something really dramatic, like going to the North Pole by snowmobile."

Ralph looked at his companion with an odd expression that Art could not quite place—something between determination and pugnaciousness. "Okay, then," said Ralph, "maybe I will!"

Art laughed it off, and Ralph laughed with him. The conversation soon passed to other topics. It was a glorious spring day in a pretty little city whose hills and bridges had reminded more than one visitor of San Francisco in miniature. Thoughts of winter seemed almost sacrilegious on a day like this one. Ralph insisted on paying the tab as they left the bar, and the two new friends parted with a hearty handshake.

Aufderheide made his trip to Bathurst Inlet that month, using dogs as he had planned. When he returned to his home in Duluth and sorted through his accumulated mail, one business-sized letter caught his eye. Opening it, the professionally printed letterhead showed a red silhouette of a snowmobile emblazoned over a blue map of the North Pole. It announced: "Plaisted Polar Expedition 1967—Ralph Plaisted, Leader—Dr. Art Aufderheide, Co-Leader."

Dr. Art Aufderheide

Art inhaled sharply and sat back as he read and re-read Plaisted's letter. He was amazed by everything Ralph had accomplished in just a few weeks. Plaisted had already recruited two other friends of his to go north, with prospects for more in the offing. He was working on corporate sponsorship from Bombardier, the Canadian manufacturer of Ski-Doo snowmobiles, and had begun the process of requesting help from hundred other corporations too. Another acquaintance from WCCO in Minneapolis might be interested in filming the expedition. A secretary from his insurance agency was working nearly full time to keep up with expedition correspondence.

At that moment, Art realized that his new friend was a man of boundless determination. He already knew Ralph's natural gifts as a salesman made him a hard man to refuse. There was no doubt in Art's mind that Ralph Plaisted was going to the North Pole by snowmobile. And Art knew he was going with him, because he too found it impossible to refuse a man as persuasive as Plaisted. But how was he going to tell his wife, Mary, that he was going to the North Pole?

...

THE TOWN OF ELY STANDS AS A SYMBOL in Minnesota of a true far north location. Literally at the end of the road for most of its existence, in 1965 the town still held onto its image as the last stop in far northern Minnesota, a place you go in the summer to get away, to live for a week or two in a cabin with your children, catching frogs, chasing spiders on the boat docks and roasting hotdogs over a driftwood fire. To Ralph Plaisted, Ely was the perfect weekend getaway. He took his young family every summer weekend to the island land he purchased where they fished, cooked out and shared the dream of life in the woods held by many who call this place their second home.

It was one of those thirty-degree-below-zero mornings in January 1965, when Plaisted stepped out of his cabin and pulled the starter cord on his 9½ horsepower Ski-Doo Olympic snowmobile. He gunned the little single cylinder engine and nosed through the accumulated snow toward the roadside and a destination far to the south. Dr. Hall, a retired neighbor living in Ely, came out to witness the time of his departure and suggested to the bundled up man on the motor sled it might be too cold to go.

The map says it's about 250 miles from Ely to St. Paul but, as Plaisted and other early snowmobilers were learning, distances are magnified by the zig-zag routes these little vehicles use to find their way through the winter world. It was a trip of five hours in a car, but how long on a snowmobile?

Yes, it was cold, but Plaisted was prepared. His friend Roy Halvorson, the Duluth distributor for Ski-Doos like the one he was riding, had found him a cold temperature suit in the Neiman Marcus catalog and had it shipped up from Texas just for this ride. It was a refrigeration suit designed to keep workers like meat packers and fish sellers warm in their big freezers and Plaisted figured it would keep him, if not warm, at least alive as he made tracks toward his destination to the south.

It was at his annual deer camp two years before that he had first heard about snowmobiles. These were newly introduced motorized scooters for the snow from Canada, his campmates explained, and they could go almost anywhere over the snow in winter. Sometimes they got stuck and sometimes they broke down, but a determined traveler could use one to go where he wanted to go over the winter snow. The idea captivated Plaisted. Winter had prevented him from doing the things he loved to do outdoors many times in the past. Maybe the new snowmobiles were just the thing to help him spend more time out of doors in the winter. With vehicles that could travel through deep snow, he could visit his isolated cabin, travel onto frozen lakes for fishing, entice the family to spend more time doing the things they had learned to love during their many warm weather trips to hunt and fish in the north woods of Minnesota.

Plaisted soon found a dealer in nearby Wisconsin who had them for sale. He bought one, then another, and soon he and his family were out in the evening and on weekends putt-putting in the snowdrifted fields and roadsides near their home in the outskirts of St. Paul. Shortly there were a few adventurous neighbors joining the fun and the newly fledged enthusiast quickly learned what he needed to know about keeping the little contraptions running in the cold and ice.

The outdoor loving Plaisted family took to the machines naturally and some of his neighboring families, the Woolseys and Powelleks, bought snowmobiles to join in the fun. On weekend rides around the neighborhood and sometimes in the country at Plaisted's deer camp cabin, they imagined themselves riding the machines on longer, more ambitious adventures. They thought of themselves as the new Eskimoes, bundled up for the cold and experiencing outdoor adventures like never before. Plaisted was totally entranced. He couldn't break away from persistent daydreams about other treks they could take someday.

These were the thoughts that propelled him to pursue his first long-distance trip and that frigid day, as he bumped along in the snow alongside the winding two-lane highway leading out of Ely. It was an adventure but Plaisted wasn't a wild-eyed dreamer out to risk it all. Ever practical, he had arranged to have one of his trusted employees, an agent with Plaisted Insurance Agency, drive one of the company Plymouths as near as possible along the planned route in support. And the automobile would be able to rendezvous if the Ski-Doo malfunctioned to a point beyond repair along the way, which Plaisted knew from experience with the crude and often stubborn machines, was a possibility.

His planned route took him along township and county roads west from Ely until he reached the nearby mining town of Tower. Here he hooked up to an old mining railroad grade and headed south for maybe fifty miles. Between the old rail bed and the electric power lines that transected the terrain along his route, Plaisted was able to thread his way south, zig-zagging through Minnesota's Iron Range country, stopping for fuel in the town of Virginia as planned.

A hasty rendezvous with his support driver, a fill-up of five gallons of fuel mixed with oil and Plaisted was off again, winding his way south to a final destination on Lake Phalen, a small lake on the northern edge of St. Paul. He had left Ely at seven in the morning and was passing through the Minnesota Iron Range sixty miles to the south at a few minutes after ten. He was making good time.

Snowmobiles are opportunist vehicles. They find their way on frozen lakes and streams, on unplowed back roads, in snow-filled roadside ditches, under the wires on power line rights-of-way and down old logging railroad grades like those that criss-cross Minnesota. Plaisted knew as long as he kept the sun in his eyes he was heading more or less south and, while he didn't sketch an exact route for the trip, he had a general notion which routes he would likely take.

About halfway into his journey, he came across an unfinished section of Minnesota's north-south interstate highway that he planned to follow. When his travels took him far enough south that the unfinished grade ended and he encountered traffic, he simply nosed his Ski-Doo into the center median and kept going as cars passed by in the nearby lanes going north and south.

It wasn't long before this strategy attracted the attention of a county sheriff. Dutifully stopping for the cruiser with the flashing red lights, Plaisted fished in his pocket for a packet of papers he had brought along. Anticipating there might be questions from the authorities in the various jurisdictions he was passing through, he had taken the precaution of applying for a license before he began the trek. There was no such thing as a snowmobile license in Minnesota then, so the puzzled officials in St. Paul had given Plaisted a license like those given to rural postal drivers who sometimes used tracked vehicles to deliver mail in remote areas. It was permission for driving off the pavement and exhibiting other normally unacceptable vehicle behavior to facilitate the delivery of mail.

Between the official-looking permission documentation, his friendly manner, and the plausible reason for his journey, the sheriff had little choice but to grant Plaisted passage. He could continue on the freeway until the next exit, the deputy said, but then he had to find another way to complete his trek.

Fortunately, Plaisted had logged enough miles south by this time that he was able to pick up another vacated railroad line discovered earlier while riding on weekends near his home. Once on this route, Plaisted knew he was going to succeed. The rail line right-of-way would take him within a mile of his home in the St. Paul suburb of White Bear Lake and, by the looks of things, he would have the ride completed in just over thirteen hours, riding the final six hours in darkness.

Another stop for fuel a few miles north of the city, a final rendezvous with his support vehicle to document the time and mileage and the snowmobile adventure was complete—except for the publicity. In the morning after overnighting at his home, Plaisted placed a telephone call to alert officials of the St. Paul Winter Carnival he was near. One more hour on his snowmobile and Plaisted was threading his way along a creekbed to the surface of Lake Phalen, right on the edge of the city. His trek complete, he rode across the snow-covered lake to a welcoming committee of Winter Carnival officials, TV reporters, clicking camera shutters and a gaggle of shivering onlookers not nearly as well dressed for the cold as he.

Plaisted was a celebrity that day, a conquering winter hero who dared to travel all the way to St. Paul from near the Canadian border on that strange little putt-putt machine.

Plaisted knew a little celebrity in his hometown would be fine for business and he found the publicity oddly gratifying. The reasons for the journey had been adventure, of course, and to demonstrate of the capability of the snowmobile. The machine had fulfilled its mission, traveling perhaps 500 snowy, zig-zag miles in a single, long, cold day while missing nary a beat.

Publicity from the Ely trip found favor as well with officials at the Ski-Doo company. Dealer Roy Halvorson's relationship with Plaisted grew quickly after the Ely trip and the colorful customer from St. Paul became a close personal friend. The snowmobile industry was hungry for publicity, and men like Plaisted with vision and a talent for attracting attention were valuable and necessary. Plaisted's easygoing, natural friendliness and interest in the outdoors were things Halvorson could appreciate and Plaisted's dignified, thorough approach, as demonstrated on the successful ride from Ely, gave the pioneer snowmobile distributor confidence. He told the budding adventurer his company would be happy to supply snowmobiles and whatever help it could to support any new snowmobiling ideas Plaisted might dream up.

...

A NEW SNOWMOBILE EVENT IN THE PLANNING STAGES for the St. Paul Winter Carnival in the coming winter of 1966, based as it was on Plaisted's long-distance ride the previous year, began to involve him in new and unexpected ways during the summer of 1965. The popular civic event included many of the city's movers and shakers in those days, people who took part as volunteers in the event planning, the sponsorship programs and the execution of various elements of the citywide festival. It was an interesting and influential assortment of people, all involved one way of another in creating this complex civic publicity extravaganza.

The public relations men, the company presidents, the local politicians and the volunteers, they all brought their skills and talents to bear as part of the Winter Carnival and Plaisted watched and learned as he prepared for the first Carnival sponsored snowmobile ride—the proudly named International 500, now planned to go from Winnipeg, Manitoba, to St. Paul's Lake Phalen. Involved in most of the action in the weeks running up to the 1966 Carnival, Plaisted was the snowmobile event point man. He had prestigious sponsorship from Bombardier, the Ski-Doo snowmobile manufacturer, and he was usually introduced as the man to be credited with planting the seed that got this new snowmobile event started.

Swept along in the booster atmosphere that was always part of carnival activity, in January of 1966 Plaisted found himself traveling to Winnipeg with his newest snowmobile to participate in the inaugural race. It was thirty-five below zero in a brisk, snowy wind when the first of fifty-four snowmobiles were flagged off to start the competition and the starting number Plaisted drew made him one of the last to leave. The race course, like his route from Ely the previous year, weaved a crooked path as it first followed a river, then wound along farm fields and several unplowed country roadways before reaching the border and heading south along the two-lane highway to East Grand Forks, Minnesota.

Plaisted's heart was never really into the racing; he wished the event had continued to be billed as a ride. But he did well on the first leg, crossing the border in seventeenth position. His Ski-Doo, however, was in rough shape. The miles of pounding along in the ruts formed by the leading riders had taken their toll, and his snowmobile broke down a mile or two short of the first day's finish line. Many of the drivers had received help in various forms, including spare parts, gas, even rides in the back of pick-up trucks by this time. After Plaisted and his broken machine were transported into town and repairs made, he was encouraged to rejoin the fray as it made its way to St. Paul. What difference would missing those two or three miles make as long as he was there for the finish in St. Paul?

But it made a difference to Ralph. He had gone less than a mile before he stopped in his tracks. He pulled back his hood, spit in the snow, and turned around. He wasn't going to win by cheating, he wasn't going to lose by cheating, and he sure as hell wasn't going to lose his self-respect for any damn race. This wasn't the way he expected or wanted it to be. The race wasn't the man-against-nature experience he craved and the drive to win or at least finish in front of the Twin Cities' press felt by many of the competitors left Plaisted cold. Disgusted, he dropped out of the race and boarded a train for home. His racing days started and ended right there, but, as his rail car bumped along on its way south, he knew his snowmobiling adventuring was far from over.

Yet it took a random comment from Art Aufderheide in a Duluth bar a couple of months later to crystallize in Plaisted's mind what he really wanted to do. The North Pole beckoned him, as it had so many others before.

...

PLAISTED WAS ENOUGH OF A BUSINESSMAN to realize he needed to form a company for the specific purpose of snowmobiling to the Pole. He would be its president, and he asked George Cavouras, a friend from the insurance business, to be its treasurer. Among the first people Plaisted talked to were his neighbors, Don Powellek and Bumps Woolsey. They both thought it was a fabulous idea. Don was keen to go along, and his experience as an electronic engineer would be useful in establishing radio communications. Although Woolsey was also keen to go, his professional skills as a dentist would be less useful in the Arctic, and it would take some arranging to leave his one-man practice for the months required. Nevertheless, Woolsey did not hesitate to sign on with Plaisted, confident he could work out the details.

One of the people Ralph Plaisted met during his involvement with the St. Paul Winter Carnival was a TV newsman named Gordy Mikkelson. A news director at WCCO, the Twin Cities' largest TV station at the time, Mikkelson was skeptical at first of Plaisted's announced plan to go the North Pole and he invited the would-be explorer to the station for an intensive interview.

Mikkelson and two other people in the WCCO newsroom fired questions at Plaisted for nearly two hours and when he finally left the station he was shaken and apprehensive. Was his idea so outlandish that he wouldn't be taken seriously? Plaisted recognized that the support of Mikkelson and the powerful media outlet the newsman represented would be crucial to his plans and, if he had failed the test, it would be a major setback.

But Mikkelson was impressed by the earnest and guileless Plaisted. The man made no boasts and had more questions than answers during the interview where he gave the impression of a serious and businesslike determined to pursue his plan as far as he could. There was no questioning Plaisted's outdoor credentials. He seemed more than convinced of the practicality of snowmobiles to traverse winter environments and his own exploits spoke to the fact he was as experienced in the outdoors and as knowledgeable about snowmobiling as anyone in 1966.

Mikkelson thought it over, consulted with his colleagues and finally decided to lend his and his station's support to a big, friendly outdoorsman and his idea. Snowmobiling was popular in Minnesota and it was clear the winter activity would be a continuing story on the station. Besides, the hopeful explorer hadn't asked for anything beyond information anyway. If his plan fell apart it was going to happen for some other reason because, once he was convinced of Plaisted's integrity and dedication, Mikkelson pitched in enthusiastically, willing to help the expedition anyway he could. He also tried to gain the interest of CBS, his network partner.

What Plaisted needed most from Mikkelson was advice and information. The first thing the newsman did was use his extensive contacts to help Plaisted start filling in the necessary details he would need to sort out with government. Introductions to Minnesota's U.S. Congressional delegation were made and, in May of 1966, Plaisted arranged to go to Washington, D.C., to meet Minnesota's Fifth District Representative Don Fraser and senators Walter Mondale and Eugene McCarthy.

If you're going to ask for help in Washington, few things are more important than a good introduction, and Plaisted's good connections in the

Twin Cities got him the reception he needed at the Capitol. Representative Fraser spent a few moments chatting with his fellow Minnesotan and, although the two Senators didn't provide personal audiences, each of them arranged to have members of their staffs work with Plaisted to help him thread his way through the maze of bureaus whose help, guidance and permission would be necessary if the expedition was to become a reality.

After listening to Plaisted's story, Congressional staffers directed him to the Navy Department at the Pentagon. Calls were made and an appointment with an Navy undersecretary was quickly arranged. The polar regions, as had been the case for decades, were not any kind of priority for the U.S. military, limited at the time to bases in Alaska and Greenland, Distant Early Warning (DEW Line) activity and occasional submarine voyages under the ice. The Navy could have been a major hurdle, but once again Plaisted's natural friendliness and easygoing sincerity penetrated what might have very easily been an administrative brush-off. After a few minutes of listening to the earnest Minnesotan, the Navy men realized Plaisted was serious. But, they informed him, any serious expeditionary activities in those far northern regions were going to require the assistance and acquiescence of the government of Canada.

The Navy knew exactly where to tell Plaisted to start. When he left the Pentagon in the late afternoon after several hours of meetings, he had the names of the key people in Canadian polar bureaucracy who were in the positions to entertain such a plan. Graham Rowley, head of Canada's Northern Affairs Office, and Dr. Geoffrey Hattersley-Smith, head of the Defense Research Board. Once again, good connections paid off for Plaisted; The Navy agreed to contact the Canadians and help set up a face-to-face meeting in the weeks to come.

While good connections had helped put Plaisted in the right offices and in front of people in the U.S. government who could help him, not everything he attempted went as smoothly on this first trip to the Capitol. The National Geographic Society had gotten wind of his proposed expedition, and had written to Plaisted asking for an interview. When he was a child, the Society's magazine had occupied a place of honor in the living room, its importance second only to the Bible in the mind of the youngster, and he was eager to make a good impression and gain their support.

He was ushered into an imposing conference room with walls paneled in dark-stained wood, and was met with a steely indifference by the men gathered there. Why, he was asked, would he want to do such a thing, anyway? Didn't Plaisted realize that the North Pole had already been conquered, by Admiral Robert E. Peary, on an expedition under the aegis of the Society in 1909? Plaisted didn't doubt Peary's claim, did he? To do so would be seen as un-American by the Society. There was no interest in a me-too, especially by a group headed by a man with no scholarly or scientific credentials. And you've never actually been to beyond the Arctic Circle before, Mr. Plaisted? What makes you think you can take a group of your Minnesota cronies to the North Pole? They'll drop out the first time it gets really cold. Sure they're your friends, and that's the problem: if you want to make it to the North Pole. You have to drive your men so hard that they hate you for it. You just haven't got what it takes to drive your men as hard as they need to be driven to get to the North Pole, Mr. Plaisted. You're too nice of a guy. They won't make it, and neither will you.

Plaisted managed to suppress his disgust until he left the building on M Street. He certainly didn't doubt Peary had gotten to the Pole—in those days, nobody did. And what about that crack about his "Minnesota cronies"? It was an insult to his home state and enough to make Ralph's blood boil. In the months to come, the memory of this meeting would be a constant spur to Plaisted. He would *not* give the National Geographic Society the satisfaction of being right—about Minnesotans, or about himself. He decided then and there that would drive the men as hard as he needed to, even if it meant being as unpopular as a drill sergeant in boot camp.

The National Geographic visit was a disappointment, but the other people and agencies had given him more than enough reason to believe an expedition to the North Pole on snowmobiles could happen. Plaisted wasn't going to let one snub shake his faith. Aware of the many hurdles that lay ahead he boarded a plane for home, his head spinning with plans and ideas and, most of all, questions that still needed answers.

...

ANOTHER RACER COMPETING IN THE 1966 RACE had similar problems getting his machine repaired and ready to go after the rough first leg into Grand Forks. He too worked outdoors in the bitter cold, the feeling in his fingers going numb as he replaced a broken spring and straightened out his twisted steering gear. But for this Winnipeg-to-St. Paul competitor, the only challenge was to make his snowmobile survive the brutal contest to the very end. Walt Pederson entered the race with the same kind of motivation that infused everything he did; he had something to prove and, for him, it was first about making it to the finish line and then about finishing with a fast time, maybe the fastest time.

Walt Pederson

He was competing as part of a three-rider team running under the name of his snowmobile business in St. Cloud, Minnesota. Pederson's Honda House motorsports shop was one of the largest and fastest-growing snowmobile dealerships in the state, and Pederson knew the publicity he could potentially garner from a respectable showing in this highly publicized event would help sales of the Ski-Doos he had in stock.

Pederson was a wiry bundle of energy and, although his teammates were forced by breakdowns to drop out of the race, he was able to perform the necessary repairs and fixes along the trail to stay in the race to the end. Although he finished in seventh place to some high-powered custom sleds, his was the first Ski-Doo across the line in a three-day snowmobile race that attracted a surprising amount of publicity, even garnering significant attention at the national level.

The competition had the expected effect on business and Honda House was sold out of snowmobiles soon after the race. Pederson also enjoyed a bit of notoriety at Ski-Doo. Roy Halvorson made a personal telephone call to congratulate him on his success and offer the support of the distribution company for future forays into snowmobile adventure. A few months later, as Pederson was picking up a new machine at the Duluth distributorship, Halvorson mentioned that a friend of his, Ralph Plaisted, was going to the North Pole by snowmobile. Pederson was immediately smitten by the idea. He called Plaisted the next day, introduced himself, and asked to go along. After a brief chat, Plaisted was convinced that Walt Pederson would be a superb addition to the team.

...

ONCE HE BEGAN TO ATTRACT MEDIA ATTENTION, Ralph Plaisted was often described in press accounts as "an insurance man from St. Paul." But insight into the man begins when Plaisted is described more precisely: He was a *successful* insurance agency owner. The fact was, were he not a business owner and had the business not been thriving in 1965, he wouldn't have been in a position to imagine devoting the necessary time to something that, especially at the beginning, must have seemed unlikely to everyone, including himself. In some ways, the insurance business also provided a template for developing and applying some of the skills that would later be proven invaluable, especially during the time when Plaisted was making preparations for a polar expedition.

Insurance is an intangible. If you're going to sell it to someone, the concept must be given substance, made to seem palpable and vital to the people whose decisions are required to put a policy in place. Selling an insurance policy requires the salesman to routinely encounter people he has never talked to before and find a way to sell them what is essentially an idea . . . and an elusive one at that. Difficult or impossible for most people, it was something that came naturally to Plaisted. An instinctive communicator who harbored a genuine interest in people, he translated these insights into insurance sales with apparent ease. He became so good at closing a deal, he was good-naturedly accused by jealous colleagues of using hypnosis.

But it wasn't hypnosis. Plaisted had come by his skills honestly and he employed them the same way. If there is any truth to the adage salesmen are born, not made, then he was born to sell.

Growing up in the tiny east-central Minnesota town of Bruno, Plaisted spent his younger years nurturing his lifelong love of hunting, fishing and being outdoors. To him, school was just something to mark the time between days on the lake angling for fish or time in the woods spent tramping around in search of game. Convinced life held more for him than studies, he decided he could read and write well enough by the time he reached the tenth grade. Against the wishes and arguments of his parents and teachers, he left school for good and struck out for the nearby "big town" of Superior, Wisconsin, to seek his fortune. He took a job delivering ice, supplementing his pay by working nights as a bouncer at a local pool hall.

Making money in the ice business requires the deliveryman to "sell his shrinkage." Every daily load of ice was factored for some amount of the product to melt as the iceman made his rounds—his shrinkage. But the sharp and speedy operator found ways to sell the built-in overage every day, pocketing the proceeds as a reward for fast work and salesmanship. Plaisted's shrinkage fund grew rapidly as the weeks passed, thanks to his go-getter approach to the job, his gregarious nature and genuine talent for sales.

He was also a natural peacekeeper at the billiard hall where he spent his evenings. When the inevitable disagreement at the tables would begin to escalate to fists and swinging pool cues on the odd evening, Plaisted knew how to step in and encourage a shift to cooler heads. Well over six feet and rippling with 250 pounds of ice-hauling muscle, Plaisted might have used threats and menace to maintain order. But he rarely doubled a fist, relying instead on negotiation. By adroitly pointing out to the players how much they had to lose by misbehaving and offering to lend a fair-minded hand in any argument, Plaisted was generally able to quell any bad behavior quickly and smoothly.

He took pride in keeping the peace in the rough and tumble atmosphere of the pool hall while never even raising his voice and this rare skill endeared him to the owner who, never guessing the big, gentle kid was only sixteen, let him stay rent free in a back room of the establishment, It was an arrangement that provided cheap overnight protection for the business and saved the young bouncer money he would otherwise have had to spend at a rooming house.

The skills that made Plaisted a bonus-earning iceman and an inspired pool hall bouncer as a younger man were the same ones he employed to succeed at insurance sales years later. Like the pride he felt in negotiating peace in a pool hall, Plaisted genuinely enjoyed insurance sales and the process of moving prospects from arched eyebrow skepticism to a relaxed handshake. He never tried the easy way—selling to friends or family. Instead he approached working with strangers as a game, honing his skills in reading and qualifying his customers and carefully applying the proven approaches and techniques of his profession.

Certainly every insurance salesman uses the same basic methods, but Plaisted was a virtuoso who transcended mere sales. He usually made a friend at the same time he was closing a sale. Emphasizing the importance of protecting a family and its assets by preparing for the unknown, he would fill a family need while his calm, unhurried manner reassured his newfound friends they were being well taken care of.

He would often say, while the expeditions were in the process of forming in 1967 and 1968, that he wasn't qualified to be a member of the expedition that bore his name except for the fact he was along to cook the meals. But the reality was the skillful salesmanship and magnetic ability to connect to people that came so naturally to Plaisted were key factors that fueled many of the events that made this big dream seem real and ultimately, become real.

The plan had started out in Plaisted's mind as an adventure for he and some of his snowmobiling friends but this image of a polar holiday faded quickly as the realities of mounting such an expedition took form. It wasn't long before early planning meetings with the his growing group of polar hopefuls revealed some of the key issues, and key talents, that would be necessary to make this dream into reality. Beyond being able to ride a snowmobile, the expedition members were going to have to bring some real expertise to the challenge, things like mechanical skills, knowledge of radio and communications, ability to navigate on a frozen ocean.

And it was going to cost a lot of money. As a plan began to form during the spring and summer of 1966, it became quickly clear the attempt was going to require probably a dozen individuals. This meant substantial costs for transportation, food, clothing and equipment.

...

Plaisted recognized from the beginning that the job of raising the money was going to fall to him and it was a job he was equipped to tackle. The expedition hoped to count on the support of Bombardier as a core sponsor. It was, after all, the maker of the snowmobiles they planned to use. Thanks in part to Plaisted's strong relationship with Roy Halvorson, there were ever improving relations with the Quebec manufacturer. In the midst of an enormous surge in sales after the introduction of the small Ski-Doo models in 1959, Bombardier had money, and much to gain from the publicity the expedition was likely to generate. Plaisted's earlier Winter Carnival successes in publicizing the machines and their uses had not gone unnoticed and after some negotiation, Bombardier was willing to pledge the snowmobiles needed for the attempt. When only cash would do, the company could usually be counted on to step up and provide it. There was no doubt from the expedition side there were going to be some strings attached, but with Halvorson handling the duties of diplomat on his regular flights back and forth to Canada on this and other business, this part of the fundraising effort remained a constant.

One of the strings Bombardier sought was sending a company representative to the Pole along with Plaisted. Ralph was hesitant at first; every member of the team so far was a personal friend of his, or at worst, like Walt Pederson, a friend of a friend. He knew he could get along with each of them, which was, he felt, the great strength of his team. How would a stranger fit in?

But after a few phone calls, his doubts were substantially relieved. The man they proposed sending was Jean-Luc Bombardier, a nephew of the com-

Jean-Luc Bombardier

pany founder. Young, handsome and strong, Jean-Luc's imagination had been fired when he first heard of Plaisted's audacious plan. Much like Walt Pederson, he had extensive experience as a snowmobile driver and an intense desire to see the expedition succeed. And, much to Ralph's relief, he pledged to follow Plaisted's authority as expedition leader without question. In the end, Bombardier's energy and daring would prove irreplaceable to Plaisted.

But it was clear that the Bombardier Company was not going to bankroll the entire expedition. Plaisted attacked this challenge the same way he approached an insurance sale. For him, it was a game in which he would learn the rules and skillfully apply them to achieve the needed results. He eagerly went to work finding other sponsors and he questioned everyone in hopes of finding the best ways to attract sponsors.

With the help of Pat Carr, attorney for one of the Plaisted Agency's major clients, Plaisted developed a credible and appealing sponsorship pitch. Carr drafted a bulletproof hold harmless agreement and counseled the enthusiastic fundraiser on the details of asking for money and material.

At one point in their relationship during that summer of 1966, Carr asked Plaisted if he was sure it a good idea to name the expedition after himself. Carr pointed out it might be safer to give the expedition some lower profile name in the event of a failure or some other embarrassing outcome. Plaisted thought this over carefully, finally reaching the conclusion that he was bound to be connected to the project no matter how it was named. He decided attaching his name to it signaled commitment and, the fact was, he had no intention of failing.

Employed in his office at this time was a woman perfect to assist in the job of finding sponsors. Bertha Levy was already retired once, having spent a lifetime as a personal secretary. Her husband had made a fortune in chemicals and she didn't have to work. But like many talented and congenitally busy people, Levy needed something to keep her active and out of the house when she went to work part time at Plaisted Insurance. It took no coaxing to get her to agree to work on the sponsorship program and, although her hours were supposed to be limited, she dove into the project with gusto. Plaisted would go to her to help compose letters, keep records, locate addresses and phone numbers and handle subsequent correspondence and the many details attached to a project like this, all tasks Mrs. Levy handled admirably.

Other expedition members were involved in this effort too. Bumps Woolsey had a thriving dental practice in St. Paul, and one of his patients happened to be William L. McKnight, chairman of the board of the 3M Corporation. During an office visit that summer, Woolsey told McKnight that he would be gone for a few months, to the North Pole. McKnight was interested. "Drop by the St. Paul Athletic Club next Thursday night at eight," McKnight said, "there are some people I play poker with that I want you to meet."

Bumps showed up at the appointed time and told the doorman that he had an appointment with Mr. McKnight. He was taken in an elevator to an upper floor, where a number of poker tables were filled with players. McKnight greeted him warmly. "Come on in," he said, "we've just finished dinner. Let me introduce you around."

It seemed to Bumps that presidents, vice-presidents or board members of every important company in Minnesota were there: Munsingwear, Pillsbury, General Mills, Dayton-Hudson, and of course 3M. Although McKnight's poker pals were not experts in the Arctic, they asked intelligent questions, which Bumps fielded as best as he could. And he was frank about the need for funding. Sponsorships for equipment were all well and good, but the expedition needed money to buy and transport fuel. As Woolsey left that evening McKnight pulled him aside and told him quietly, "I think you'll get what you need."

A few days later, Bumps received a registered letter from McKnight at his office. His eyes bugged out when he opened it. He was holding the largest check he had ever seen.

...

IN THE HUNDREDS OF LETTERS THAT WENT OUT on Plaisted Polar Expedition stationary were requests for everything from camera equipment and weather instruments to wool socks and packages of cheese. Of course, most of these requests were turned down or ignored. But as the weeks went on, pledges of equipment continued to mount up until the expedition could list more than sixty sponsors large and small. As Plaisted's garage filled with gear, it became increasingly clear that the expedition was not just a pipe dream. He was going to the Pole.

2

Hard Lessons

Geopolitics was the farthest thing from Ralph Plaisted's mind in July of 1966, when he made his first flight to Canada. He was looking for a permit to explore and his trip to Ottawa was his singular opportunity to meet with the Canadian officials charged with looking after the nation's far north and developing its future. He was planning to personally ask for permission to take an expedition across Canada's polar ice to the top of the world. For him, issues of sovereignty and exploitation were not a part of his quest; his interest was only challenge and experience.

Canada had already seen more than a few explorers crossing its territory on the way to discovery, exploitation, and glory. Recent explorers had generally made a mess, leaving dead expedition members and shattered plans for the tightly stretched northern authorities to clean up. This was the reason the nation demanded all those with far north exploration plans obtain a permit. There were criteria to meet, papers to file, hoops to jump through. Plaisted had made inquiries and filed the necessary documents—the personnel list, the resumes, the physical examinations, funding details and more—but there was one more big hurdle to clear.

As the airliner slid in under the east Ontario cloud deck and touched down on a slick runway in Ottawa, Plaisted wondered if he was ready for the face-to-face meeting. This was the big moment, one that could scuttle his plans with a whisper. And there were many questions he knew he couldn't answer. In the few months he had been pursuing the idea, he had made what he believed was real progress. His enthusiasm had attracted people with real talent in areas he believed were crucial to the attempt. His contacts with possible sponsors up to this time convinced him he could raise the money and material to launch a credible expedition. But could he convince the Canadians?

With all the problems of looking after the many challenges that accrued with keeping things together in these harsh and demanding places, tourists on a lark were not likely to get serious agenda space with these leaders. Plaisted knew he wasn't going to get much audience in that well-heated room in Ottawa unless he could quickly convince the gathered officials what he was bringing had merit in the far north context and that he was someone who could deliver.

The American had come well-represented with messages from the offices of elected U.S. federal officials, connections to major broadcast media, and strong Canadian backing from Bombardier, the snowmobile manufacturer in Quebec. Would it be enough?

The first indication things could maybe go his way was the length of the meeting. It lasted three hours, a marathon grilling that at first seemed almost as difficult as his meeting with the National Geographic Society. Had Plaisted any experience in the far north? What did the American think were the advantages he could bring to such an attempt? What were the skills of the people this hopeful expedition leader had marshaled to make this attempt? Why would a businessman from Minnesota be qualified for such a permit? What did Plaisted, who had never stood on the ice of the polar sea, think his biggest problems were going to be?

The toughest questions came in a crossfire from the two men whose decisions would most determine the outcome of this lengthy meeting with the American. Graham Rowley, a soft spoken but intense man nearing the end of a long career in northern service, was chief of the Canadian department known as Northern Affairs, the offices that oversaw the workings of all who toiled and traveled in the north. If Plaisted were to fail, lose a man or some men and require a rescue from the pitiless polar ice, there was no question the responsibility would fall to Rowley.

The other man, Dr. Geoffrey Hattersley-Smith, headed the Defense Research Board. Like Rowley, his career was marked by decades of extensive Arctic experience. Both men had been to the most distant reaches of their country's far northern holdings, traveling by icebreaker and dogsled, bush plane, and snowshoe. These were the old hands of the Canadian Arctic and both were acutely aware of the challenges and dangers that were part of any activity undertaken in these frigid, all but unmapped regions. Hattersley-Smith had traveled several times on expeditions himself, among other things visiting some of the shrines of early polar exploration, the stone cairns built as markers of visitation by explorers like Fridtjof Nansen, Otto Sverdrup, and Robert Peary. He had once even traveled to Norway to meet an aged and impoverished Sverdrup and negotiate a settlement of the potential claims Sverdrup might have made on the territory he had explored and charted in the previous century. If there was an issue of sovereignty, it was felt most strongly by Hattersley-Smith.

Plaisted was not as prepared as he wanted to be, and the questions were as tough and rapid-fire as he had imagined they might be. Although he had read some of the polar literature and tried to prepare a careful and thoughtful plan, he knew there would be questions for which he had no answer. If there was an embarrassed silence or worse, laughter, he knew he was finished. He hoped to draw on his background as a salesman to stay in the game.

He had some good answers. Yes, he had some northern experience. After the war, he had taken a contract for work in the Aleutians. Freshly mustered out of the U.S. Navy where he was trained as a baker and just out of his teens at the time, he had taken and completed his contract to work in those remote Alaska islands. He worked a little longer, too, until he realized the company would keep him as long as they could and wouldn't arrange to ship him out until he quit working. A little more than thirteen months in the Bering Sea and he came back to Oregon to honor the wishes of his new wife and take her and his new baby girl back to Minnesota.

The Aleutians company wanted him back, of course, and he also had a offer to go to work in Greenland some years later. A year or two in Thule had tempted him, Plaisted said, and the money was good. But a growing family and business ruled out this experience.

Why was he ready to tackle this Arctic trek now? His insurance business in Minnesota was thriving, he explained, the company had several crack agents and a busy office that could run itself for a time. Of course, his income from personal insurance sales would be reduced but the agency could keep an adequate cash flow, he had support from his friends and family and he planned to find the necessary money to fund the entire trip.

What made him think he and a crew of inexperienced adventurers from Minnesota could travel across the ice like this, to reach the North Pole? His people didn't have any direct experience with polar travel, Plaisted admitted, but they were experts in important other ways. Jerry Pitzl was a former Marine aviation officer and a skilled navigator who honed his skills on military duty. Walt Pederson was a highly respected technician and mechanic in Minnesota known for his abilities with machinery and especially snowmobiles. He owned a successful Ski-Doo snowmobile business, Plaisted told them, and he came highly recommended by Bombardier, one of his primary sponsors. Communications were going to be the responsibility of Don Powellek, a man with a track record in electronics plus good connections at Collins Radio, an expected sponsor. Some details of equipment and frequency use were still to be worked out, but Powellek was working with authorities in Ottawa, the U.S. and the Strategic Air Command to iron out the last details.

He had a doctor, Art Aufderheide, with some real Arctic experience, having traveled with Inuit on Victoria Island hunting musk ox and doing research in his field of paleopathology. Plaisted related the story of how Aufderheide had actually been the one who suggested the North Pole trip as the pair shared a drink in a bar in Duluth a few months earlier. "Art told me if those snowmobiles were as good for winter travel as I said they were," Plaisted explained, "I should try to ride them to the North Pole."

But often Plaisted didn't know the answer to a question, and after one such embarrassing silence, he looked around the room, contemplating at the chilly faces of the assembled Arctic experience he had to impress, and decided to give up trying to be impressive and just be honest instead. "I don't know," he replied, opening his hands. "What do you think I should do?"

Ralph immediately sensed a change in attitude with his frank reply. Hattersley-Smith launched into a mini-lecture on various ways of avoiding carbon monoxide poisoning while using a gasoline heater in a small tent at fifty below zero. Others in the room chimed in with their opinions as Ralph nodded and took notes. Within a few minutes Plaisted had turned a grilling into a college-level seminar on Arctic travel with the finest professors in the world, offering sound advice on everything from clothing to food to logistics. Plaisted soaked it all up, asking frequent follow-up questions. What kind of shelters should we investigate for use on the ice, and at base camp? How can we go about arranging the all-important air support? What are the problems we face obtaining and delivering men and materials to the farthest edge of land for the attempt?

Rowley asked, "Plaisted, what do you think is the number one problem your expedition will face?"

"Fuel," he said without hesitation. "We need our gas brought up on your icebreaker because the *McDonald* is only ship available for the task."

One of the men from Northern Affairs, Trevor Harwood, spoke just then. "The *McDonald* leaves in August," he said. "If you want to make that schedule, your fuel will have to be arranged in the next few weeks."

The meeting was finally over. Plaisted could feel the sweat drying on his shirt as the conversation turned genial and dinner plans were discussed. "We need to talk this over among ourselves, Plaisted," Rowley told him, "but you'll have your decision before you leave, one way or the other."

"We'll pick you up at your hotel for dinner," Hattersley-Smith said. "My house."

The gathering ended slowly, garnished with a half hour of informalities that allowed Plaisted to hear details about some interesting Arctic realities and to tell a personal story or two. When he left the building to make his way back to his hotel, he almost dared to be hopeful. He had survived the grilling with a minimum of embarrassing moments and all had treated him with a welcome if unexpected amount of respect.

Back at the hotel, Plaisted hardly had time to pace the room more than a couple of times before the room phone rang. It was Rowley's man, Trevor Harwood. "Would you like to meet me in the hotel bar for a drink?" he asked. Plaisted was downstairs a few minutes later.

Harwood was a genial, outgoing man several years younger than Rowley and Hattersley-Smith, who were both in their sixties. And he was quick with his broad smile and an easy flowing banter, the kind of man Plaisted could warm up to. They sat at the bar and stirred their scotches as Harwood reviewed a few of the key moments of the meeting. "Well, Plaisted," he said finally, "you've got your gas. We'll look after getting it on the *McDonald* and delivered to Eureka this summer."

The news left Plaisted momentarily speechless. He took a long draw on his highball and let the news settle for a moment. This meant he was going to get the go-ahead. His expedition would have the fuel they needed where they meant to begin their trek in early spring the following year. Did this mean the Canadian government was now going to be a sponsor of the expedition?

"No, no," Harwood said, wincing for a moment with the thought. "You don't get the fuel from us. It just gets there—and you can use it. It's best we don't say any more about it. Canada can't be part of your expedition and officially we can only give you permission, nothing more." The two men shared a knowing look and turned back to their drinks. It was almost time for dinner.

Rowley told Plaisted how easy it would've been to just say no. "We could have told you to go home and not have to worry about it," Rowley said over dessert, "but that's not how you make progress. We need to open and expand the north in this country and it doesn't happen if we're timid. We're taking a chance on you, Plaisted, and I believe you can come through."

Pride must be a factor in any undertakings of this kind and this, too, was fulfilled by the fact that the young scion of the robust and rapidly growing Bombardier empire was signed on with Plaisted. Jean-Luc Bombardier would be among the travelers as they crossed the ice to the Pole and he would be there if and when the attempt proved successful to plant the brand-new Maple Leaf Flag next to the Stars and Stripes.

...

For any reasonable person, Resolute would be considered the end of the line on the road to nowhere. Resolute may be coldest place on Earth that has scheduled air service. It gets so cold there in the winter that, even when you include the summertime highs, the average annual temperature is still less than three degrees Fahrenheit. To get to Resolute, you have to cross the Arctic Circle and then keep going north for another 600 miles, only to arrive

Resolute

at a tiny hamlet of less than 200 people perched on an island in Canada's arctic archipelago. When the Canadian government moved native Inuit to Resolute in the 1950s, they hated the place: it was too cold and too far north for them. But for bush pilot Weldy Phipps, Resolute was his New York City. From his base there, he flew to places even colder, smaller, and more remote.

Weldy wasn't much of a talker until you got to know him. Maybe pilots get that way after years of talking on radio and intercom, using their words sparely. Maybe, too, a bush pilot like Phipps develops a natural reserve, disinclined to show concern, reveal doubts or suggest vulnerabilities. Certainly few of Phipps' passengers had the slightest clue how many narrow escapes their pilot experienced over the years. And the man at the controls certainly never provided much detail when they were thrown by circumstance into one of those close shaves in the Canadian bush.

After a couple hours of "yeps" and "nopes" from Phipps as his noisy De-Havilland DHC-2 Beaver winged north from Resolute to Eureka and then on to Lake Hazen on the very northern reaches of Ellesmere Island, Plaisted wondered if he would ever learn anything from the gruff and all but silent pilot. He was there in July 1966 at the suggestion of Geoffrey Hattersley-Smith to learn what he could about the size of the challenges his expedition would face in the coming year. But Phipps wasn't being much help. Maybe it was just as well, Plaisted told himself, the views alone would provide plenty of information.

From the window of the Beaver as they flew out over the fjords and channels, he found himself looking at broken up, floating sea ice. The only concessions to summer were the open water leads that laced through the ice as far as the eye could see.

"It won't look like that when you come back in April," Phipps said, seeing the puzzled look on his passenger's face. "It'll be frozen over almost completely. You'll still see some open water leads. But they won't be near as many."

Plaisted thought it looked like the shell on a hardboiled egg would appear up close after you rolled it under your hand on a table, making hundreds of little cracks.

"It looks like you could move okay. though," Plaisted said hopefully, "find places where you could get a Ski-Doo through. Do you think so?"

"You can't tell how big those ridges are from up here," Weldy explained, "and the clouds and haze makes it even worse. Some of those ridges could have walls thirty feet high or more. You just can't tell. Not from up here. "

"Lots of haze all the time, too, Weldy?"

"All the time . . . almost . . . or fog or blowing snow."

"In the winter, too?"

"Maybe more, Plaisted, maybe more . . ."

They finally flew into an area where the ice below seemed more compacted. There were fewer leads and the patches of ice seemed bigger between the ridges. The crumpled ice, in ridges that curved and curled in every insane direction, seemed bigger here, too.

"Some of the books say there are big areas where the ice is smooth. Does that happen in the winter?"

"Never seen it. But I don't look neither. Too busy, eh." He shook his head and gazed out at the crazily patterned ice. "Do you see anything that looks that smooth now?"

Plaisted admitted he didn't.

After the Beaver slid to a stop on the rough, still snow-guarded landing field at Lake Hazen, Phipps sat in the now silent cockpit writing in his log. Plaisted spoke up again.

"We're going to need a plane, Weldy, you know that. We've got some interest from CBS. They want to do a documentary. They don't want to finance any of the expedition, it's not the way they do things, but they said they could pay for the plane since they'll need it to do their filming."

"Heard that."

"Are you available to help us in April, then?"

"I'm available for any sort of mad adventure, Plaisted, as long as you've can come up with the dollars."

"We're going to need a bigger plane—"

"And I'm taking delivery of one this year, a new Twin Otter. It'll be plenty big enough for your crew and your gear, don't worry about that. Just keep your eye on the $300 an hour. It'll be expensive, Plaisted, and we'll need extra fuel."

"Graham Rowley promised me fuel would be dropped at Eureka this summer. On its way now—icebreaker *McDonald*."

...

Weldy was acutely aware of these airplane and fuel issues. The closest runway to the Pole was at Eureka. The Beaver—called the Truck of the Arctic—was rated for a range of 455 miles. But it was 600 miles from Eureka to the Pole and, of course, you had to be able to fly back. Somehow, a fuel cache would have to be set up and supplied somewhere on the ice itself. There were rules to be followed for reserve fuel, plus the dense air of the polar winter made engines extra thirsty and this cut the actual range still further. Then there was the issue of payload. The Beaver was rated for six passengers and a useful load of 2,100 pounds. You could get a Ski-Doo inside, some men and gear, but the amount of supplies and fuel an expedition would require?

The much-anticipated turbine engine Twin Otter was a bigger plane and would improve on these numbers, but the trackless ice between takeoff and the North Pole remained a mighty challenge.

"That fuel . . . that fuel," Phipps repeated, "that has to happen for this to work at all."

Later, after another recon flight on the polar ice cut short by fog, Plaisted and Phipps were back at Weldy's home base in Resolute. Plaisted was flying out the next day and he was enjoying a farewell dinner in the double-wide trailer Phipps, his wife, Fran, and their six kids called home. Dinner was a boisterous affair, all clanking dishes and elbows, but the kids melted away after dinner, leaving Plaisted, Phipps, and Fran sitting at the cleared-away dinner table.

"You know, Fran," Weldy said as he leaned back to enjoy a rye with his guest from the states, "Ralph has a plan to ride Ski-Doos to the North Pole. Leaving from Eureka in April, he says."

"If everything goes as planned, that is," Plaisted ventured, "There's more to do between now and then, you know, but we've been promised the fuel, Bombardier has said they are going to supply the Ski-Doos, and I've already raised most of the money and equipment ..."

The conversation tailed off just then, Plaisted thinking about how deep into this thing he had gotten, when Phipps spoke again.

"You know, Fran," he said, "I think they just might make it."

...

WELLAND WILFRED PHIPPS WAS PUSHING FIFTY, an advanced age for a bush pilot. The new plane was needed for Phipps' flying service in Resolute, but for him it was also a symbol. The new deHavilland was tangible proof he was at the top of a very risky and daring profession, witness that people he admired and re-

Weldy Phipps

spected recognized it. Mere money wouldn't get you one of these planes, but Phipps was in line for Number Three despite the Canadian military, the postal service, a long list of flight services, emergency and exploration teams in Canada and around the world all standing in line, eagerly awaiting the day they could take delivery of one of the new high-performance twin-turbine bush planes.

Phipps was getting one of the very first planes because he had the credentials . . . and the necessary connections. He had earned it all.

Born in Ottawa in 1922, he joined the Royal Canadian Air Force and served as a flight engineer for part of World War II until his Halifax bomber was shot down over Europe. The tough twenty-one-year-old parachuted safely from the crippled plane before it crashed, but he was taken prisoner and held for two years in a German camp until 1944 when he finally escaped with another airman during a forced march. The pair made their way safely across hostile territory to Allied lines.

Back in Ottawa, Phipps became a commercial pilot and flight instructor, quickly earning the respect of aviators across the country for his obvious skills and for his willingness to tackle the tough assignments. He flew the high-altitude photography missions the government needed around the country and he got damaged planes out of impossible situations on missions that saved both lives and valuable flying equipment. By 1955, he started flying charter assignments into the Arctic and was quickly seduced by the challenge and by the serious money that could be made.

The notion of flying where there are no weather stations, marginal radio communications, useless magnetic compass headings and often no real runways on which to land finds favor with only the wild-eyed few, and Weldy Phipps discovered he was one of them. During the first six years he flew in and out of the Arctic, he mastered the skills and techniques needed to survive in one of the world's most dangerous occupations. Flying up in the Arctic bush, he learned to land on the upgrade so the plane would stop in time, take off on the downgrade to pick up airspeed more quickly. He learned how to take off and land often heavily laden aircraft in impossibly small distances, and exactly what the limits of each aircraft were. He learned to live with life and death situations that sometimes could only end badly when visibility went right down to the ground, ending any hope of flight.

Beyond handling the aircraft, Phipps learned the basic but supremely difficult skills of airborne navigation using a sextant, gauging the surface winds and choosing possible landing sites from aloft and taking the calculated risk in crosswind gusts and low visibility. He figured out a way to mount huge, underinflated DC-3 tires on his aircraft to make even more difficult landings and take-offs possible. His reputation as the Arctic's finest was made well before he finally reached his zenith as the skilled pilot who operated out of Resolute.

Known by the 1950s all across the country for his many triumphs in the air, Phipps' recognition as one of the greatest bush pilots ever produced in Canada was cemented in 1961 when he drew out his savings, bought a pair of planes and moved his large and growing family to Resolute on Cornwallis Island, Northwest Territories, where he established his flying service at one of the northernmost locations for a civilian aviation operation in the world. The name he chose for the new venture perhaps says something about the nerveless pilot's personal view of the world of bush flying. As the only link to civilization for literally all the people living above seventy-five degrees north in Canada's central Arctic, Phipps' Atlas Aviation Service very much carried the weight of the world on its shoulders.

Phipps reputation as a trusty, Arctic-experienced pilot, his background as a decorated war hero, his willingness to accept the risky assignments and fly day after day when necessary resulted in his being respected in many quarters as a tremendous asset, especially by people whose responsibilities included the far north. When the Canadian prime minister needed to fly into the Arctic bush, it was Phipps who got the call. Landing on a rough strip in foul weather at Grise Fjord, Pierre Trudeau was shaken but impressed with the talent and courage shown by this unflappable pilot.

By 1966 when he first met Ralph Plaisted, Phipps was operating a deHavilland Beaver and Otter, a Beechcraft and a pair of Pipers and with the help of two other pilots and a crew of mechanics. His flying service was operating year round, making the supply runs, taking the emergency calls, transporting the managers of Canada's northern companies and government bureaus. Sometimes he would fly out to the polar ice with scientists and the occasional adventurer.

If there was a pilot in the world who could actually operate an airborne supply line for a traverse to the North Pole on snowmobiles, it was Weldy Phipps. The final piece of the puzzle of polar travel fell into place when he flew the new Twin Otter to Resolute. Painted on the fuselage were registration letters to match his initials: CF-WWP, call sign Whiskey Whiskey Papa. It was an amazingly capable airplane. The Twin Otter was powered by two 620-horsepower Pratt & Whitney PT6A-20 turboprop engines. Developed in Montreal, the new turbine engines were the first to use a modular design that separated the hot combustion side of the turbine from the cool compression side, making the engine very durable and, more importantly for its planned deployment in remote areas, capable of being overhauled in sections, often right in place on the wing, rather than as a whole component as had been the case with other aircraft turbine designs that came before.

...

THE PLAISTED EXPEDITION'S PLAN was the kind of thing that excited people's imagination and, especially in the optimistic 1960s, encouraged belief the feat could be accomplished. These snowmobiles could go thirty miles per hour, and with air support on deck for the necessary supplies and fuel, this trek just might turn out to be a brisk adventure ride instead of the frigid ordeal some predicted. There was no one who could say with any certainty what kind of distance a snowmobiling party moving across the polar ice could expect to make in a day or week, traveling this way. When the Plaisted Expedition arrived in the Canadian Arctic in late March of 1967, it was the first attempt of this kind ever. Everyone and anyone had a guess.

The Royal Canadian Air Force agreed to ferry the expedition, their snowmobiles and all their gear to Eureka. Populated by a handful of Canadians with military assignments, Eureka was deemed an excellent headquarters and starting point for the expedition due to its having an airstrip and several empty buildings that could be pressed into service as expedition headquarters, mess hall, and bunkhouse. Located on a fjord near Nansen Sound on a more or less direct route to the edge of the polar ice, Eureka also offered the ready access to the frozen ocean that would provide the route the expedition hoped to follow on their trek north.

Plaisted had flown over this trackless, icy world in Weldy Phipps' Beaver bushplane, but he never set foot on the ice itself. Based on his experience with snowmobiles in Minnesota, he figured his crew could make the 500 miles to the North Pole in a month. Allowing for storms and occasional open water and other setbacks, it seemed reasonable to believe the swift and agile little snowmobiles would be able to skirt around many of the larger obstacles and make at least an occasional fifty-mile day possible. Doing the math, twelve of these would put the expedition at the Pole. The literature and the polar experts he consulted all agreed April was the best time for such a trek, so the expedition planned to leave Eureka by the first day of April, arrive at the Pole before the first day of May.

...

RIGHT AWAY, THE DELAYS AND DISAPPOINTMENTS always a part of existence in the far north began cropping up to make this attempt more frustrating and difficult than it appeared back in the lower forty-eight. The ten snowmobiles provided by Bombardier, Ltd., had to be uncrated and set up. The cargo sleds had to be selected, hitched up and packed. The base station radio link had to be wired up to its power and antenna and tested. The boxes and crates of supplies had to be sorted and organized. All of this would be taking place in twenty- to thirty-below-zero temperatures in the half-light of the Arctic dawn.

The weather didn't cooperate either. Low visibility and a twenty-five-knot wind kept the departure impossible until a slight break in the weather and a modicum of readiness was achieved on March 28. Eight impatient men left the cluster of buildings at Eureka and headed up the frozen fjord to Nansen Sound and their destiny.

The words of the skeptics at National Geographic, who said Plaisted couldn't expect to bring a group of his cronies up to the Arctic sea and travel to the North Pole were ringing in Plaisted's ears as the confusion and frustration mounted. There were so many questions still unanswered as the expedition prepared to get underway. How much food and fuel to bring? How much extra gear, clothes, and spares for the snowmobiles were needed? Which cargo sleds to use and how to pack them? Which parka to wear? Not having the answers, the men did what they could, packed plenty of redundancy and hooked up at least one of every kind of cargo sled as they prepared for the trek.

Packing for the first day's travel was chaos, delaying the party until after two in the afternoon. Setting up the first night's camp after the ride to the edge of Nansen Sound was even greater chaos as the crew struggled to find the essentials they had packed earlier in the day with few clues as to what and when they would need them. Having never set foot on the ice of the high Arctic before, the men struggled with all the new things that would become everyday challenges for them in the days to come.

Beyond the gear and logistics challenges they faced was the pressing need to develop skills for traveling the polar ice. They experienced the first heavy overcast on the Sound their second day on the ice. They didn't know how to navigate in the low visibility they encountered. The near-dawn twilight obliterated the horizon and robbed vision of contrast and perspective. Just staying more or less in line and keeping the rider ahead in view was a near-impossibility. Uneven surfaces on the ice were encountered without warning, causing tip-overs and spilling the gear sleds.

Plaisted was riding out in front using techniques he relied on as an outdoorsman in Minnesota. Keep a distant landmark in position as you go, he figured, and you'll keep a steady course. The problem was he had no idea the iceberg he was sighting in on was far closer than it appeared. After three hours of riding, the party discovered they had circled the "distant" iceberg

Jack Austed

and were turned completely around, heading back in the direction of Eureka. After the first full day of travel on the ice of Nansen Sound, they had made just fifteen miles.

The next day they received their first visit from Phipps and his airplane. He brought more fuel and the Canadian Army instructor and Arctic expert Jack Austed, joining the trek with his two pet sled dogs after being delayed with Phipps in Resolute by three days of bad weather. After the rendezvous and the arrival of an Arctic veteran, the weather improved and the mood improved as the party made brisk headway for an entire day. But the painful reality that this was a group of Arctic rookies was never far from view. That evening, there were problems with the tent used for cooking and eating, there was a near-disastrous fire in one of the other tents and the temperature dropped to forty below, making it a miserable night for the crew, some sleeping in sleeping bags soaked with dog urine, some in bags burned through by the earlier fire.

Still, there was reason for hope, even optimism. By the end of the traveling day on April 1st the group had traveled 100 miles, reaching the mouth of Nansen Sound and the edge of the Arctic sea after five days on the ice. If they could continue to average that twenty miles a day toward their goal, the Pole would be theirs in just over three weeks time.

Already things were going more smoothly as routine began to make at least some of the daily struggle less frustrating and arduous. Despite these improvements, it was clear to all the ice party was over manned and overloaded. If the expedition was going to make time across the difficult sea ice in the coming days, it would require the party to get smaller and lighter. On April 3, frustrated with their pace, Plaisted decided to pare the ice party down to eight men—four snowmobiles with four cargo sleds in tow. A second visit by Phipps' airplane lifted the returning members off the ice along with some of the supplies now deemed overload. An Air Force weather flight transmitting ice condition reports to submarines traveling under the frozen surface gave ice party some insight into the first big obstacle they would soon encounter on the open ocean—the Big Lead.

Since Peary's time, the existence of the Big Lead was well-documented in the Arctic annals. It occurs at the place where the sea ice frozen hard to land finally reaches water deep enough for currents and tides to force it into motion. At this point the moving, floating sea ice takes over, making the junction is an uneasy one. As the sea ice moves, a giant open water lead alternately opens and closes, sometimes creating a span of open water miles wide, sometimes crashing together to form miles of rubble. The ice rubble forms when the fresher ice that freezes in the lead is crumpled together by the unimaginably heavy floating floe ice, ramming against the anchored shore ice.

In the few miles between the last of land just south of the Big Lead, the ice was actually relatively smooth and the expedition made fifty miles traveling northeast along the lead in search of a place to cross in that single day. Approaching and crossing the lead was full of new experiences. One was the sound of the moving sea ice. When the ice is moving, which is usually, the air is filled with sound often described as artillery fire, a busy iron foundry or a freight train. When the movement is nearby, the cracking and rumbling is deafening, making communication possible only by shouting over the din. When the movement is more distant, groans are heard, punctuated with occasional sharp snaps and reports.

Another new experience was thin sea ice. Salt water ice is different than fresh water ice. Fresh water ice on lakes is stiff but brittle, it will support weight up to a point, then shatter like glass as it gives way. Salt water ice is much more pliable and rubbery. While it isn't believed to support any more weight per inch of thickness than the fresh water kind, new sea ice stretches and bends before breaking, making determining its safety an art onto itself. Jack Austed taught the crew how to determine a safe crossing by probing the ice with a five-foot iron rod. This was how they finally crossed the new ice in the Big Lead and this was the technique they would use on newly frozen ice all the time they were on the polar sea. That is, when they couldn't rely on color.

It is said the Inuit have a hundred words for snow and perhaps they would have as many for ice if they traveled on the frozen sea like the men of the Plaisted Expedition. The travelers learned newly frozen ice is gray, less so as it thickens. Old sea ice is blue because cycles of thaw and refreezing leaches out the salt and actually makes the ice close to fresh and close to fresh water ice in appearance, too. Yellow ice is also old sea ice but it still has salt in it. Sea ice can be shades of white, some tending toward yellow, some tending toward blue, some glinting like jewels, some milky and opaque. As the men traveled north, they learned how each kind of ice behaved when hit by axes or poles and what kind of ice harbored cracks under the snow and more. The rookies, despite their frustrations, were becoming something only a handful of earthlings could claim to be: they were slowly becoming seasoned sea ice travelers.

...

THEY ALSO LEARNED PATIENCE. They were hardly across the Big Lead before they found themselves marooned on a floating ice floe with no way off except to wait for the floe to drift up next to larger nearby ice surfaces. This unanticipated island sojourn cost the expedition two full days before the floe finally moved into a position where the men could drive their snowmobiles off. Then, finally moving again, it wasn't more than a dozen miles to the next stop at open water. After two more days of waiting, the men made the first of what would be many daring runs across too-thin ice. This was going to be their world for the entire time they were on the open Arctic Ocean: ice-walled pressure ridges interspersed with open water and thin ice.

All the while, the men were learning. Days of working and traveling and sleeping in temperatures ranging from fifteen- to forty-five-below zero had taught them strategies for staying reasonably warm and dry, ways to select the best routes through the many and varying conditions, ways to measure their effort so as to remain on the job and on task for day after demanding day. Still the lack of progress was demoralizing. After a week on the sea ice, the North Pole hopefuls were only twenty miles away from land, still 470 miles from their goal.

They thought they were traveling light when they pared down to four snowmobiles and eight riders but it was already April 11 and there were still more than 400 miles to go. They made another crew change, sending Pederson, Pitzl, Austed and Powellek back to base camp and soldiering on with Plaisted, Bumps Woolsey, Art Aufderheide, and Jean-Luc Bombardier comprising the remaining ice party. With fresh men came the hope of increased mileage but the sea ice had other plans and the group of four struggled through a rubble field of several square miles in size, averaging only a mile in six hours over two days before encountering an ice obstacle they could only call the Big Ridge. This was a sheer wall of ice over forty feet in height that stretched to the east and west horizon. An overflight during a supply visit by Phipps' airplane indicated there was no way around. Refusing to

Cutting a road across a ridge

Charles Kuralt

admit defeat, the four men spent two days grinding stair steps into the sloping side and chipping ice chunks off the top to build a ramp on the steep side.

After a visit by the plane the next day—it was now twenty-four hours of daylight—the Plaisted Polar Expedition set off northward again, this time comprising Plaisted, Powellek, Bombardier, Aufderheide, and Austed. On April 17, the expedition had been on the sea ice for two weeks but had advanced only fifty-three miles from the Arctic Ocean shore. This was less than four miles per day on average. Speeds picked up a bit after the Big Ridge and, except for a storm delay on April 20-21, the expedition made steady progress, making eighty-three degrees north on April 23.

By now the ice party was far enough out on the ice that locating them reliably became a worry. To answer this concern, a piece of World War II equipment called a SARAH (Search And Rescue Antenna Homing) beacon was put into play and it worked admirably, allowing Phipps to home in on the ice party without searching as he had been forced to do on occasion previously when light conditions were bad.

For a few days, the expedition made steady progress, covering twenty miles one day, nearly all of it north, thirteen another day, eleven on the third day. At eighty-three degrees twenty minutes they were less than 400 miles from the Pole and the way ahead was good, sometimes even allowing some full speed running, At times they were traveling so fast they had to stop to allow Austed's dogs to catch up.

...

THEN CAME THE BIG BLOW. STARTING ON APRIL 27, a wind that was part of a typical Arctic spring storm came up, sometimes blowing more than fifty miles per hour. The ice party had no choice but to lace down their tents and wait it out. They knew if anything untoward happened, like a tent breaking its ropes and blowing away, they might perish. The generator took this opportunity to blow a piston, ending radio contact. Fuel for the tent heaters was growing short. Sitting in the tent day after day, the groaning and cracking of the ice under them reinforced how far the spring breakup of the pack ice had advanced. The expedition had faced many dangers since venturing out on the bay ice in March, but this storm threatened the ultimate. They feared for their lives.

Plaisted recorded in his diary this was the moment when any thoughts of reaching the Pole ended. Now he wanted only to survive and keep his men alive. The responsibility for getting these men into this situation weighed heavily on his mind as the tent flapped wildly, no end to the fearsome storm in sight. All feared the next thing to happen would be the ice breaking up under them, a likelihood in strong, sustained winds like they were experiencing.

It was a tense seven-day siege that lasted until May 3 when, in the middle of the day, the wind died down in fifteen minutes from a raging gale to nothing. The exhausted men crawled from their snowed-over tents to see a brilliant blue sky and just a few wisps of clouds. They were shocked to discover just how close to their tents a new, large crack in the ice had advanced.

But the Big Blow ended it. Following through on your promises is one thing, thought Ralph, but suicide is another. The ice under their feet had clearly become too mobile and uncertain for safe travel. The ice party moved to a patch of smooth ice to await the plane. When they lifted off for the 1½ hour return flight to Eureka, the spot where they had waited out the Big Blow looked like a spider web laced with cracks of open water leading in every direction. They had spent thirty-seven days traveling on the ice and had made good 216 miles north to reach a furthest north of eighty-three degrees, thirty-six minutes. When they lifted off the ice in the Twin Otter on May 4, 1967, there were still 384 miles of ice between them and the goal that had eluded all comers for centuries.

They didn't feel like failures, despite the way the numbers looked. After all, they were all still alive and the fresh ambitions of a month earlier had ripened into polar wisdom. The 1967 expedition ended in disappointment. The whole affair might've ended right there, but something happened as the men got off the plane in Eureka that hardened their resolve and set the tone for the coming year.

...

ON THE TARMAC, WALT PEDERSON AND JEAN-LUC BOMBARDIER stood together, both bitterly disappointed. Of all the expedition members, these two were the most determined to reach the goal. They knew after their experiences over five weeks on the ice all the reasons why they didn't reach the Pole. There were mistakes, regrets, and plenty of what-ifs. But it was the end of the trip and they were going home without making the goal.

"I hate that storm," Bombardier said in a smoky exhale. "We were going good 'til then."

"We started too late," Pederson said quietly. "How could we know? But we did some things right, didn't we?"

"Yes, we could make it, we could make it all the way. I know we can do it." Huddled against the breeze blowing clouds over the low sun, the Canadian's French accent made it sound like an oath.

They were joined by a tired and defeated-looking Plaisted, who stood in the lee of the bushplane with the other men, looking out at the ice in the fjord.

Plaisted said they would try again. "I've made a list. I spent the time in the trip back here writing up all the things that went right—and wrong. One thing, we had pretty good luck with the gear, but we need to stick to the plastic sleds."

The other men nodded in agreement.

"And we need to start sooner before the ice starts to break up. That really finished it."

"We have to start further north, Ralph," Pederson said, "if we had that week back . . ." His voice tailed off wistfully.

"We know what we're doing now," Bombardier said as he lit another cigarette. "We could have really moved except for that storm. I hate that storm."

"And the Big Lead," Pederson added, "and the Big Ridge."

"Well, you kept the Ski-Doos going all the way, Walt," Plaisted said, looking at his notebook where he had jotted his end of trip notes. "We know we can count on them, thanks to you. We can make it on snowmobiles, we know that for sure now. We came up here and survived on the ice for a month, boys. We made two hundred miles across the ice and no one was hurt or killed. We got through the Big Blow. We deserve another chance and I'm going to get it for us. I think I can raise the money and Bombardier will stick with us, don't you think Jean-Luc?"

"I'll talk to them. I don't think the family will give up too easy, and I know I won't. We will get the machines I think, but it's tough to go home now . . ."

As Jean-Luc's voice trailed off, they all fell into silence. For a few moments all the details of the past month were running through their minds. None wanted to leave with the job unfinished, the goal still out of reach. The three men standing along in the swirling early evening wind swore an oath. They would return to the polar ice again and this time they would keep going until they made it . . . no matter what. Their mitts clasped as each man tried to imagine what the future he had just committed himself to would hold.

While most would return for the second attempt in 1968, some said emphatically they would not return. Bumps Woolsey wanted to, but he knew his one-man dental practice would not survive another two-month "vacation" the following year. He reluctantly begged off. *The CBS News* team of Charles Kuralt and two technicians had shot enough film for their television documentary, which aired in prime time a few months later. Once again, Ralph Plaisted was briefly famous, now on a national stage. But CBS declined

Conquering a ridge

to send Kuralt again, which meant Plaisted would have to find other ways to raise the $300 per hour that Weldy Phipps' Twin Otter demanded. The fame he garnered from the CBS documentary would help him enormously in that fundraising effort.

When they returned to try again, it would be with a wealth of knowledge about travel on the Arctic polar icecap no one else on Earth possessed. They knew what changes would have to be made in their timetable, their equipment, their procedure and more. Plaisted had already zeroed in on Ward Hunt Island at the more logical starting point. Pederson was already thinking of the snowmobile modifications he would make for the next trip. They knew what kind of cargo sled they needed. The small fiberglass Sno-Champ sleds made in Minnesota were light and had performed admirably. Special versions of this solid bottom design would be best, made just a bit bigger to accommodate the tent poles.

The men had learned from this five weeks on the ice that the snowmobiles need sturdy but loose hitches to enable smooth starts from rest and keep the cargo sleds from overturning the tow machine in tipovers. They needed smaller, easier to fill fuel tanks, as fueling was dangerous and messy. There were many other things.

Maybe it was true in May of 1966 that Ralph Plaisted couldn't gather up "a bunch of his cronies" and make a trek to the North Pole. But in May of 1967, those cronies were newly made experts in the arcane art of travel on the polar ice, the best in the world. Maybe the most important piece of the puzzle was now in place. And now they had the ability and experience as well.

But there would be one final element in the mix when they returned the following March. Call it Polar Fever—the rare but virulent disease contracted by some who travel in the very high latitudes, a life-threatening malady suffered by many others before them. They would return to take their snowmobiles to the North Pole or die trying.

3

EVERY CIRCUS NEEDS A RINGMASTER

THE SIGN OVER THE DOOR TO NORDAIR'S RAMP at the Montreal airport carried the message in orderly, bold letters: "DEPARTURE OF PLAISTED POLAR EXPEDITION FEB 20, 1968." But pandemonium reigned inside. A bar at one end of the room was almost obscured by reporters who appeared to be fascinated by each other, ignoring the others in the room. People of all shapes, nationality, color, and sex milled about, clustering intermittently around the scattered exhibits: the expedition members themselves. A middle-aged man of medium build wearing a medium gray suit was introducing a couple to Ralph Plaisted. He was directing a film of the expedition. A cub reporter was asking Jerry Pitzl how he would know when they arrived at the North Pole.

"It is hard, because it's just a theoretical dot in the ocean and the ice looks the same there as anywhere else," Pitzl explained. "I'll use a series of sun elevation measurements made with a marine sextant, and compute our position from mathematical tables."

The reporter made her way over to where Walt Pederson was explaining snowmobiles to a curious onlooker.

"The front end is held up by two steerable skis," he explained, "while the rear consists of an endless track—like on a military tank. It's driven by a sixteen-horsepower, air-cooled engine and weighs about 250 pounds. They're really made for recreational use."

"But," she inquired wide-eyed, "what will you do if you get a flat tire?"

A large well-dressed man spared Pederson by interrupting and introducing himself. "Name's Johnsen," he said. "I represent Zenox Corporation. We make a new tape recorder. Like to have you take this one along and try it out on the ice. Send us a letter about it when you get back."

Thanking him Pederson dropped the tape recorder into a bag he was carrying which already contained those of two other brands as well as a small camera, two quarts of snowmobile oil samples, a pair of gloves obviously provided by distributors anxious for product endorsements. Noting a salesman explaining the operation of a watch to Powellek he excused himself and moved over in his direction.

"The calendar feature of the watch is useful," Don Powellek was assuring the beaming salesman. "You see, it's easy to become confused about the date up there. The sun is just now coming back after an almost five-month continuous polar night. We'll move out onto the ice as soon as we can see. A month later the sun will be shining twenty-four hours a day. By the end of April the pack ice will be broken up. That gives us less than two months to reach the North Pole."

"All expedition members over here!" the loud voice of the director ordered imperatively as hot, brilliant lights flooded one corner of the room where the expedition flag was taped to the wall. CBS and Charles Kuralt would not be along this year; but a Canadian production company had paid Plaisted for the film rights to the 1968 trip. The production company would

Jerry Pitzl

Andy Horton

send producer Fred Clark and two Swiss cameramen, the brothers Hans and Ernst Michel, farther north to film the whole thing.

There were other personnel changes as well. Jack Austed's dog team would not be needed, as Plaisted was now more convinced than ever that the snowmobile was the future of Arctic travel. A friend had suggested Andy Horton, who had been added as a radio operator for their new base camp at Ward Hunt Island. Art Aufderheide was concerned that an injury at base camp would force him to leave the ice, and wanted a second doctor along. After a nationwide search, Dr. Weston Cook, a South Carolina surgeon, was chosen to serve as the base camp physician.

Setting a smile on his face the director stepped in front of the expedition members, turned his back to the people in the room and faced the television cameras.

"Ladies and gentlemen," he announced to the wall behind the cameras, "we are happy so many friends of the expedition came down here spontaneously to see them off tonight. As you know, a year ago these men attempted to drive snowmobiles to the North Pole. Beset by storms and open water leads, this group of amateurs fought their way 200 miles off shore before

Dr. Weston Cook

the breakup of the pack forced them off the ice. Starting a month sooner than last time they're going back to try it again. With last year's experiences to help them, they're confident they'll make it this year."

Nudged into attention by his companion, a glassy-eyed reporter dutifully raised his hand and asked, "Do you expect to find a monument left by Peary at the North Pole in 1909, Mr. Plaisted?"

Turning to the television camera with the glowing red light above it Plaisted explained, "No. You see, the top of the world is an ocean and the North Pole is just an imaginary spot in the middle of it. The ocean is covered with ice but because of the currents, winds, and tides this ice is moving constantly. It breaks up and then the pieces are forced together again until the surface is just a rugged mass of jumbled ice. Anything left on that ice would just gradually drift southward into the Atlantic Ocean and sink as the ice melted."

On and on the interviews went as the various governmental representatives and political luminaries successively stepped into the camera's view. Plaisted explained to the television world how they would fly to Ellesmere Island, the most northern of the islands in the Arctic Ocean off Canada's mainland. A supply aircraft capable of landing on the ocean ice would help them establish base camp at the northern end of this island, and this plane would be used to deliver gasoline and needed supplies to the ice party. Traversing the 450 miles of rough pack ice of the Arctic Ocean to the North Pole in open snowmobiles, they would be evacuated back to base camp by the supply aircraft.

Suddenly a shrill cacophony rent the stale air of the room as a brilliantly uniformed bagpiping band of kilted Highland pipers burst into sound. Marching precisely about the main lobby of the airport they advanced down the ramp to the room of the Plaisted party. The sudden appearance of this group had its desired effect as hordes of idle, bored travelers followed this curious group.

The pipers marched through the room three times before the camera crews were satisfied, then moved through the rear door and formed a double line out to the waiting aircraft, still perpetuating their ear-splitting dissonance.

"Lights," shouted the director. "Get the lights on 'em!" And when the group was appropriately illuminated he hustled the expedition members forward. "Now go," he ordered. "Walk right down between the pipers, up the steps and into the airplane. You first, Ralph."

Awkwardly the men in the fluorescent-blue jackets moved down the aisle formed by the pipers, resembling nothing more closely than an aging basketball team. One by one they began to enter the aircraft.

But even the best-laid plans of professional men can come to naught. The film company had underestimated Walt Pederson. A small group of men were surrounding Pederson at the rear door of the room, obviously protesting vociferously and gesticulating freely.

"What's the matter?" the director demanded as he rushed over to the group, alarmed at this interruption of his otherwise flawlessly staged production.

"Walt won't sign the expedition agreement," Plaisted snorted. "The agreement would prohibit him from endorsing any product competitive to the Bombardier Ski-Doo snowmobiles we're using. Walt says he makes his living selling snowmobiles and can't tie himself up like that."

"My God, can't you settle that inside the plane?" the director pleaded, but no one paid him any heed as the bickering waxed more heated.

On and on they argued; and on the pipers played and on and on the people waited. The icy wind whistled across the concrete field, whipping the snow around the bare, unadorned and slowly bluing legs of the musicians. Several times they faltered as their eyes, but never their heads, turned toward the little knot of wrangling people. Finally a cameraman was heard muttering an irreverent "Oh, to hell with it," as he turned off his camera.

As if on signal the pipers ceased and straggled back into the terminal. The bar closed soon after and the last spectators promptly melted away. Someone inside the aircraft was heard to yell: "Close the goddamned door! It's cold in here!"

An hour later, all differences eventually resolved, the plane taxied to takeoff position and the 1968 Plaisted Polar Expedition made an inglorious, unphotographed departure from civilization.

...

THE MOOD INSIDE THE CANADAIR DC-4 was boisterous as the reality of their departure gripped the expedition. They were going! Really going to the North Pole! Art Aufderheide laughed at the jokes of his seatmate, Don Powellek, but he couldn't help but notice that in the row ahead of him, Ralph Plaisted was quietly staring out the window, unaffected by the high spirits around him.

Art had seen the same thing last year, at about the same time. The burden of command was beginning to weigh on Plaisted, he realized, dragging their leader's mood down at the same time everyone else was being buoyed. Leaving civilization, everything was on Ralph's shoulders now: food, shelter, communication, even the very lives of the expedition members. Art didn't envy him in

Don Powellek

the slightest. He had himself disliked the title of co-leader that Ralph had bestowed upon him the previous year. And though Ralph had the real responsibility, even the idea of command was foreign to Art's quiet personality. So he was more than grateful when Ralph had tactfully suggested that Don Powellek might do well in the role of expedition co-leader for their 1968 attempt.

But what mostly worried Art now was the personality change he had seen in Ralph the previous year, one he hoped—but did not really expect—could be avoided this time out. Art recalled the prediction made by a member of the National Geographic society, that Ralph would have to drive his men so hard that they would hate him for it. Ralph repeated that story often, perhaps using it as a talisman to himself, a way of explaining why the normally jovial salesman could became so surly and short-tempered after crossing the Arctic Circle.

But Art suspected otherwise. It was not Plaisted himself choosing to be disagreeable; rather, Art thought, the crushing burden of responsibility had weighed his personality like a millstone, causing an unnatural psychological stoop. Fortunately, Art also knew that the other men were aware of Ralph's responsibilities and more than willing to forgive his moodishness, as long as their goal was reached. The fact that nearly everyone here was a veteran of 1967 and had volunteered again was an excellent sign. The men knew him and trusted him, they understood his ways. Yes, Art thought, the men would be fine. But Ralph? He wasn't so sure.

...

PLAISTED STOOD AT THE WINDOW of one of the Eureka weather station's buildings, watching the storm rearrange Ellesmere Island's snow cover for still another day. Only his hands clenched tightly behind him betrayed his massive effort to quell the frustration rising inside him. Less than a year previously he had stood at this same window staring at the same scene. He remembered how they had left at the first sign of that storm's abatement, childishly eager to begin their trek. He almost blushed as he recalled their naiveté, for they had done almost everything wrong. Crouching in his tent on the pack ice during the storm that ended their 1967 attempt at the pole, he had pondered the causes of their failure. And after their return he had confronted most of the eighty-seven skeptical sponsors of his first effort, arguing that the experience gained on that undertaking would ensure success on the next.

He emphasized, each day was so valuable that they would start as soon as the sun returned after the long Arctic night, near the end of February, regardless of the temperature. They would shorten the distance by starting at Ellesmere Island's most northern tip, near Cape Columbia, from which point Peary had departed in 1909. The enormous mass of supplies which creation of a base camp there required would be flown up by the supply aircraft during the last two weeks of February. In fact, with the continued unofficial assistance of the Canadian government, he had already arranged during the subsequent summer to have the icebreaker *McDonald* move the unused gasoline from his 1967 expedition from Eureka as far north as possible—a remote inlet called Tanquary Fjord.

Only four snowmobiles with minimal loads would be used, operated by men now familiar with pack ice travel. More snowmobiles only meant more chance that one would break down, and the expedition was only as fast as its slowest machine.

Throughout the spring, summer, and fall he had argued, persisted and cajoled until he found himself the following Christmas with the financial backing necessary to launch his second attempt to reach the pole. He felt a deep responsibility to the trust these supporters had in his judgment, and flinched when he reviewed the events of the past two weeks.

Certainly, he reflected, no one could have expected him to anticipate the breakdown of one of their transport aircraft's engines, which caused them nearly a week's delay at Resolute on the way up; nor the tempestuous weather at Eureka after their arrival, which had grounded their supply plane for another week. Those two weeks had been intended for the transport of the supplies from Eureka and Tanquary Fjord across the mountains to the northern shore of Ellesmere Island where they were to set up base camp on a small outcrop of rock called Ward Hunt Island. He squirmed when he glanced at the March 5th date indicated on the wall calendar. Instead of being a week's travel out on the pack ice, they were still at Eureka, base camp construction had not even begun and their supplies were still buried under ever-deepening snowdrifts at Tanquary Fjord.

Sighing, he turned to watch Don Powellek and Jerry Pitzl. Powellek was a tall, somewhat overweight man of about forty with thinning, blond hair and a perpetual twinkle in his eyes invisibly coupled to a mischievous grin. He was playing solitaire and chatting idly with Pitzl.

"Been with the company fifteen years now," he was telling Pitzl. "Ever since I finished electronics school."

"Then why are you quitting when we get back?" Pitzl inquired. "Seems to me being an industrial sales engineer is a pretty good job."

"I started electronics in the Navy because I like to put electrical things together," Powellek explained, "and instead, for fifteen years I've been selling the electronic products the company puts together. That's why I came along with Plaisted."

"You mean the challenge of the expedition's communication problems lured you up here?"

"Right!" exclaimed Powellek, demonstrating some animation for the first time that day. "The problems are enormous. Just think—a radio light enough to be carried by the ice party, powerful enough to reach at least 500 miles back to base camp, yet durable enough to operate at sixty below zero!"

"Well, I'm glad you're coming along again this year, Don. After the failures we had last year with the navigating beacon, I feel better knowing you put together the one we're using this year."

"If only I'd had time to test it before we left," Don commented hesitantly, then added: "Just think, though, when we get to the North Pole, WCCO in Minneapolis has arranged for me to carry out a pole-to-pole radio transmission to the South Pole in Antarctica. That's never been done, you know."

"Oh?" Pitzl stifled a yawn as he squinted through the sextant with which he was toying. A man of average height in his early thirties, his lean, muscular body belied his urban life. Friendly, alert eyes reflected his interest in his environment, but a slight, premature frown imparted a sufficiently troubled expression to suggest more than average concern over his course in life.

"Where'd you learn to navigate, Jerry?" Powellek asked him.

"Marine Air Reserve," Pitzl answered, characteristically laconic, "Joined it after my divorce." And after a few pensive moments he added: "George tell you? I quit my job teaching Geography at University High School."

"Why?" Powellek inquired, surprised.

"Getting tired of it. Figure I ought to go on to get my master's degree in Geography when we get back."

"Where?"

"Probably at the University of Minnesota. My dad and step-mother are planning on moving back to St. Paul anyway."

Plaisted watched Pitzl record his sextant's readings, consult a book of navigational tables and then draw a line on a map before him. Plaisted knew nothing about radio or navigation, but he knew a lot about Powellek and Pitzl. And that was enough.

Ralph considered the qualities of the other men. He had had a problem understanding Aufderheide initially. Neither the glory of polar conquests, the promises of public adulation or the flattery of publicity seemed to elicit the response Plaisted needed. For he wanted the man—as much for his arctic knowledge as for the dignity his medical degree would lend Plaisted's pleas for financial support. He had not believed that it could be possible for a man educated to nearly age thirty and a successful doctor to be so childishly vain about such a simple, self-taught skill as photography. But when Plaisted did recognize it, he had only to outline the challenges of this lure before he recruited him as the first avid member to the expedition.

Ironically, he found Art so little interested in the medical aspects that, to get him, he had to agree to staff the base camp with another physician, though insisting he be able to operate a radio as well.

They had been fortunate to find Wes Cook. Twenty-five years of practice as a medical specialist in orthopedics in Columbia, South Carolina, had developed skills potentially useful to the group. But Cook's lifetime interest in radio and hunting Alaskan animals suited him perfectly for the position of base camp physician and radio operator.

He watched George Cavouras and wondered at his wisdom in bringing this man north with him. Now vice-president of the insurance firm with which Plaisted conducted his business, he looked back upon a life as orderly as a crossword puzzle. Married but without children he parked his car in the rented space of a heated garage beneath his high-rise apartment (complete with security guard), shunning even the need to shovel snow from a driveway. After volunteering as treasurer for Plaisted's expedition the previous year he had invited himself along the second time.

No explorer ever selected an expedition member with a more improbable background, Plaisted thought to himself. Yet two months later he was to look back with pride at the man's performance and his own judgment in including him.

The room's tranquility was abruptly shattered when the door burst open and, enveloped in a cloud of swirling snow, the two bodies of Walt Pederson and John Moriarty catapulted into the building.

"Got it beat, Ralph!" Pederson exulted. "By heating the carburetor with a torch I can start any one of those machines any time at any temperature."

"Great, Walt. I knew you'd figure it out," Plaisted replied. And he did know it. He had learned quickly of Pederson's almost incredible mechanical genius. He had needed someone like that and recognized later it would be almost predictable that Pederson would seek him out as soon as he heard about the expedition. Raised near Duluth, Minnesota, in a house too small

George Cavouras

for four, he found himself one of eight children. This may have been the origin of his enormous competitive drive, supporting him through what often seemed to him a lifetime of struggle. Cloaking his enterprising motivation in amiability had led him at age forty to a successful, settled life in a modest-sized central Minnesota community as a businessman (motorcycle and snowmobile sales) with a devoted wife and family. But a lifetime of struggle had apparently left him with uncontrollable competitive instincts, for no degree of attained security seemed to free him from the need to challenge himself again and again. For Pederson even a stroll became a race. With this combination of will and skill Plaisted had the man he needed.

John Moriarty's addition to the group had been nearly as lucky. John had applied his biology education from the University of Minnesota to the problems of food processing for a large Minneapolis firm. He had prepared the dehydrated food for the expedition's first attempt. A highly intelligent, sensitive and artistic young man, he found himself bored with the apparent irrelevance of his work. When Plaisted discovered Moriarty's avocational mechanical interests he agreed to take him along as base camp mechanic. Even without actual experience, Moriarty had already proved to be an ideal choice.

"Why don't you sit down and relax, Ralph?" Jean-Luc Bombardier suggested. "You know we can't move until the storm stops." He was lounging in the corner of the room, casually recording popular tunes from the weather station's phonograph on the small tape recorder he intended to take along on the ice. Even though he had shared the previous expedition's experiences with this man, there was much about him Plaisted did not know. Now approaching age thirty, while not particularly tall, he was strikingly handsome with delicate features, jet-black hair, dark brown eyes, an occasional wispy mustache and a friendly, almost intimate smile. As a scion of the Bombardier family that manufactured the snowmobiles used by the expedition, Plaisted knew Jean-Luc felt a deep responsibility in his participation. The Canadian public viewed him as their representative. There were times when Plaisted suspected the man might be trying also to prove something more: to himself? To his family? To his wife? To his company or his country? He didn't know because, while generally jovial as well as kind and considerate, Bombardier revealed little about himself to others. Before they met, Plaisted had imagined him as a shallow, dissipated playboy. On the ice they had learned to know him as a man of paradoxical qualities. At times demonstrating an almost adolescent pleasure in riding snowmobiles over rough terrain or concern over the appearance of his developing beard, he astonished everyone with such a display of raw courage, dedication to the expedition's goal and endurance of physical hardships, that he earned their almost awesome respect. While he might not understand him completely, Plaisted was fervently grateful for his inclusion in the group.

John Moriarty

"Got Minneapolis on the air for you, Ralph," Andy Horton called out from the adjoining radio room. Nearing fifty, Lieutenant Colonel Andrew Horton was approaching retirement from the United States Air Force when he had heard of Plaisted's plan and invited himself into the group. As an attorney his military duties had provided only an occasional opportunity for exciting duty, but an assignment to Thule, Greenland, had whetted what proved to be a lifetime interest in the arctic. Anxious for an opportunity to return to the north he agreed to renew his amateur radio license and accept the position as one of the expedition's base camp radio operators. While he sometimes incurred the group's good-natured jests when he betrayed his deep devotion to his family on the air during radio contacts with them, he also earned the members' complete trust and fidelity by his unyielding commitment to expedition duties, willing helpfulness and perpetual geniality. Plaisted was happy Horton was along again this time.

This, then was Plaisted's way: to plan for the big things; to promote the financial support; to find, recognize and recruit men with superlative ability in the necessary technical skills; to forge them into an effective unit and hold them by using each man's own special interest as his sole motivating factor; and to depend on them to solve the technical problems as they arose. Their success was his—and so were their failures. It wasn't the ordinary way of the discipline of military command, but it was Plaisted's way. And he intended to take them to the North Pole with it.

Arising to enter the radio room Plaisted turned around briefly to view the group once more. He had the right men, he told himself. satisfied. Now if only the weather would let up!

...

"HOW MUCH FARTHER?" Plaisted shouted into Weldy Phipps ear as he watched the pilot stare alternately at his instrument panel and then out the window.

"Don't know," Weldy replied. If they could have flown directly over the mountains they would have found Ward Hunt Island easily at the end of the pass. But with this thick weather the only way they could get there was to stay a hundred feet off the ice, fly down Nansen Sound and hug the northern shore of Ellesmere until they got there. It was a route Weldy had flown before, but not often, and now the weather and the twilight obscured all but the closest landmarks.

"In this poor light I don't understand how you'll know when we're there," Plaisted commented.

"Looks like we might not be able to," Weldy admitted. "There's a cone-shaped hill on it but it's not high enough to be real useful as a landmark in this dusky light. According to my instruments we should have been there ten minutes ago."

Plaisted stared out the window. It was still a few days too early for the sun to rise above the mountains and the end of the storm still obliterated most of the sun's glow. The higher mountains were lost in a gray haze but the base of those at the shore's edge were still visible. The shadowless diffusion of light blended it all into a foreboding menace. He shuddered. The expedition now depended on a slender supply line that stretched from Montreal to Resolute Bay, to Eureka, to Tanquary Fjord—a line that now had to be stretched one more step, to their anticipated base camp at tiny Ward Hunt Island, just off the northern tip of its gigantic neighbor Ellesmere.

The fuel dump at Tanquary was vital, and Weldy had flown George Cavouras and Wes Cook there the previous day to begin the laborious process of digging last year's fuel drums out from under this winter's snow drifts, and transporting the drums one at a time from the rocky coast half a mile inland to an area flat enough to land an airplane. It was a thankless task, but critical to the entire operation. From Tanquary, Weldy would have to fly the fuel to Ward Hunt Island—if it could be found—and on to the ice party, perhaps with a stop at an anticipated on-ice refueling cache as well, which they figured would need to be set up halfway from Ward Hunt to the Pole. Assuming, of course, that they made it that far.

Suddenly Ralph felt the plane bank steeply and head back in the direction from which they had come. Alarmed, he asked anxiously: "Aren't giving up and going home, are we?"

"No," Weldy replied. "I just recognized the steep bluff of Cape Columbia. We've gone fifteen miles too far. We'll fly back for twelve minutes and try to find Ward Hunt Island."

Plaisted continued to stare out the window but it all looked alike to him. Even after they found it, landing might be difficult. The plane, he felt, was overloaded. Besides himself and Ernst Michel, the motion picture photographer, there were Powellek, Bombardier, and Pederson, three snowmobiles and a variety of gear. Weldy had wanted him to wait another day for the storm to abate but Plaisted had insisted.

Again he felt the plane bank. This time there was a more cheerful note in Weldy's voice as he announced: "That's it. There's the cone-shaped hill. It's too dark to see them but those huts must be right at its base."

"Will you land on the little lake behind the hill?" asked co-pilot Ken Lee.

"No. Can't take a chance with the hills around it in the dark. Have to set down on the shelf ice in front of the huts," Weldy explained.

"But you can't see well enough to check the surface first," Lee objected.

"Wouldn't help anyway," Weldy countered. "At these temperatures we're leaving a wake of ice vapor behind us fifty feet wide which would fog out any place we'd fly over first. Buckle up tight. We have to go in blind!"

Walt Pederson was looking out the window, talking into his tape recorder.

"I can see the mountains now," he reported to the microphone. "We're about fifty feet off the ground. There are the huts. I see them now. They're almost covered with snow. Man, they look lonesome. And the wind is really blowing yet. I can see plumes of snow skimming off the roofs. Down to about twenty feet now. There's the surface. Say—it looks rough. Just about touchdown. A little more and—that's the roughest—oops, we bounced off and hit again—HEY! That was a hard one. The gear is being tossed around in here like—ouch!—a salad—There's another—and another . . ."

He never finished the recording as a sleeping bag, caroming off the wall, tore the microphone from his hand.

Weldy was fighting the wheel. As soon as he felt the craft rebound from the initial touchdown he had slammed it forward to hold the nose ski down. It had held for a moment but the surface was obviously badly hummocked. When the right ski struck one nearly two feet high it was only because of their low speed that he was able to bring the wing back down again to avoid a ground loop. Again and again the skis collided with the hard-edged snowdrifts. First the left ski, then the nose, then the left again. The wildly convulsive movements themselves endangered the craft for the heavy machines were being hurled about inside with enough force to threaten not only the occupants but the fuselage itself. Gradually he felt the impacts lessen as their forward speed slowed and with enormous relief he switched off the power to the engines as the plane coasted to a stop. Glancing out the window Weldy saw the fragmented ends of the ropes controlling the left ski flapping in the wind.

With a single-mindedness, irksome to Weldy now, but which he came to admire later, Plaisted ignored the dangers they had all just survived, leaned over Weldy's shoulder and suggested: "I'll help you fix the ski while the others get the huts in shape. You can leave early in the morning. If you can get the four sleds, one more machine and Aufderheide in here by noon we'll leave for the North Pole tomorrow!"

4

We've Got to Get Organized

THROUGH THE WINDOW THEY COULD SEE WALT racing down the slope from the smallest hut toward the plane, a red sled roped behind his snowmobile following along convulsively. *Walt*, Art thought to himself, *always seems to race any machine he drives*. Even before the whine of the Twin Otter's turbines had subsided he jerked the door open, shouting exultantly: "It's sixty-two below here this morning!" And no one questioned it, when Moriarty's first searing breath of that cold air triggered a paroxysm of coughing.

After unloading the supplies they had brought, John and Art dragged their bags of personal gear up to the larger of the two huts emanating chimney smoke. The scene revealed when they opened the door startled them into the realization they really were on an expedition.

A janeway hut at Ward Hunt

These were "janeway huts," of the same half-round shape as the familiar Quonset huts of World War II fame, but less permanently constructed. They had a wooden skeleton covered by a thick-double layer of quilted canvas enclosing insulating material; while an airlock style double door kept the Arctic weather at bay. The buildings had once been new; now shreds of canvas hanging from the arched roof disgorged a gentle shower of insulating material with each shuddering gust of wind. Four cots were crowded close together along the sidewalls, the head of each toward the warmer central part of the building, creating a narrow aisle down the center. Piled indiscriminately on top, between and beneath the cots as well as hanging from nails above everywhere were the several tons of items imagined necessary to reach the North Pole. Powellek, Plaisted, Bombardier, and Ernst Michel were clustered at the far end around an inconspicuous stove. Their breath and clothing testified to the heater's inadequacy, as did occasional mounds of sifting snow deposited on some of the cots. Upon their entry Plaisted whirled, glared and greeted them by crying:

"All right, now everybody get your stuff together. We're leaving for the North Pole in half an hour with whoever's ready!"

One and one half hours later they were ready—or at least thought they were. The weeks of frustrating delay now compounded the rising excitement as the moment of departure approached. Plaisted charged about the room performing a perpetual series of activities—moving a box to another cot, hanging up one of a thousand items lying on the floor, remixing piles of mixed-up supplies—all accompanied by a stream-of-consciousness almost shouted rhetorically.

"Goddam it! It'll be one o'clock before we get goin' today. Why can't you guys have your stuff ready? Been sittin' around for two weeks doin' nothin'. You're gonna work this year or get off the ice. Whose socks are these? Ain't never gonna be warm in here 'less John shovels snow as high as he can around the outside of these buildings. Keep your eye on that generator, John. Read the book so you can fix it if it fouls up. Without it we got no radio. Damn it, Art, don't take so many extra clothes along; you got to share a bag with Ernst. Christ, I froze my knees yesterday kneeling down fixing the carburetor and we ain't even on the ice yet. Who's got a piece of rope? I don't want none of . . ."

Like the rest, Weldy was ignoring Ralph's ravings. He reclined atop the supplies on the cot adjacent to the one Art had chosen and amusedly watched him rearrange the contents of his bag into photographic, navigational, medical and personal supplies. Although he didn't say a word, the eloquence of his expression declared his conviction that this disorganized, confused group of suburbanites weren't going to get any farther this year than last. "And I'll have to bail them out of trouble in the end," he thought.

Packing completed, Art zipped up his field parka and went out. It was pure pandemonium outside. The unmuffled engines of at least one of the four machines was always running, challenging any attempt at conversation. Walt was crouched over the engine of a machine, coaxing its stubborn carburetor with the flame of a gasoline-soaked rag. After about a minute he vainly tried starting the motor again.

"These going to run in this cold weather, Walt?" Art shouted in his ear.

"Ski-Doos are okay. It's the gas."

"What's the matter with it?" Art inquired naively.

Walt's disgust was evident as he answered: "We haven't got any of our own gas up here yet so we're using a drum of World War II gas I found behind the building. Weldy will have to drop us our own on the ice when this stuff runs out. Trouble with this stuff is that it's so cold the colored dye has clumped out and is clogging up the lines."

Dismayed at the lack of planning to provide gasoline at the advance camp for the machines, Art stared at the gasoline passing through the transparent plastic fuel line, watching the red precipitated dye particles pass into the carburetor. Suddenly a large glob of ice passed through the line and when it reached the carburetor the engine choked and stopped.

"Plenty of water in that old gas too, Walt," he commented.

"Most of that's from the hydraulic fluid," Walt answered.

"The what?"

"We don't have the oil up here yet either that we need to mix with the gas for lubrication, so I'm using the fluid from the hydraulic line drained out of that old tractor by the other hut. It's pretty bad but I'll keep 'em running!"

Dazed by the knowledge they were going out on the Arctic Ocean's pack ice with twenty five year old gasoline lubricated with ice-clogged used hydraulic fluid in weather of sixty degrees below zero, Art turned to Powellek who was carefully padding the radio container in a sled with a sleeping bag.

"Where do I pack my stuff, Don?" Art inquired.

"Wherever you want to. Nobody's planned how the sleds should be packed."

Viewing the mountains of items piled outside awaiting packing into the four small sleds, Art stood there mentally arranging the gear into appropriate combinations, and concluded nine more sleds would be required to accommodate it all. His indecision was terminated when Plaisted burst from the hut, shouting: "All right, you guys. Help me get this stuff loaded up. Who brought this out—we ain't takin' that. Don, go get the other tent. We haven't got enough rubber straps to hold this stuff on with. Count the sleeping bags—we got all six of 'em? Let's take an extra lantern along. John, that oatmeal we had for breakfast was good—go get a couple of boxes and throw 'em in. How about that . . ."

It was a remarkably haphazard way to pack for an expedition but it was remarkably Plaisted's way. Back in Minnesota they all knew it would be this way when the time came and he didn't disappoint them. Detecting his expression he came over to Art and said, "I know what you want to say, Art, but if we wait here until everything is ready we won't leave 'til June. If we move out there on that ice and run out of gas they'll *have* to get the stuff up here. So we're going with what we have and let them catch up with us!"

Unloading the Twin Otter at Ward Hunt Island

Ten minutes later the four sleds were loaded to the point of upset and Ralph announced departure time had arrived. Jean-Luc asked, "What about the rest of the stuff, Ralph?"

"We ain't got room for it so we ain't takin' it!" Plaisted declared.

Looking over the pile of unpacked items Art retrieved the sextant and tied it on one of the sleds. Bombardier and Pederson finally got all four machines running at the same time so they left—three times. The first two departures were for the photographers, much to Walt's dismay, since he was having great problems keeping the idling engines operational.

It was 1:30 p.m. when six excited men left Ward Hunt Island on March 7, 1968, bound for the North Pole. Weldy, staring at the tiny figures disappearing over the distant icescape turned to Moriarty and commented: "They act like a bunch of Cub Scouts going to the zoo!" and several minutes later added, "I told Plaisted to go dead north. I saw a couple of big floes out there that'll help him. But look at them—going straight northwest. It's going to be just as fouled up as last year!"

The first five miles north of Ward Hunt Island is relatively smooth shelf ice. This was ground-based ice more than one hundred feet thick, the Ward Hunt Ice Shelf (now gone because of global warming). Over this shelf ice Bombardier, like last year, led the group, followed by Plaisted, then Powellek and finally Pederson. While Ernst rode on Plaisted's sled, Art found himself clinging to the one behind Powellek. These sleds were little more than eight foot fiberglass toboggans with slightly raised sides and the first five miles of travel confirmed Art's fears that they would defy all efforts to ride on them. Already top-heavy with excessive gear, they could be kept upright only if the passenger shifted his weight and rode them much like a bicycle. But to do this it was necessary to kneel on them and hang on to a strap or rope. The resulting compression at these spots for even as little as five minutes in these temperatures caused frozen knees and fingers, relieved only when an unanticipated lurch would pitch the rider from the sled, allowing a moment of exercise. Then, too, the engine of each machine stopped at least once during that time, and Pederson had to teach each of them how to thaw out the ice trapped in the carburetor. Condensed exhaust moisture also left a trail of ice ten feet wide behind each machine, obscuring it and all surface features, preventing tandem operation of the caravan. Their exhilaration somewhat cooled by these initial problems they were more appropriately prepared emotionally for the realities which awaited them as the edge of the pack ice neared.

They had expected rough ice here—but not ice like this. The waters of the Arctic Ocean were covered by a thin crust of ice, from three to fifteen feet thick. But it was not the smooth, rarely broken surface characterizing most inland lakes in winter. Like all oceans, the Arctic's waters were driven by currents, tides, and winds that kept its ice cover broken up and moving much of the time. Such fragments might vary from twenty feet to five miles in diameter. Where the moving pack ice was driven against the unyielding shore, the pileup created the world's roughest and wildest ice surface.

Bombardier had parked his machine at the edge of the pack at the foot of the highest mound apparent so that, from its top, it would afford him an overview of the area from which to choose a route. Scrambling up the various blocks of ice, carefully avoiding the more jagged edges, all joined him at its summit and surveyed the first part of their journey. They had expected some bad ice but this was the worst they had ever seen. The pile on which they were standing inclined steeply downward at least fifty feet into a pit-like area,

All you have to do is cut a road and it's easy

the floor of which contained irregular boulders of ice with cracks between them large enough to swallow the entire machines. Beyond this lay ice fragments of countless shapes and sizes tumbled in every imaginable plane. There was no flat, horizontal surface the size of a kitchen table within their vision.

Ernst was the first to break the silence. “God, we can never cross that!” he exclaimed.

“It’s got more snow on it than last year’s ice,” Pederson noted, groping for some optimistic thought. “We can get onto it by that big block over there,” he pointed, “fill in the crack beyond it with snow and work our way over to that area where the pieces are smaller.” But even as he spoke his voice trailed off in doubt.

Standing at the edge of the pack ice, Ralph Plaisted stared out at that rubble of icy obstacles. Just the memory of those agonizing hours the previous year made him shudder. “Why did I come back again?” he asked himself. “We got away alive last year. No man knows what that ice will do. This year when the ice moves again maybe we’ll be on the wrong floe. These men trust me; yet I don’t know what will happen out there.”

Bombardier was looking out over the pack too, but turning from side to side. Pointing finally to the right he told Plaisted, “If we chisel down that small one over there and fill in the crevice behind with snow we can work our way over to that part there where it doesn’t look so bad.”

The sudden throb of the Otter’s engines intruded upon their reverie. Weldy was leaving Ward Hunt Island to go back to Eureka. “Look at Weldy,” Pederson called out. “He’s flying out over the pack ice. What’s he doing that for?”

No one answered him as they watched the plane leave the island and, instead of flying south to Eureka, pass directly north and head out over the pack ice.

A mile out it turned, flew back over the island and then headed in the same track out over the pack again. Suddenly Don realized what Weldy was saying.

“He’s trying to tell us we’re off course—that we should enter the pack over there and head out in the direction he’s flying,” he called.

Leaping aboard the nearest snowmobile he raced over along the edge of the pack in the direction indicated and arrived just as Weldy passed over the third and last time. While waving to him a tumbling, small red object became visible in the sky above, fluttering to the snow nearby. Inside the package of cigarettes, which is what it proved to be, was a scrap of paper bearing the message: "You're forty-five degrees off course. Enter the pack here. Best ice ahead. Two pans eight miles due north."

Don grinned as he read it. "When we can't even stay on course for the first five miles over smooth ice I wonder what Weldy expects from us over the next 450?" he murmured.

"Forget it and let's go!" shouted Walt as he impulsively drove his machine off the smooth shelf ice and entered the pack though a narrow channel between two ice boulders. Almost immediately he disappeared. They all rushed forward simultaneously, thoroughly alarmed. Both the machine and the sled were lying on their sides, while Walt was straining to right them. He had driven right off the edge of a flat-topped block, dropped about three feet, struck another at an angle and upset. Unhurt, he looked up sheepishly.

Furious, Plaisted strode over, reached down and turned off the engine. Turning to the rest he shouted: "All right, come off it; this is an expedition, not a Boy Scout campout. Let's get a couple of things straight right now. And listen good so I only have to say it once. Jean-Luc—you go first. You pick the way and the rest of us go where you tell us. We'll keep you loaded lightest so you can scout out the best path. Walt, you stay last. You're the only one who can really keep these machines going in this weather with that gooped-up gas. If you're up ahead and one of us breaks down we'll lose a lot of time trying to catch up with you and send you back. So you stay last, see? Don, you drive a machine behind Jean-Luc. Try to keep a little behind him and give him a chance to move around to find the best path. Don't push him too hard. He's loaded lighter than you are so you might get stuck while he's scouting if you follow too close. Art, ride on Don's sled. That way you can take pictures when you want to and help him push and shovel when he gets stuck. I'll follow in the other machine behind you. Ernst, you ride on the sled behind my machine and hop off to take movies whenever you want to. Now listen, Ernst, and everybody—nobody runs on the ice. These pans got lots of cracks in 'em one or two feet wide. You can't see 'em because they're filled with snow. But if you run and your foot goes down into a crack you'll break a leg. I don't have to tell you that you can't put on enough clothes to stay warm out here if you don't move. Break a leg and you can't move. Figure out the rest yourself. So everybody walks—and carefully. Got that?"

The group nodded soberly. Nobody had to say it aloud: a broken leg was a death sentence in the Arctic. Plaisted continued, "Another thing: somebody gets stuck, everybody pushes. And watch the axes and chisels when you're working on the pressure ridges. You guys haven't swung an axe since last year so watch your feet and the next fella's. Watch your breathing, too. It's sixty below. You work too hard and you'll breathe too fast and deep. Do that and you'll freeze your lungs. And let's keep an eye on each other's face for frostbite. We're goin' all the way this year. We won't get there with anybody who's fooling around, getting careless or not doing his share. So remember that. All of it: Now, Jean-Luc, get out there and pick a path. And the rest of us, let's go."

They had needed that. With the pecking order reestablished, each man proceeded to his duties in an orderly manner, eager now to begin the real purpose of the expedition. Trailing his lightly loaded sled Bombardier led the group. Within fifty feet he was stopped by a litter of broken ice fragments piled fifteen feet high. The others did not even start their engines but removed the tools from their sleds, walked up to the obstruction and spent a vigorous twenty minutes with ice chisels, axes and shovels, clearing and leveling a path through the area. The task did not appear to be more than half completed when Jean-Luc raised his hand, waved them clear and returned to his machine. Viewing the littered chunks of ice, the sixty percent grade, the irregular surface and the height of the rise they could hardly believe he would attempt it. Yet it was with awe that they witnessed the verification of his judgment. He started the machine, and, with its track spinning and clutching at the ice, the entire unit careening from side to side with the following sled caroming off the sides of ice boulders, he guided his snowmobile up the steep, icy slope, across the top and plunged down the far side.

"You're a tin can cowboy, Jean-Luc!" yelled Don. "A performance like that on a motorcycle back home will get you a blue ribbon at our state fair next fall."

"Jean-Luc, we'll save more time if you go back and drive the other three across yourself," Ralph ordered. "The rest of us can't drive that well and at least one will drop his machine off the 'road'. Even if he doesn't get hurt it would cost us another half hour getting it back up again."

While they repaired the "road" damage created by each transit, Bombardier brought the other three machines with sleds through the obstacle.

For the next two hours they pushed, heaved, yanked, shoveled, chiseled, lifted and carried those machines and equipment through the most chaotic ice in the world. While icicles dangled from their beards, they were soaking their clothing in sweat. They were literally inching their way along now, very gradually threading a sinuous path through this nightmarish surface. When an iced-up engine stopped Art's machine at 3:45 p.m. he looked about to find the sun gone and the sky the peculiar grainy texture reminiscent of a ground glass surface. Uneasy, he turned to Plaisted and remarked:

"I don't like the sky, Ralph. It looks heavy, like it often does before a blow."

"Damn, we're just getting started. I hate to quit already," he replied. "How sure are you?"

"Not sure at all; just worried. But you can't fight the light much longer anyway. The days are short now, and within half an hour it will gray out. You won't be able to move then anyway."

Plaisted studied the terrain ahead. It all looked as uninviting as what they had come through. There was no real floe where they were now but the irregularities of the icy surface had been somewhat smoothed by heavy snow.

Long, hard work

"All right, Art," he agreed reluctantly. "We'll camp. This spot okay?"

"Has to be. Nothing better around."

Ralph shut off his engine, as did Don, and they began unloading the sleds. Jean-Luc ahead turned, saw them and understood, coming back to join them. Walt hurried up from the rear and, without turning off his engine, ran up to Ralph, grabbed his arm and demanded, "Why are we quitting already? We can still see and we've got plenty of gas. Let's go on a while yet."

"Art says it might blow and we got less than half an hour travel left anyway."

"If we got half an hour let's use half an hour. If it blows we'll quit,"

"Easier said than done, "Art answered. "This flat spot is big enough for us. From the top of that pressure ridge I could see there's no camping spot anyplace we'll be for the next hour."

"We'll stay here tonight, Walt," declared Plaisted. "Now get your sled unpacked and service the machines so they'll run tomorrow."

Reluctantly Pederson obeyed. The two tents were dragged out. The men were rather clumsy setting them up, not having done so for nearly a year. After misplacing the supporting poles several times they eventually managed its erection and Art walked over to the nearest sled containing a shovel. Turning back toward the tent the sight made the intervening eleven months fade into a day.

The tent was shaped like a four-sided teepee. It was entered through a circular opening part way up the sloping front wall. To seal it from the wind a thirty-inch long canvas sleeve was sewn to the edge of the opening that could be withdrawn into the double-walled tent, twisted and tied. Plaisted had never really mastered that sleeve entrance during the entire previous expedition and, as if on signal, the men stopped now and watched. Again they weren't disappointed. He stomped over to the tent, dropped down to his knees and picked up the sleeve. Drawing it over his head and chest he propelled himself forward with his feet. Instantly the peaceful air of that part of the Arctic Ocean was split by a muffled, sputtering sequence of oaths distinctly unflattering to the tent designer.

It required two of them to extract him from his predicament and get him appropriately entombed in its interior. Thereupon he promptly demanded they begin handing in the sleeping bags, stove and other camping equipment. It wasn't easy for Don and Art to keep up with the continuous flow of conflicting orders emerging from inside.

This confused type of camp activity was exactly what they had come to expect, and so it now imparted an air of comfortable reassurance. Secretly all of them forgave him for any display of intemperance, for all knew he really did have the coldest, most unpleasant duty of the group. Kneeling down in snow and air of more than sixty degrees below zero, unable to move much, he found it necessary to carry out many of the chores with bare hands handling cold metal. With gasoline's notorious reluctance to vaporize at these temperatures, even starting a balky stove inevitably resulted in brittle, white fingers before success was achieved. Those frozen hands just simply seemed to warm a little faster if addressed with the appropriate vigor. The progressive series of frustrations inevitably led to a gradually rising tempo and volume with which his spontaneous rhetoric was delivered. Those doing chores outside and listening had found it possible to gauge the stage of completion of duties inside by the vehemence of his curses.

It was a surprise, therefore, when they stopped abruptly. They looked up reflexively to see Walt kneeling down, his head thrust through the sleeve entrance talking to Plaisted. Walt was speaking in such low tones they couldn't hear him at all but periodically they could understand an occasional phrase of Ralph's answer. "what? the tools? . . . but you can't . . . tomorrow . . . go ahead . . ."

Walt backed out, stuffed the sleeve into the entrance and walked over to his machine. Unhooking the sled, he jerked the starter rope petulantly and to their astonishment disappeared down the trail they had made back toward base camp. In a few moments only the ice fog trail created by his machine betrayed his departure.

Slowly and clumsily the erection of the second tent, the radio antenna and other camp chores were completed. As Plaisted's complaints about the cold gradually decreased in volume, frequency and intensity they recognized the supper hour approaching, and when he demanded they refill all the pots with snow it was obviously time to come in. Stowing their parkas in the sled outside with the other gear to prevent their thawing, they eagerly wriggled through the sleeve entrance.

As the welcome blast of warm air from the gasoline stove enveloped their faces they felt the fatigue engendered by the day's efforts. Gratefully they sat on the rolled up sleeping bags. Plaisted thrust a cup into Don's hands and poured the cold water of melted snow into it, for he had learned last year the extent to which a day's work on the ice in cold temperatures can dehydrate a man. While Don was gulping the water, Jean-Luc asked Plaisted the obvious question.

"Where did Walt go?"

"Back to Ward Hunt Island."

"Back to—but why?"

"He forgot his tools."

No one spoke. But all had similar thoughts. An expedition proposing to go to the North Pole—and the mechanic forgot his tools!

The silence was interrupted only by an oath from Plaisted as he cut his right index finger while opening a tin of chocolate. Thrusting it into Art's lap he demanded, "Damn it, Art, fix it, will you?"

Inspecting the wound, Art replied "It's not much, Ralph, but we can't afford an infection now so wash it up while I get the suture kit from the sled. We'll thaw that out while we eat, and I'll sew up the cut after dinner."

The remainder of the water was sacrificed to the cause of Plaisted's injury. Art returned after an inordinately long delay outside. He carried no bag or kit but instead reached into his pocket, tore a fragment from his handkerchief and bandaged the finger with it. When a roll of tape appeared from the other pocket Plaisted inquired,"Ain't you gonna sew it up?"

"Can't."

Why not?"

"Looks like the suture kit and the medical bag didn't get packed on the sled when we left."

"My God," Plaisted snorted, "Can't I depend on you guys for anything? Don, get on the radio, see if you can contact Moriarty at base camp and tell him to send the medical kit out with Walt."

"I can't," Don muttered dejectedly.

"Why not?"

"We've got all the radio equipment along but nobody brought the generators that we designed to be run off the Ski-Doos."

"Jesus Christ, do I have to do everything myself?" Plaisted stormed. "You guys had a whole year to get ready. If you hadn't spent so much time posing for newspaper pictures and making like Arctic heroes you'd have been better off. Now we'll lose another half day sending Walt back for the rest of the stuff after he gets back here tomorrow. My God, you'd think we're on a picnic instead of goin' to the North Pole, the way you guys forget your stuff."

And dipping a cup into the soup bowl angrily he thrust it at Ernst.

"Here, hurry up and drink your soup so we can go to bed," he commanded. "It'll be a long day tomorrow!"

"Can I have a spoon, please?" Ernst inquired.

"Shut up and drink it," Ralph growled. "I forgot the silverware."

...

JOHN MORIARTY HAD NEVER BEEN NORTH of Minnesota before. Even before the thrill of the ice party's noisy departure had subsided, Weldy had turned to him and said, "John, have Ken show you how to run the radio, but don't take too long. We have to get two men to Tanquary Fjord dig out those gasoline barrels and build a runway there so we can keep supplying the ice party. Ken and I will take Andy Horton and Fred Clark and drop them off at Tanquary for a few days."

The fifteen available minutes had hardly seemed long enough for a complete course in radio operation as well as instructions for generator maintenance and repair of the space heaters. When Weldy had left, just a few minutes after the ice party departed, Jesus before Pilate could not have felt as abandoned as did Moriarty. Alone in the Arctic, in a partly snowclogged shack at sixty degrees below zero, John clutched the radio microphone as fervently as a drowning man would a life preserver. He listened desperately to Weldy's routine communications with Eureka, tried talking to Weldy himself, then reluctantly turned it off later as only static poured from the speaker.

He was, he realized a few hours later, officially the loneliest man on earth. The six-man ice party was to his north, getting farther away by the minute. To the south, he guessed that the nearest human beings might have been Andy Horton and Fred Clark, camped 120 miles away at Tanquary Fjord—if Weldy had gotten them there. If not, the nearest actual settlement was Eureka, population ten, another 140 miles beyond that. The "Mayor of Ward Hunt Island" had won his election in a landslide, 1 to 0, a unanimous vote with 100 percent turnout. Somehow, Moriarty didn't feel like celebrating.

His biggest worry was that a polar bear would find him. He was sitting on top of perhaps the largest cache of food in a radius of several hundred miles, the supplies waiting to be ferried out to the ice party when needed. The expedition had two rifles, one with the ice party, and the other would be with Andy and Fred at Tanquary. John had no gun, and, looking around the hut, there was nothing much useful to make a weapon with. And he was keenly aware that the canvas walls of the janeway hut would be no match for a hungry bear. Even if he managed to scare the bear away, it was still entirely possible for an animal of that size to destroy the hut and its contents, leaving him with no chance to survive the Arctic elements.

Recognizing his dependence upon the electrical generator, he went outside to the generator shack, checked its gasoline supply and wiring. The abrupt rising of the wind surprised him and drove him back into the "warm" hut, taking the maintenance instruction booklet with him. Lighting a gas lantern he sat down and began studying the directions. He found it difficult to concentrate though. Having had no previous experiences with polar bears, every sound of the wind was misinterpreted.

John kicked around the empty hut, fixed himself dinner, tried to read the manual again, then gave up and made up a cot, thinking he'd turn in early. But it was cold in here, he realized, and checking the catalytic heater, it had stopped. He would have to fix it himself, since he knew he could not survive without it. But he knew nothing about the heater. He would have to teach himself from the manuals, and perhaps even from disassembling the device itself. He dug around to find the manual and began to read, but once again he had a hard time concentrating in the gathering cold.

The wind howled outside, rattling the canvas walls. He was utterly, totally alone. There was no telling how far away the ice party was. Ten miles maybe? Twenty? Even if it were only one mile, that would still be too far for rescue if a polar bear should wander by.

Suddenly a loud crash pounded against the outside of the hut. The canvas walls shook. John's heart froze. As he quickly looked around the hut for a weapon, the inner door of the airlock burst open with another loud clatter. A large furry head poked into the dark room.

It was Walt Pederson in his parka. "I forgot my tools," he said casually. It might have been several minutes later before John's heart started beating again.

5

AIR SUPPLY

IT WAS NINE BEFORE THE ICE PARTY AROSE. It had been a miserable night for, in the absence of available caribou hides, even the catalytic heater had not been able to overcome the effect of the uninsulated floor. They were all pleased to hear Don Powellek outside a few minutes later suddenly call out excitedly:

"Ralph! Ralph! I found the emergency Honda generator in the sled with Walt's stuff!"

"That's great. Warm it up, get it started and get on that radio. Find out why Walt ain't back yet. I'll make breakfast."

Twenty minutes later after a few abortive attempts, the encouraging purr of the operating generator penetrated the tent wall and a minute later the electric crackle as the radio came alive. Since the tents were pitched adjacent to each other all could hear Don's calm, professional voice calling, "CJU 942 this is Mobile One. CJU 942 this is Mobile One."

Surprisingly within half a minute, Wes Cook's quiet answer floated from Eureka across the mountains to the pack ice and poured from the set's little speaker. "Mobile One, this is CJU 942, Wes here. Go ahead, Don. How's everything out there?"

"Under control here, Wes, but we sent Walt back for tools last night and he hasn't come back. Know anything about it?"

"Yes, Don. I talked to John at base camp last night. Seems as though Walt thought he saw a polar bear coming in last night and he won't go out again without a gun until the wind goes down."

"Stand by, Wes," Don replied, and then, shouting to the other tent he asked, "Hear that, Ralph? What'll I tell him?"

Plaisted was silent for a moment, muttering to himself, then answered: "Talk to Walt, tell him you and Jean-Luc will meet him at the edge of the pack with a gun at noon sharp. Tell him to bring the other stuff we forgot—and give Wes the list of stuff for Weldy to drop to us this afternoon."

"CJU 942, this is Mobile One," Don resumed. And when Wes answered again he learned that Wes had a schedule with base camp at 09:45. Don relayed Plaisted's instructions and emphasized their need for caribou hides, ice picks and a shovel or two. After signing clear, it was with almost loving care that he packed up the equipment, proud of its unprecedented performance at these temperatures.

When they heard Powellek and Bombardier leave, Plaisted told Art, "Knock their tent down and pack up as much as you can while I make breakfast. Eat as soon as they get back and then take off."

Art dressed and went outside. The bitter cold made him cough and even mild exertion caused his heart to race. The sun wasn't up yet but the bare ice of the ridges reflected a gray light already tinged with pink. Art walked over to the sled, removed his camera and checked the temperature. The thermometer registered minus fifty-eight degrees Fahrenheit Pulling off his heavy mitts, he operated the shutter skeptically, but was surprised to hear the mechanism grind slowly through its sequence. Several tries later, the camera emitted a "click" familiar to normal operation. Leaning forward slightly he plunged his now white, numb, bare hands behind his belt, into his trousers and down between his thighs. Several minutes later he straightened up, replaced his warmed hands into his mittens and happily prowled the area for photographic opportunities. The tent was still up, the gear still unpacked and Art was still taking pictures when Powellek and Bombardier returned an hour later with Walt.

...

JEAN-LUC BOMBARDIER WAS BREATHLESS when he reached the top of the pressure ridge. This ridge had been unusually high. He was grateful for the snow that had been blown between many of the ice fragments, for the support it provided the snowmobiles proved of great advantage. But it did create a treacherous walking surface, for thin snow bridges frequently collapsed under his feet and it was only his heavy clothing that prevented injury in some of such falls.

His view of the surface beyond this ridge was his first encouraging experience since entering the pack ice yesterday. Immediately before him lay a flat, unbroken, snow-covered surface which extended northward at least five hundred feet.

"A floe!" he exclaimed, "A real pack floe!"

Its surface, riding several feet above the level of the surrounding ice, betrayed its thickness and age. The high pressure ridge completely encircled it, a silent record of the pressure it had resisted from the surrounding ice fragments and a mute testimonial to its own enormous strength.

All day yesterday and today Jean-Luc had dreamed of floes as he was forced instead to fight his way through the chaos of jumbled ice. Foot by foot he had had to pick his way as gingerly as though he was crossing a floor of broken glass barefooted. It was not only a matter of struggling through the area himself; the following sleds would pick the same path so he must judge each possible alternative route by the ability of the least competent driver in the group. Again and again he traversed a problem area successfully only to stop beyond it and use his ice axe to smooth a surface too threatening for the other machines. He knew the two miles of progress such methods permitted daily would bring them no nearer the pole this year than last. He had longed for the terrain he hoped they would find farther out on the pack ice—larger, discrete, rather flat floes of ice separated from each other by pressure ridges. True, such ridges were higher than this jumbled ice near the shore, but once crossed the smoother surfaces of the floes permitted more rapid traverse. It had been that way near the end of last year's trip. He remembered it was somewhat like crossing a series of fields, climbing the high fences that enclosed them.

"Now here's our first floe," he said out loud. "We ought to be able to move a little faster after this."

Whether it was the optimism inspired by the floe or the incongruity of a man alone on the Arctic Ocean's pack ice speaking out loud was not clear but he began to chuckle. Bombardier had found himself talking out loud last year too, and when relating this to a friend upon return from the expedition, had been reminded that this was a common reaction in men in isolated circumstances. Joshua Slocum, Charles Lindbergh, and even Richard Byrd had yielded to the compulsion.

And it certainly was a lonely role he was playing. In the morning Jean-Luc left a half hour or so before the rest and his lightly loaded sled quickly carried him out of sight of the group. It was he who first faced the unknown ice ahead. It was he who risked encountering a polar bear alone and unarmed. Each morning he wondered whether this was the day he would break through thin ice and, alone, be unable to get out. Or the day a wind would obliterate his path. If so he knew he and the party would never find each other again.

Fortunately the attention demanded by his chores permitted him little time for speculation of such dismal possibilities. Scanning the pressure ridge of the far side of the floe his practiced eye was drawn to a depression in its skyline. Several large fragments in this area were lying flat and he accepted this as a probable exit route from the floe. But would it be the appropriate direction—north? Lacking an instinctive sense of direction he found it a nettlesome bother. As Jean-Luc gazed about him aimlessly he became aware of Ellesmere's mountain range outlined low against the horizon to his left. No longer visible from the ice surface, he could now still visualize them clearly from the top of the pressure ridge where he stood. He had thought he was facing north, yet if he was, those mountains should be directly behind him.

"Damn," he declared aloud. "Drifted west again. I'll have to wait here until the rest catch up and find out how far off we are. Art will get me squared away again, and I can take off while they're hacking a way through this pressure ridge to the floe."

Bombardier sat down on an ice slab, extracted a cigarette from his pocket and lit it. The dry, bitterly cold air inhaled in rapid breaths caused by his exertions had dried his throat passages so that the first puff of smoke triggered a paroxysm of coughing violent enough to make him feel the ice under his feet vibrate. Disgusted that even this simple pleasure was denied him, he flipped the still burning cigarette from the ridge. His eye idly followed the trailing arc of smoke as the cigarette bounced and disappeared between several ice boulders into a dark crack. A slight movement of the crack held his attention, and he stared in horror at the realization that the ice vibration he had felt resulted not from his coughing but from the fact the floe had cracked at the edge. It had become detached now from its adjoining ice, and the black water of the underlying Arctic Ocean was being exposed in the slowly widening lead, which separated him from his machine and the remainder of the party.

...

THE HUMMOCK LOOMING IN FRONT OF DON POWELLEK'S machine appeared formidably rough. Once again he slowed down and once again his machine

A barely averted catastrophe

bogged down. And once again Art jumped off Powellek's sled which he had been riding and helped push the reluctant snowmobile. Ernst (with Plaisted riding the sled) directed his machine around them, accelerated instead of slowing down, and easily crossed the difficult area. Stopping beyond, he and Plaisted walked back to assist the others.

"Goddamit, Don, you gotta give her guts when you come to a steep climb. If you slow down like this you'll hang it up every time," declared Plaisted impatiently.

"Lay off him, Ralph," Art declared. "He knows that, but he knows too that if he does I stand a good chance of being bounced off the trailing sled and might get hurt. And he cares a lot about that."

"Well, we won't get to the Pole this way. We could get there faster by walking."

"Forget it; we'll work out a system. But have you noticed something else? Every time Bombardier comes to an obstruction in his path he chooses the left alternative. He's gradually swung around now so that we're heading for a west pole, not the North Pole!"

"Art, you've got to do something about that. Can't you teach him how to use a compass or something?"

"Not practical, Ralph. Like I showed you last year, the magnetic North Pole is not at the top of the world where the geographic pole is. Instead, it's down at about seventy-five degrees north latitude and we're at about eighty-sour. In other words, we're more than 500 miles north of the magnetic pole so our compass points south from here. Even so we could correct for that but it's so close that the compass is sluggish and requires about five minutes to settle down and register a reliable reading. That's too long. However, if he would just alternate every time—go left once and choose the right direction the next time he might hold a lot better course than this. I'll talk to him."

"He's getting too far out ahead anyway. He shouldn't be that far away alone. He could get hurt." Ralph replied as he returned to his sled.

"You drive for a while and I'll try riding the sled," Powellek requested of Art.

"All right. Be sure to change your position often or you'll freeze your hands and knees hanging on back there," Art answered as he pulled the starter rope.

The snowmobile engine reluctantly coughed itself into action again. They were still operating on the twenty-five-year-old gasoline they had salvaged at base camp and lubricated with hydraulic fluid. The gasoline had enough water in it so that the resulting ice was a nuisance. He watched it apprehensively for the machine was approaching a steep incline. Accelerating, the snowmobile readily climbed half way to the top of the rise when the ice chunk entered the carburetor. The motor stopped as abruptly as though it had been turned off. Art jumped off and quietly cursed the dirty fuel under his breath, for he knew the machine would now have to be pushed to the top even after the motor was started again. When he saw Walt ahead of him instead of behind him he stood helplessly by the machine until Plaisted, ahead, detected their breakdown. He saw Plaisted accelerate to try to catch Walt but it required nearly five minutes to achieve it. Although they were too far away to be heard, it was obvious an infuriated Plaisted was chastising an impatient Pederson bitterly for not following his orders and remaining in the rear for just such a situation. An embittered Pederson then disconnected his sled and returned on his snowmobile.

"What's the matter with it?" he asked Art.

"Ice in the carburetor. What do we do?" Art replied.

Walt pulled a rag from his pocket, wrapped a wire around it, dipped it into the gas tank and then lit it. A huge flame burst from the homemade torch as he thrust it beneath the carburetor the flame enveloped the entire engine.

"Got to melt it out of there," he exclaimed. "Just keep the flame off the fuel line—it's plastic and melts," he added. Walt held it there for about two minutes until the flame had decreased to only a few inches in height.

"Now pull the starter rope while I hold the flame in front of the air intake so the flame gets sucked right into the carburetor," he ordered.

With a simplicity that belied the tortured hours Walt had spent devising this technique to start a frozen motor in temperatures of sixty below, the engine roared into eager operation again. And as Walt rather clumsily replaced his tools in the container, Art noted parenthetically that white, frozen fingers were getting to be an almost normal condition for the uncomplaining mechanical engineer as he reacted to the challenge of keeping the machines operational.

...

IT WAS PLAISTED WHO, two hours and many breakdowns later, first caught sight of Bombardier atop the ridge in the distance.

"Don," he ordered, "disconnect your sled and catch up with him. Hold him there. He's swung completely west. We'll lose a half day if we don't turn him back north pretty soon."

Eager simply to be traveling fast again, Don obeyed with juvenile alacrity. When the others arrived there a few minutes later both were bent low over the snow inspecting the crack in the ice at the edge of the floe.

"It scared the hell out of me when it cracked," Bombardier explained. "I thought it would open fast, and I would be stranded over here. But it only opened about three inches and then stopped."

Art inspected the crack carefully, stepped back and walked a hundred yards in each direction. returning, he remarked, "The floe is intact. It merely detached itself from the thinner ice which was adhesive to its periphery. We've seen cracks like this ever since we left shore but they've been frozen. They must occur off and on again all winter. I doubt any one knows why for certain but possibly the tide lifts the ice just enough so that its own weight causes it to crack. In spite of what we've been told, the ice we've been on these past two days gives every sign that it hasn't really moved since it all froze up last fall. The snow covering it is heavy, hard and has obviously been through many windstorms. But this has more the appearance of ice which has been lifted from below, cracked loose from the surrounding pieces, and then been allowed to settle back and freeze into the same position again. Look—this one is only an hour or so old and already has a thin crust of new ice over it. In a few days this big floe will have been cemented firmly to its neighboring ice chunks again."

"I haven't been looking at the ice that way, Professor," Don commented, "but it is true. This stuff looks as though it's been here awhile."

"Most of it hasn't seen a summer," Art continued. "The days get warm enough here to melt for a few weeks in summer and it even rains a little here. That rounds off the sharp edges of the ice chunks. Most of the ones we've seen these past two days are sharp-edged, so that it would seem this ice was broken up after the melting season last summer but hasn't moved much all winter. Of course, remember we're still only about ten miles off shore. Farther out it will probably look mostly like this floe. This one has gone through at least one summer. That flat spot near the center that looks like a small skating pond was probably a pool of melt water last summer. The hummocks are all rounded from thawing and the floe 'rides high.' Its surface is about two feet higher than the rest. That means it's about twelve or more feet thick so this one must be a number of years old. Anyway, as long as it stays this cold I don't think we'll get much ice movement this close to shore."

"Maybe so but all the same, Jean-Luc shouldn't go so far ahead," Plaisted declared. "Besides, Art, can't you help Jean-Luc hold north better?"

"You think maybe it's easy to go in a straight line here with all this rough ice?" Jean-Luc demanded defensively. "I got to go where I can, that's all."

"We all know that," Art answered, attempting to soothe his friend's offended spirit, "but it's a natural tendency to turn left in the northern hemisphere. A man lost in the woods will usually walk in a counter clockwise circle. When you come to pressure ridges and have to go around them try to keep track and alternate your choices, left once, right the next, and so on. Maybe it will help."

Bombardier was clearly not completely happy but promised he would try and prepared to depart again when Powellek called out:

"It's nearly three, Ralph. I've got a sched with Moriarty at base camp to see if Weldy is coming out for the air drop. It will take about fifteen minutes to set up the aerial and get the set ready. Shall I try it now?"

Walt had just returned from retrieving a sled in time to hear Don and promptly objected.

"To heck with it. We've still got gas and good weather. Let's go and let him find us when he comes."

Don looked pleadingly at Plaisted who was studying the terrain ahead. He wanted to move but knew the party was inconspicuous in the rough ice. Furthermore they would need to do considerable more ice chopping through the ridge on each side of the floe. This would not only take time but he knew Don was willing but not excessively skillful with an ice axe and, therefore, a threat both to himself and those around him when he used it. Last of all though he realized Weldy needed a flat area like this floe as an airdrop target.

"Okay, Don," Plaisted decided. "Weldy probably can't find us without help so get on the radio, but I'll tell you now once and for all. I don't like radio schedules, and we won't keep 'em if it slows us down."

Happy to be able to keep faith with his schedule, Don retreated to his sled and began to set up his equipment while the others attacked the lowest point in the pressure ridge with axes, chisels, and picks.

Fifteen minutes later a passage had been created through the pressure ridge, providing access to the floe. Only one large block of ice still remained to be removed. An enthusiastic Ernst plunged his ice chisel under it and yanked on the end, attempting to lift it out of place. The heavy ice chunk refused to budge but the chisel instead yielded to Ernst's massive strength and bent sharply.

"Jesus Christ, Ernst," Plaisted yelled. "Break up the ice, don't pry it with your bar. We only got a few of these chisels and it's still a long way to the North Pole. Swing your axes and chisels but don't pry with 'em. You're too strong to use these tools that way."

Before Ernst could answer Don ran over and announced "John says Weldy just left base camp to come out here. He came in from Eureka, stopped at Tanquary Fjord to pick up a few barrels of fuel the fellows there had dug out and also the stuff we asked for. He stopped at base camp at Ward Hunt, pumped the extra fuel from the barrels into his tanks and is on his way here now. Oh, yes, he brought Pitzl in from Eureka to work with John at base camp. John sounded awfully happy about that."

Plaisted was pleased that something was working out properly and ordered, "Good. Stay on the radio and guide him in to us as soon as you can hear or see him. But wait—tell him we're by the first big floe. He'll be able to spot that easily from the air."

"Okay," Don answered, "but I can't talk to Weldy directly. He hasn't got the crystal installed for our wavelength yet in his plane, but Wes at Eureka can reach his frequency. I'll stay in touch with Wes and he can relay our messages to Weldy."

But Weldy didn't need anyone's help. After takeoff from Ward Hunt Island he had told his copilot Ken Lee, "We'll take her to three thousand and head straight northwest. Bombardier always starts out north and then swings west. In seven minutes we'll start looking for a small floe in the middle of that crushed ice."

Just as the last snowmobile and sled were being helped across the ridge onto the floe, the familiar sound of Weldy's engines reached the ears of the ice party. Almost instinctively Walt leapt to his machine, jerked the engine into life and roared out onto the floe, directing the machine into a series of wild contortions to help attract Weldy's attention. A moment later the Twin Otter aircraft passed over the floe, banked and descended to about one hundred feet above the ice. From the surface the men could see the small rear camera hatch open and a ten-gallon gasoline drum emerge from the plane's belly.

The plane had already passed overhead when the gasoline hit the hard surface of the floe. Still propelled by the impetus of the forward speed of the plane (nearly ninety miles per hour), it struck on end, split and then arched upward in a long arc, spinning end over end and spewing its contents into the frigid air. Instantly Walt, who had parked on the far side of the floe, pursued it, attempting to reach it before all the gasoline had drained out in the hope of salvaging at least a part of its contents. Plaisted reacted by dashing to a sled, snatching a caribou hide from it and thrusting it at Bombardier.

"Go out there and use this to mark the softest spot you can find so Weldy can use it as a drop target."

Walt returned after several minutes with the deformed gasoline container, announcing: "It hit on the rim and split the top. Only a couple of quarts left in it. This was white gas for the stoves and heater."

As he finished transferring its contents into their own partially depleted white gas container, Bombardier returned from his task. As the Otter approached for another pass it was obvious that Weldy was not risking a stall at this altitude for the plane passed overhead no slower than before. Again a ten-gallon drum of gasoline was thrust from the opening. It struck just beyond the caribou hide target. A cloud of loose snow marked its impact point, and although it rolled for another hundred feet it did not bounce again and appeared intact. Walt dashed out after it and, after a brief inspection stood erect and waved both his arms to inform Powellek of a successful drop. He barely had time to get out of the drop zone when he saw Weldy was already on his next approach.

Again and again the plane flew over the floe, dropping first a succession of fuel drums and then a heterogeneous collection of tools and "tentware."

Art stared in amazement as food boxes, ice chisels, shovels, caribou hides and even whisk brooms rained from the sky to litter the surface of the floe. A vision from two years previously unexpectedly surfaced in his consciousness and once again he and his Eskimo traveling companion, Nangoaq, were traveling by dog sled down Bathurst Inlet in the central Canadian Arctic. All they needed was on that one sled. The only item carried for shelter was not a tent but a snow knife, for an igloo had proved to be more comfortable and convenient that a tent. "Fuel" for both men and dogs could be guaranteed by carrying merely a rifle. It seemed so much less complex than this. But then he had to remind himself that there were no seal or caribou out here at this time of year, and that the thin snow cover of the floes infrequently provided the necessary type of drift for igloo construction. Furthermore tents saved valuable igloo construction time that could then be used for traveling. Nevertheless, their passive dependence on that aircraft was a disquieting experience for those accustomed to solving their own problems in an active way.

It was fully an hour before Don reported, "Weldy's dropped all he has for us. He's on his way back to Eureka."

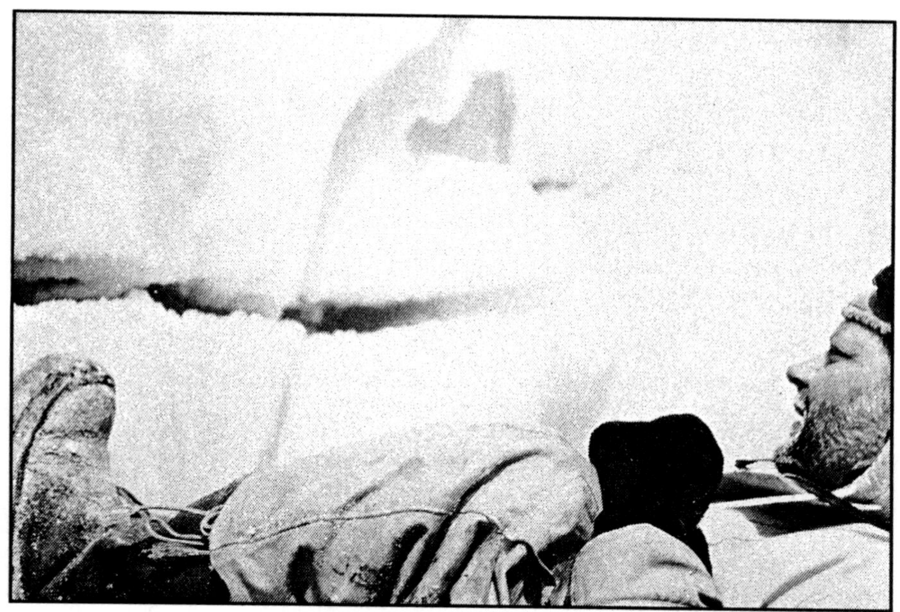

Don examines a newly formed crack

"Tell him to fly ahead of us and look over the ice for us," Plaisted asked.

"He can't, Ralph," Don rejoined. "He used up all his spare fuel. He just said it looked like lots more rough ice ahead."

It had required an unanticipatedly long time for the air drop. Since the camera hatch was only about twenty inches in diameter and since the craft flew so fast, only one item could be dropped on each pass, the plane itself had to fly a one-mile circle to get into position for another pass. No one needed to be reminded this would create a fuel problem as the party progressed to the outer margins of the plane's fuel supply.

Like the others, Plaisted welcomed the end of the airdrop. Standing quietly for an hour in these low temperatures he had noticed first the irritability and then the gradual depression that came over him so regularly when he became seriously chilled. It was not really the pain or annoyance of numb toes or shivering trunk that was disturbing. He knew the exercise involved in retrieving the dropped items would soon correct that. But even when he recognized the reason for his emotional depression and knew that physical activity would soon rewarm him, the temptation was still great to yield to the lethargy such a chill created. Yet he heard himself shouting; "Awright, let's get this stuff picked up and stashed. We got a couple of hours travel left yet today."

But it was another half hour before the newly acquired gear was all packed appropriately on the sleds and an exit path had been created off the floe. Immediately they found themselves back in the rough ice, picking their way from piece to piece, doing more dragging, pulling, heaving and lifting than riding. With overheated blood now surging through his face, hands, and feet virtually begging to be cooled, Plaisted found his mood rising so that even the frustration of their slow progress depressed him less than usual.

Attempting to smooth a passage across several small hummocks, Powellek was hacking at an upended slab of ice adjacent to Plaisted. The axe struck the flat surface of the slab tangentially, caromed off the ice and buried itself in the snow beside Plaisted's foot. Jerking his foot back violently, he swore at Powellek, "Christ, Don, be careful with that axe, will you? We're just about done here anyway so why don't you go bring up your machine and sled?" He sighed with relief as Don trudged off toward his snowmobile.

Art had been watching the light and turned now to Plaisted, suggesting, "I don't like the way it looks, Ralph. It looks like it did the night before our big blow last year. Maybe it's time to set up camp for the night."

Walt ceased chiseling and protested instantly.

"We got all the gas we need now. We can make camp in the dark if we have to. Let's go while we can."

"Maybe so," Art admitted, "but traveling in this progressive grayout is dangerous. You can't tell a hummock from its shadow now and the one thing we can't afford out here is a broken leg."

Walt began to answer but his voice was drowned out by Don's arrival on the machine. The prepared path led across several small hummocks and contained a sharp turn near the center to avoid a five-foot drop down an angulated slab of ice partly buried in the snow. Don progressed easily down the leveled surface but, confused by the treacherous light, did not detect the curve and steered straight ahead, immediately disappearing from sight. Although all the men sprang forward instantly they found Don below, already extracting himself from beneath the loaded sled. Fortunately he had been hurled from the machine into rather soft snow and the following sled had fallen partly upon the snowmobile, preventing its full weight from crushing

Powellek's body. He was unhurt, but after his machine and sled were replaced on the intended track no further coaxing was necessary to make camp.

"Where do we stay tonight?" Plaisted asked.

Art looked about him. No floe was available, so he simply selected an area where the snow had filled in a place flat enough to support the two tents, and declared: "Right here. It's all small pieces of ice here with no real support in the event of ice movement, but I don't expect any for a week anyway until spring tides at full moon—if our theory is right."

Art had learned that this could be the most unpleasant part of the day. The cramped quarters in the tent resulted in rapid chilling. He did not envy Plaisted's task inside. The exertion involved in setting up the tents, preparing protective snowbanks and other chores kept him warm outside and offered him tempting opportunities for low light photos. By the time he entered the tent, therefore, the group was already making plans for the next few days.

"Walt, how much gas have we got?" asked Plaisted.

"Five gallons in each of the four machines and two ten-gallon drums besides."

"How much white gas? We're using almost two gallons a day."

"We lost ten gallons today when that first drum Weldy dropped split, but we've still got about seven gallons left."

"All the machines in good shape?"

"Of course!" Walt replied with emphatic satisfaction.

"We got enough food for ten days," Plaisted went on. "We gotta get better organized. Why carry ten days of food and three days of gas? We got to move better than we are or we'll never get to the Pole. We got about fifty days to make four hundred miles north. That's nine miles a day average. Say ten. But two days are gone already and we only averaged half that. And we ain't out of the rough ice yet. We just gotta move faster, that's all. After this we carry three days' gas and five days' food with us. And we still got too much stuff. I want everybody to go over their stuff tonight, and the first chance Weldy gets to land we're gonna send back all the extra parkas, shirts, and things we don't need. If we don't cut this load down we'll never get to the pole."

"I can get rid of six pounds of navigation table books if we just radio my sextant readings to base camp and let Pitzl work them out there and radio back our position to us," suggested Art.

"Great. You really don't need all that film either. Send some of it back and call for it when you need it."

"The Honda generator is working so well I could send back the two generators that run off the snowmobiles," Walt volunteered. "They're about ten pounds each."

More suggestions led to about one hundred fifty pounds reduction. Plaisted insisted on twice that but seemed willing to start with those items.

After their meal of rehydrated chicken with rice had been finished Plaisted ordered Powellek, "Tell Wes at Eureka we'll need fifty-five gallons of mixed gas and ten gallons of white gas day after tomorrow. No more food and nothing else. We'll confirm the night before and if we're in big floe country by then Weldy should set down and take the extra stuff back with him. And don't make any daytime radio schedules!"

...

"THEY SURE LOOK SMALL DOWN THERE, don't they?" commented Ken Lee as they passed over base camp at Ward Hunt Island on their way back to Eureka.

Weldy looked out the window on his side. From their height of 6,500 feet the three diminutive, partly snow-covered janeway huts resembled just three more rocks in the landscape.

"Look at the ice pattern in front of base camp," Weldy remarked. "The wavy surface of the shelf ice is flat in front of Ward Hunt Island, as though the front of the island is in the lee of a wave-swept lake. It's easy to understand why Canadian glaciologists want to study this area; there's nothing like it anywhere else in the arctic." After a few moments of silent thought he added, "We'll push on up to 9,700 feet. The peaks here are close to 10,000 and even though the pass we're using isn't much over 8,000, I like the safety factor to be on our side."

The monotonous drone of the engines was almost hypnotic. The steep pitch of the blades caused the propellers to bite deeply into air rendered so dense by the bitter cold that it was almost tangible. Weldy could literally feel the enormous power of those turbine engines and was proud of them; their steady throb spelled his security in a land where every view threatened disaster. His eye habitually swept the dials of his instrument panel, lingering for a moment on the altimeter to reassure himself of its progressive rise. Reaching for the microphone he depressed the button and called:

"Eureka, this is Whiskey Whiskey Papa. How do you copy?"

"Loud and clear, Weldy," answered Hans' quietly reassuring voice. "Eureka here. Where are you?"

"Just passed over Ward Hunt and in the pass on the way to Tanquary. 7,500 now and climbing. Weather clear. ETA about one hour—that's about 18:00. What's your weather?"

"Pretty good. Ceiling 4,000 with ice crystals above; visibility five miles; wind northwest at thirteen, a little blowing snow."

"Thanks Hans. Tell Wes to put a can of Plaisted's beer in the refrigerator. It's been a long day. Signing clear."

Weldy stared out the window and thought idly of the many things that still needed to be done. The plane's radio had to be modified so that he could communicate directly with the ice party. Also the ice party carried a small, battery powered, electronic navigation signal transmitter but the receiving unit still needed to be installed in Weldy's plane and tested.

"Tested—and how!" Weldy thought. Last year they had used a similar system of different make—the SARAH beacon. Weldy was partial to this one because it was an old, reliable unit used by the Canadian Air Force for years. Weldy liked reliable things up here. "Don't take toys to the Arctic" was one of his favorite aphorisms, a belief reflecting a philosophy perhaps explaining why he was still flying when so many of his bush pilot friends were already buried. But he knew the value of testing too—the unit had never been reliably operational last year, and several times he had found them through sheer luck, even though they had never penetrated more than one hundred miles from shore. This year Powellek had staked his faith (and survival) on a new, tiny, cigarette package size unit. Although he had profound respect for Don, Weldy was uneasy about this, especially when he learned it had only been bench-tested, not field tested. Judging from the progress of the group so far this year it seemed as though he had at least several weeks time before finding the ice party without an aid would become a problem. By that time the weather would be a little warmer and it would be a little more pleasant to work in the cold aircraft during installation.

The big hang-up though would be the fuel supply. Seventy-five tons of aircraft fuel was buried under rock-hard snowdrifts at Tanquary Fjord where the Canadian icebreaker *McDonald* had managed to push it last summer. Although only about 120 miles south of Ward Hunt Island where base camp

Buried fuel drums at Tanquary Fjord. Three hundred barrels had to be dug out and moved half a mile.

was meant to be, the 10,000 foot high peaks of Ellesmere's northern mountain range separated the two. And for every six of the fifty-five-gallon gasoline drums the Twin Otter could carry over the mountains, two were consumed by the plane itself. And, as usual in the Arctic, Tanquary Fjord was subject to frequent vision-obscuring gales or ice fog which were independent of the general area's weather. Even Andy and Fred could not dig out enough drums to keep the plane supplied on its longer flights later. And to land the fully loaded Otter, flattened air strips would have to be created at both Tanquary Fjord and Ward Hunt Island.

Weldy began to arrange the problems in a priority list in his mind, for this was his whole life in the arctic. His daily routine always involved a series of problems which, because of their interdependence must be solved in a certain sequence. For here there were no alternatives, no other choices, no other people. A burned out igniter, a faulty control, a bent ski, an unexpected squall or thaw—these and a thousand other things could prevent his flight. And when Weldy didn't fly, nothing moved. There were no other planes, no boats, no buses, cars, trains or repair shops. To all in the eastern high arctic in winter, Weldy was not merely "Atlas Aviation Company." He was "Outside."

As they passed over the peak with the familiar black rock face, Weldy turned to the altimeter again, for he had learned from previous flights that he generally reached the desired height at this point. Gratified at seeing the needle hover over 9,700 feet he reached forward and adjusted the propeller's pitch to an angle designed for level flight. Instantly the whine of the right turbine engine began to rise. Alarmed, Weldy looked quickly out the right window, then at the instrument panel. The tachometer confirmed his fears of a runaway engine. The whine continued to rise, unresponsive to an adjustment of the propeller's pitch. The engine, turning at a speed for which its mountings were never designed, began to vibrate now, and the trembling wing was shaking the fuselage. Desperately he yanked at the right engine's throttle control, but the whine merely rose higher and the fuselage convulsed more violently. The engine clearly was totally out of control, and almost without hesitation he slapped the electrical switches to the engine. Immediately the siren-like scream of the turbine began its decrescendo and the shaking subsided. Within a minute it was silent. Ken Lee had once dreamed this sort of thing happened and had awakened in a cold sweat. Now he knew this was no dream and, although the blood had drained from his face he had not spoken. Now he merely stared at Weldy inquiringly.

Weldy, in turn, was studying the altimeter. He glanced briefly down to reconfirm his position, then returned his gaze to the instrument panel. Without looking up he felt Ken's silent stare and answered his unspoken question.

"We can't hold this altitude with only one engine but we should make it over the hump all right."

They both looked out again at the rugged terrain beneath them. Many of the arctic islands in Canada's archipelago demonstrate the low, flat monotonous surface which betrays their origin as merely former sea floor which rose above the surface when relieved of its heavy glacial ice cover. But Ellesmere is the queen of the group. Thrusting upward from the ocean bottom her mountains burst through the ocean's surface, clawing skyward for nearly two miles. Named by explorers of competing nationalities, the British Empire Range and the United States Range perpetually challenged some of the world's iciest gales, their bare rock faces gradually acquire a linear and chiseled topography testifying to the violence of these elements. The snowfall, though light by temperate zone standards, still exceeds the summer melt. Inexorably, then, the valleys between the peaks become filled with snow until the snow's sheer weight compresses that in the lower levels into ice. This ice cap, now as much as 6,000 feet thick, is perforated periodically as the higher peaks of the range penetrate it. At the ice cap's periphery its own weight pushes the plastic icy mass out into the troughs between the rocky peaks like so much excess cake frosting, forcing it into a slow motion cascade down the steep inclines as so many glaciers, where the stresses and strains crack the surface into crevasses as much as thirty feet wide and a hundred feet deep.

The many alternatives raced through Weldy's mind as he stared at that uninviting terrain. Although most of these mountains had been seen so seldom by man as to remain nameless, Weldy had created his own nicknames for many derived from his experiences with them. His eyes sought out and found what he called "Airplane Glacier." The previous summer Dave DeBlickey and Ken Lee had landed a party of scientists there, and then developed engine trouble. They had been forced to descend the glacier on foot and walk fifty miles to the scientists' camp at Tanquary Fjord to radio for help. But it had been summer then. Even so, he felt they could survive the trek at these winter temperatures if the winds would be forgiving. But the plane would be a total loss, for it could never take off from there again with only one engine, and repairs there would be unthinkable.

Tanquary Fjord had been their immediate target and when Weldy was using up fuel at the airdrop it was with the concept that he would refuel at Tanquary Fjord on the way back to Eureka. With the rigid flight discipline he had imposed upon himself long ago, however, he had allowed enough reserve for an alternate "airport"—in this instance the weather station at Alert, ninety miles east of Ward Hunt Island. To reach Alert now, however, he would have to fly back through the pass—and in the tight u-turn required in the middle of the pass, it was doubtful that he could retain sufficient altitude.

No, Alert was out. Then the full realization struck him that Tanquary Fjord was out too. Once landed there they themselves would be safe, but no complex repairs could be carried out there either. The plane might eventually be salvaged with an icebreaker supply ship next summer, but he could afford neither such a salvage operation nor the loss of the craft through the winter months.

He checked the fuel gauges once again and once again went through the necessary mental arithmetic and once again concluded that, while it was marginal, they probably could reach Eureka—if they could get through this pass. The 1,500-foot safety margin with which he routinely supplied himself here seemed none too great now. The altimeter needle was already sagging as Weldy fought for every foot of altitude, raising the plane's nose until he heard the warning whine of the stall signal's indicator. "Big Blackface" was already behind them and he was gratified to see "Grandpa Peak" approaching, which marked the summit of the pass. They were still five hundred feet above the snow when they reached it; they were so low, it was the first time he could remember looking at the peaks flanking the pass. Problems still remained, for the snow sloped only very gradually from the summit and several lower peaks remained to be circumvented. Ken Lee had been silent all this time, but when they finally emerged from the pass into the valley leading to Tanquary Fjord he expressed his enormous relief with the laconic comment:

"Thought for a minute we'd bought the farm that time!"

Without answering Weldy turned the plane away from the camp at Tanquary, directing it toward Greeley Fjord and Eureka. To Ken's surprised and inquiring glance he answered:

"We'll have to pull that engine and Eureka's the only place we can do it. The fuel is going to be close. When we get down to the denser air I think this one engine will hold her at about 5,000 feet. If it does we can cross Foscheim Peninsula—it's only about 2,500 feet—and save ten minutes of fuel. If not we'll have to follow Greeley Fjord down to Eureka Sound and follow that in to Eureka. If we run out of fuel we might be able to set down on the Sound and pull it in to Eureka with a tractor from there."

Ken did his own arithmetic and decided it *was* close, but they probably could make it. But he had reservations about landing on the sound's surface. The water in Eureka sound and Greeley Fjord had opened up last year and frozen again during a gale. Most of the surface was pocked with upended floes three to five feet high.

...

Far below, Andy Horton and Fred Clark paused in their attempts to free still another barrel from a snowdrift to watch the Twin Otter disappear down the fjord.

"Seems like you just can't depend on anybody up here," Andy muttered petulantly. "Weldy said he was refueling here on the way back. I've got a bowl of hot soup and coffee on for him in the shack and even wrote a letter to my wife to have him take along to Eureka, and now he doesn't even stop!"

Raising Eureka on the radio, Weldy reported, "Hans, we're coming in on one engine. Fuel is close. ETA 16:10 now. I'll check with you again about 16:00."

Hans' alarm was reflected in his voice as he promised "We'll monitor your frequency all the way in. Tell us what you want from us."

Tortured minutes flowed by as Tanquary Fjord flowed beneath them. With considerable anticipation, Ken leaned forward to scan the surface as they passed out of its mouth into Greeley Fjord but sat back disappointed, for its surface lent itself no more readily to an emergency landing than the other. And he knew from the area around the weather station that Eureka sound was no better. As Weldy had anticipated, the plane had stabilized its altitude at 5,500 feet. As they flew above the fjord the low-fuel light blinked, then burned steadily on the Twin Otter's instrument panel. Two hundred and fifty pounds left; usually enough for half an hour.

"Using more gas than I expected. Guess the one engine must be a lot less efficient than two. And the air is a lot thicker down here."

Surveying the ice below, he made the only decision he could and directed the Otter away from the fjord, overland in a straight line for Eureka. They would save ten minutes that way, and they needed every minute. They were committed now. Foscheim Peninsula which they were crossing was not really mountainous but it was covered with rugged hills and steep-sided, river-scarred valleys. There might be occasional places a pilot like Weldy could set down safely—but only a few, and one would have to be in the right place at the right time.

"Twenty minutes out," Weldy reported to Hans. "We have the low-fuel light."

Ken's heart began to pound as he recognized "Old Blacktop" in the distance. This was a 1,500-foot high, flat-topped, dark, rocky hill just above the weather station at Eureka. Only rough terrain lay beneath them and their target. If only the fuel would last now. Five minutes out, then four minutes ... then three . . . two . . . and one. With no opportunity to enter the usual landing pattern the Otter cleared the end of Old Blacktop with 500 feet to spare, dipped sharply and approached the airstrip. Ken could see eight of the nine weather station men at the edge of the airstrip; only the radio operator remained on duty in the camp.

A moment later the skis touched the runway smoothly and the ordeal was over. Weldy turned around at the end of the strip and taxied back to the hangar, then shut off the engine and checked his watch. He grinned; five minutes to spare. For a bush pilot, it was a piece of cake.

...

PLAISTED WAS LADLING OUT THE SOUP in the tent and, as he often did, was thinking out loud. "We got started a week late, lost time because of breakdowns from that old gas, lost more time when Walt had to go back for tools and stuff, lost a couple of hours today on the air drop and had mostly nothing but that damned rough ice so far. Two more days shot and we're only about ten miles out on the pack ice. But fellas, that floe we were on today did my heart good. Where there's one of those, there's more. We'll be hitting a lot of them soon and then we'll really move."

They were all relieved to see his generally depressed mood elevated by such optimism.

"Ralph! Ralph!" Powellek was shouting excitedly as he ran over from the other tent where he had been keeping his radio schedule with base camp. Thrusting his alarmed face through the sleeve entrance he announced, "Weldy lost an engine on the way back today. He got back to Eureka all right but figures it will be two to three weeks before he can get it replaced and operational again!"

6

What Else Could Go Wrong?

"But Ralph," Art repeated for at least the third time, "We're less than fifteen miles out now. We can run right back to base camp down our own trail and wait there until the supply line is organized again. If we continue to move out onto the pack ice until our supplies run out we'll be too far out to come back on our own in case Weldy won't be able to get supplies out to us."

"Walt, how much gas we got?" Ralph demanded again.

"At least enough for three days, maybe four. Let's go. They'll figure out something."

"And the white gas?"

"About seven gallons."

"Don, where did Wes say the single-engined Otter is?"

"Cambridge Bay. Dick DeBlickey is flying it, taking care of Weldy's routine contracts while he's with us."

"Cambridge Bay? Where's that?" asked Plaisted.

"Way down on the southern end of Victoria Island nearly a thousand miles south and four hundred miles west of here," Don answered. "Even if he doesn't eat or sleep, there are three big hops he has to make: Cambridge to Resolute to Eureka to here. Each is around 500 miles and I can hardly believe the weather over that long a stretch won't keep him pinned down somewhere. Think it over, Ralph. There are a dozen things that could keep DeBlickey from reaching us in time."

Plaisted was thinking. Of the 435 miles of ice remaining between them and the North Pole. Of the unknown but shrinking number of days available to traverse them. Of the dozens of sponsors and hundreds of supporters who had placed their faith in his knowledge and experience this time. Of the devastating demoralization he knew would overwhelm them if they were forced to return to base camp and wait there idly while valuable traverse time slipped by. He studied his men intently. Like himself, Walt Pederson lived daily the uncertainties all businessmen know. He had become accustomed to them long ago, learning to assign a risk factor to any alternative. Plaisted knew professional men carried considerable immunity from this daily type of challenge, that their risks lay in their technical fields where they could make fully informed judgments. And he was not blind to the fact that the victims of the professional man's judgment errors generally were his clients or patients, not himself. It was no surprise to him then to find Art and Don urging a conservative course upon him. The threat to themselves he had reduced to two categories: travel and survival. Pederson had promised three days of travel and he himself estimated ten days of survival supplies. Admittedly they would have to reduce white gasoline consumption below their usual daily level of two gallons. He knew water-starved men could not simply eat snow—that its low temperature would blister the mouth and rob the body of heat. Their food, too, needed to be hydrated to become edible, and their stove demanded "white" gasoline. still, they had seven gallons left. He would have to be firm in his decision, however; it was much too early in the journey to permit a schism to develop among the men.

"We came out here to go to the North Pole," he announced in a voice that declared the decision nonnegotiable, "and we won't get there by going south. DeBlickey's on his way out here. He'll get us what we need until Weldy gets his plane fixed again. Now Art, if you want to do something useful, teach Jean-Luc how to tell which way is north,"

As Art opened his mouth to protest what he regarded as an unnecessarily caustic gibe, the eloquence of Plaisted's countenance silenced him. Although transiently relieved by optimism only moments before, all the gloom of repressed anxiety and impatience had returned, deepened now by sheer despair. Don, Jean-Luc and Ernst returned to their tent and all retired without further discussion. Subconsciously the first, hesitant, reluctant step of converting an arctic outing into a true expedition had been taken. And they didn't like it.

...

"THAT GENERATOR IS CERTAINLY PERFORMING like an old workhorse," Moriarty commented to Pitzl as he pored over the maintenance directions in the rear of the devices assembly booklet. "Walt set it up out there in that tiny, unheated, wooden crate six days ago and it's been running continually in weather between fifty and sixty below ever since. The electric light in here is nice, but mostly, I'm grateful for that radio. It sure would be lonesome here without it."

When Pitzl didn't answer, Moriarty looked up to find him staring at a chart he had tacked to the inside of the shack door. The upper half was occupied by a map at the top of which the North Pole was located and the northern end of Ellesmere Island appeared at the bottom. Between the two he had drawn a straight line divided into regular, short segments. Adjacent to this line, extending from Ward Hunt Island, he had drawn an irregular, short line, only about an inch long. He was staring pensively at the end of this second line, silent and frowning. Moriarty walked over and stared at the map over Pitzl's shoulder.

"What's so interesting here that you don't even hear me, Jerry?" he inquired.

Pitzl started, laughed embarrassingly and explained. "Sorry, John, we're the only two people on northern Ellesmere Island and I don't even listen to you. But I got all absorbed here and I'm seriously worried. This line connecting our base camp to the North Pole is about 450 miles long, We'll have some inevitable delays so we'll have to average at least ten miles a day to make it."

"These segments into which you've divided that line are ten miles long, I suppose?" John asked, now interested. "And the dates next to the line represent the day when the ice party should be at each of those points?"

"Right," Jerry replied. "The ice party left March seventh, today is the tenth. They ought to be right here tonight, thirty miles out," he declared, pointing to the end of the third segment on the line. "But here is where they *really* are," and he shifted his pencil point to the end of the irregular line paralleling the other but only about an inch long, "Only about fifteen miles out, with Weldy down for at least two weeks, they'll be a hundred miles behind schedule. We'll never make that up in time!"

Shoulders drooping in despair, he slouched over to his navigational instrument container, removed the sextant and assembled it. He slid a tin can over the electric light bulb hanging from the ceiling and fastened it with a wire. Light streamed through a pinhole punched in the side of the can, simulating a star. Retreating to the rear of the hut he pointed the sextant at his artificial point of light and squinted into the eyepiece.

"Don't you ever get tired of practicing using that thing, Jerry?" inquired Moriarty, watching Pitzl's facial contortions curiously.

"Sure," Jerry admitted, "but the North Pole is just a theoretical dot in the middle of the Arctic Ocean and the ice floes on the surface there look like those anywhere else. The only way we'll know when we're there is to have good, reliable, sextant readings of the sun, so we can plot our position accurately on the charts. I want to be so familiar with this instrument, that even when I have to use it in bitter weather, I'll be able to come up with the right answers."

"What kind of a sextant is it?"

"Marine sextant, same as they use on ships," Jerry answered without taking his eye from the instrument.

"What are those wires coming out of your pocket?"

"Because of the pressure ridges on the ice I can't see any horizon there. Instead, a bubble type of artificial horizon is attached to the sextant. But I need a light inside it in order to center the bubble properly. The power for the bulb normally comes from two batteries in the handle, but last year the batteries would freeze up before I could get a reading, so this time Don fixed me up a holder with wires so I can keep the batteries warm in my pocket and just plug in the wires to the sextant."

"At least we'll know how they're doing," John stated optimistically. "Don and I have a schedule at 0200 GMT every night. That's in about five minutes so I'll get tuned-up."

Reassuring, too, was the monotonous drone of the generator's engine outside. For it was not only the convenience of light or appliances that concerned him. Without it he had no radio—no way to find out where the ice party was, what it needed and when it expected supplies; no way to tell Weldy at Eureka whether or not weather permitted landing. The steady throb of that generator long ago, subconsciously and imperceptibly, had blended with his own heartbeat.

"CJU 942 Mobile Two, this is Mobile One," he called into the microphone after the adjustments had been completed and was delighted to hear Powellek's familiar voice reply almost immediately. And after the usual exchange of greetings he was pleased to hear Don say: "And we've had a good day, John. After some rough ice we followed a frozen lead northwest for seven miles. Give us twelve miles north for the day and mark us down at . . ."

Moriarty leaped from his desk, groping in the darkness for his coat as Pitzl's alarmed cry reached him. "My God, what's that John?" The regular rhythm of the generator's exhaust had suddenly accelerated, rising in a rapid crescendo, to a screaming whine that signaled all loss of control. Coincident with this catastrophe the radio's volume suddenly rose to a megaphonic blare, then ceased abruptly, emitting the acrid smoke of an electric fire. The electric lights first flared in brilliant intensity, then extinguished in a shower of filamentous sparks.

Wrenching the door open while still half clad and plunging into the Arctic cold with bare hands, he shouted back to Jerry: "Governor on the generator let go. The increased RPM must have poured several hundred extra volts into the line and burned out the radio and lights."

...

FROM THE TOP OF THE PRESSURE RIDGE Art pointed to the tracks Bombardier's machine had imprinted in the snow as he had passed this way earlier in the day.

"Look at that, he's trying to overcome his tendency to drift to the west so much that he's overdone it. These past fifteen minutes he's been going straight east. If he turns right any more we'll be heading back towards shore!"

"He's picking a good path though," Plaisted answered. "Nobody's hung up a machine or sled all morning. If he could only figure a way to hold a north heading we'd be on our way. I think I can see him up ahead on that big ridge. If we could only stop him until we get there."

Bombardier hadn't needed stopping. He was waiting for the group atop a pressure ridge, overlooking a unique ice topography, radically different from that which they had been traversing. A few minutes later Plaisted scrambled up the ridge fuming internally at the delay engendered by the easterly direction Bombardier had taken all morning. Pederson, Powellek, and Aufderheide followed. Opening his mouth to chastise Bombardier, Plaisted suddenly became silent as he saw the ice ahead, then gasped: "The shore lead, the big shore lead that gave us so much trouble last year. And it's all frozen now!"

Powellek's eye swept the terrain and recognized the pattern. The huge pressure ridges were absent. Instead, a monotonously flat area lay ahead. It was broken up only by thin fragments up to five feet long, but these would offer little impediment to progress through the area.

"Wow, we'll really be able to make time now," declared Walt, as he reached the top of the ridge. Above his frosted mask his eyes betrayed the delight he felt at the prospect. "Let's go!"

"Jean-Luc, I came up here to give you the devil for heading so far east, but you've brought us to the best ice we've had since we left," Plaisted admitted grudgingly.

"Are you sure we ought to go ahead. Ralph?" Powellek inquired somewhat anxiously. "I'd feel better if we could have Weldy fly over it first and check it for open water.'

Plaisted remembered the open water of that shore lead last year too. He remembered that and how their floe had split when under pressure that night. It made him a little sick to remember how he had nearly fallen into the ocean water when the floe had split. But he thrust it from his mind as he answered, "The ice is thicker than it was in the lead last year. If we go now we can get across it before it opens up again. Besides, Weldy ain't coming, so we're going. All right, everybody!" he yelled. "Let's cut a road through this pressure ridge and get on to this lead ice."

It was cold enough so they were all happy to be back at work.

As they were swinging axes, chisels, and shovels, Aufderheide took their pictures.

"Put your parka back on again for a minute while I take one more shot, Walt," Art requested. "The folks back home won't believe you chop ice at fifty below in only a woolen shirt."

"Hurry up and shoot then," Walt pleaded, "or I'll get the parka all sweated up and you know we can't dry it out very well in the tent out here."

Finishing with Walt, Art moved over to photograph Ernest. The young Swiss was a tall, muscular fellow, brimming with energy, who seemed to enjoy his participation with the ice party immensely. Indeed, so much so that Plaisted occasionally felt compelled to remind him to take some motion pictures. He was swinging his axe with special vigor when a particularly heavy blow was followed by a snap as the handle broke and the metal axe head spun into the snow.

Obviously annoyed, Plaisted burst out, "Jesus Christ, that's the second one, Ernst. Can't you learn to take it easy with those axes? We haven't got that many extra handles. And don't lose the head. We'll have to fix it later."

Chagrined, Ernest groped in the snow for the axe head and, finding it, tossed it carelessly into the nearest sled with a gesture of disgust. Moments later the path through the ridge was completed and the caravan passed through, reaching the ice lead.

The lead is frozen, but how thick?

For nine miles they traveled almost at will and at top speed. Exhilaration swept them as they wore their way around the many upended fragments, the thin snow cover of the flat ice providing excellent traction.

When Plaisted saw Pederson quickly moving into the lead position he repressed his own impulse to reprimand him again, realizing Walt's urge to be first under these conditions must be irresistible for him. Although the air itself was motionless, the breeze created by their own speed chilled them so rapidly, that Art was actually grateful for the pause when he was hurled from the sled as it struck an angulated hummock and upset. Unhurt, he reassured the alarmed and apologetic Powellek who was driving the snowmobile, adding, "How thick do you think this ice is, Don?"

"Well, it's white so that means its thick enough so the dark ocean water isn't visible through it, and yet it has a very hollow ring as we pass over it. Maybe seven or eight inches?"

"Yes, I suppose so. Do you think we'll hit any open water here?"

"Hope not. Actually I sort of doubt it, because in these temperatures, open water would steam so vigorously we ought to be able to see the resulting cloud from a distance."

"That's true," Art answered. "But I'll still feel better when we're beyond this shore lead even though it will mean slower and rougher travel again."

Shortly thereafter a pressure ridge appeared to the north and a few minutes later they were at its foot. From its summit the frozen lead was seen turning eastward as far as the eye could reach.

Squinting at the odometer reading on his machine, Pederson announced exultantly, "Nine miles in just over an hour—and most all of it north too! Maybe this will be our fifty-mile day!"

"I'll settle for fifteen," Plaisted replied, beating his nearly frozen hands together. "There's no use following this lead to the east so get your chisels out. We're going back to work."

Sauntering over to where Bombardier stood, Art commented, "I've noticed something that might help Jean-Luc. The wind seems to be from the west consistently here. It aligns the snowdrifts in an east-west direction. If you simply cross them at right angles you'll be heading north."

"Or south," chuckled Pederson.

"Oh, come on," Art replied. "He doesn't get that far off. One other thing might help too," he added, turning to Bombardier again. "When the sun is out, try to keep it behind you, over your right shoulder in the morning and your left in the afternoon."

For three more hours they struggled drearily with the ice-pushing, lifting, chopping, dragging and occasionally riding briefly. The sky was graying again when they reached a small floe in late afternoon. Watching Art scan the sky again apprehensively, Plaisted reassured him once more, "Forget it Art. That's just the way the sky looks every day about this time when it's this cold, I guess. It ain't going to storm. If you think this floe is okay, let's set up here before somebody gets hurt in this bad light."

The cheerful inflection in Plaisted's voice mirrored the entire group's buoyant mood infused by their unexpectedly good progress. If they had achieved fifteen north miles that day, Plaisted reflected, it would begin to make up for the initial delays and their progress ought to improve even more as they would encounter more larger floes farther out.

It was with only a trace of irritation then as he dispatched Art to retrieve Pederson who, reluctant to stop, was already busy at work at the pressure ridge on the far side of the floe. Spurred by the warmth their efforts had generated, their camp chores were quickly completed. And when Pederson and

Aufderheide returned, they found the tents up and could hear Don on the radio inside one of them. He soon emerged, a concerned frown, replacing the happy mood of a few minutes previously. Shouting though the tent wall to Plaisted inside, all could hear as he reported, "John at base camp answered but faded out. I don't know what happened, but I suppose they lost power there. Wes at Eureka was monitoring us and broke in to say that DeBlickey only got as far as Resolute. Weather is okay there, but Eureka is socked in. Wes says Hans figures it will be better tomorrow there, but a low pressure zone is moving in toward Resolute, so he isn't putting any bets on DeBlickey coming in tomorrow either."

"Okay, we ain't gonna die if he don't get here tomorrow," Plaisted answered, though it was easy to detect a return of the depression he had felt earlier. Handing an empty kettle out through the tent entrance, he commanded:

"Fill this with snow and then tell everybody to come in and eat."

Art walked over to empty the remaining sled—his and Powellek's. Releasing the lashings he removed the first sleeping bag. Laying it on the snow he suddenly picked it up again, bent over and smelled it. Tossing it aside he jerked the other from the sled and repeated the procedures. Frantically he tore out all the other items, scattering them about indiscriminately. Inspecting the red, five gallon container carefully, he turned and walked to the tent, pushed his head through the en-trance and quietly announced to Plaisted:

"We just got another chapter for the book, Ralph. Ernest threw that broken ice axe head into our sled, and it hit the bottom of the plastic five-gallon white gas container. All the gas leaked out. Two sleeping bags are completely soaked with gasoline and useless; so are three food boxes. And we've only got about two gallons of white gas left in the other can. When is DeBlickey coming?"

...

WES COOK STARED AT WELDY ACROSS THE TABLE. His physician's eye clearly detected the fatigue nearly overwhelming this man. The pilot's bushy eyebrows sagged now, nearly meeting his swollen lower lids, His unkempt beard had not protected his face from the frigid wind adequately, and layers of peeling skin exposed the painful, red frostbites over the bridge of his nose. With head bent so low as to touch his jaw to his chest, the usually powerful shoulders now drooped wearily, while his arms and hands guided the food into his mouth with nearly mechanical rigidity. Wes had expected Weldy to claim the rest which his near disaster had earned him, but Weldy had gone directly to the radio, contacted his wife, instructing her carefully to call the aircraft factory in the morning and have a new engine flown to Resolute immediately. Ignoring normal living schedules he had then gone back to the airstrip to begin the laborious task of removing the affected engine from the plane. Since then he had seen Weldy only twice, when he came down briefly for food. The temperature had hovered near fifty degrees below zero continually and yesterday it had been windy all day. Yet Weldy and Ken Lee were forced to work out in the open on the runway, unprotected from the elements, without heat and largely with simple, manual tools.

"How's it coming up there, Weldy?" asked Wes.

After a long pause, Weldy's tired voice answered quietly, "Slow and cold. Pat Haskell welded some steel bars together in his off time into an 'A' frame for us. Couple more hours on the machine and we'll hook the block and tackle to it and pull the engine out.' After a further pause he inquired, "What do you hear from Resolute?"

"You surely hit the schedule right in Montreal. They got your engine on the weekly commercial flight into Resolute just in time. It arrived there last night. I talked to Fran yesterday. She said they were reluctant to send it—said none had ever been installed outside the factory before. They didn't think you had any chance at all of getting all the interdependent controls properly adjusted out there in the open up on the air strip. But she insisted and was careful to see that they included a trouble-shooting manual they put out for their mechanics.'

Weldy grunted, filled his mouth with a massive spoonful of mashed potatoes and chewed thoughtfully, then inquired, "What's with DeBlickey?"

"He loaded your new engine aboard the single engine Otter last night already but you know the visibility here has kept him from leaving Resolute. Weather's good there."

"Keep your eye on it here, Wes, and give him the green light as soon as you can. I think it'll clear here real soon. I saw a sliver of blue sky in the north on the way down from the strip a few minutes ago. Heard from the ice party?"

The anxiety in his voice when he asked about Plaisted's men did not escape Wes, who was touched once again by Weldy's deep concern for the safety of that party and his recognition of their dependence on him. He wanted so much to reassure him, yet was obligated to report exactly what he knew.

"Last night," he answered quietly. "But only briefly. Said everything was okay, but they were awfully short of white gas—so much that they didn't want to use any more than they had to running the generator for the radio. As soon as I told them DeBlickey was still in Resolute they said they'd check again tomorrow night and signed clear. Don't know why they should be so short—they had enough for at least ten days just day before yesterday."

Weldy stared at the salt shaker in front of him as he demolished a huge chunk of roast beef silently. Finally he asked again, "Ward Hunt still out?"

"No answer since day before yesterday," Wes affirmed reluctantly.

Weldy rose wearily, pulled on his parka and mitts. When he opened the door an icy blast propelled a heavy swirl of snow into the vestibule. As he pulled the door shut behind him Wes could hear him muttering half to himself:

"Why do I stay up here and fight this bloody country?"

...

THE FIERY RAYS OF THE RISING SUN PENETRATED the red canvas tent walls, flooding the interior with an orange color, as unreal as the scene itself. Frost covered everything in the tent. It hung from the inside walls like the cobwebs of a long unvisited attic. A knife, pencil, and pocket diary lying on a cardboard food box were covered with half an inch of the powdery stuff. It even lay upon the metal cover of the camp stove resting on the rectangular 'kitchen' box along one side, On the floor were the three motionless bodies, stuffed into the remaining two sleeping bags. The white layer of frost did not totally obscure the black, coffin-like structure of this bedding. The contents of an unopened bottle of Scotch, not six inches from the head of one of the bodies, had been rendered as solid as the ice on which the tent itself rested. Dangling from the apex of the tent inside was a cluster of mittens, boots, and liners hung there to dry, but saturated now with the crystallized vapor of breath. The very picture of abandonment and desolation, the scene was as lifeless as the pack ice itself. It was fifty-five degrees below zero inside that tent.

Walt awoke slowly, only the irregularity of his breathing betraying his waking status. Even without opening his eyes he could feel the unfamiliar presence of a body lying next to him. Only gradually did he remember the loss of the two gasoline-soaked sleeping bags and how they had zipped two bags together to create one large enough for three crowded men. He was lying on his side in an outside position and slowly he became aware his back was cold, but he knew he could not change position without jostling and waking the others. Arching his cold back sleepily, he felt his face brush painfully against a sharp, ragged edge. Wide-awake now, but motionless, he opened his eyes to the full misery of their situation. When they had crawled into the sleeping bag the night before with feigned cheerfulness, it had seemed warm enough. They had even flipped a coin for the envied center position, which Art had won. But the crowded conditions had forced them to sleep motionless all night. And all night Walt's exhaled breath had bathed the edge of the sleeping bag, which he had pulled protectively partly over his face, soaking it and converting it into a sharp-edged, ice-encrusted ridge. It was this edge's abrasive caress of his cheek that had awakened Walt.

With open eyes but motionless, Walt watched part of each breath add to this ice layer while the remainder floated gently upward. The tent was a four-sided teepee and as his breath rose, its vapor condensed into frost that adhered to the tent wall near the top. After four or five such breaths the frost layer became too heavy, detached and floated gently downward again; coming to rest on top of the sleeping bag.

Despair swept all resolve from his mind. All he wanted right now was to be as far away from this miserable place as he could be. The warm comfort of his bed at home crowded his mind. He pictured how his youngest daughter, sent by Mother to wake Daddy for work, would bound into the room and laughingly throw herself upon him with shouts of glee. And then the breakfast table with all the cheerfulness of anticipation of the day's events. Or later the quiet pleasure of reading by the blazing heat of the fireplace. And still later, the affectionate embrace of his wife's warm body. Love, warmth, and cheer filled the world he had left. And he longed for it desperately. Right now.

"Ralph?"

"Yeh, Walt?"

"Let's get up, Ralph."

"Go back to sleep, Walt."

"Why? I'm cold."

"The longer we stay in bed until everybody's ready to get up, the less fuel we'll use. The fellows in the other tent aren't ready to get up yet, so go back to sleep."

"There's a quarter inch of frost on the zipper *inside* my sleeping bag. Let's get up, Ralph."

Grudgingly Plaisted stirred. Suddenly the air exploded with, "GOD DAMN."

"What's the matter, Ralph?," an alarmed Pederson inquired.

"My beard froze to the edge of the bag during the night and I damn near tore the skin off my face just now getting it loose!"

No less ludicrous a complication could have provoked them to laughter, but this was enough. The mood was broken; they even knew what to expect now. Plaisted sat upright and instantly shivered violently. Nevertheless, he raised the stove's cover, reached for the gasoline tank and pumped about fifteen strokes of air into its chamber. The cold metal of the pump handle instantly blanched his thumb. Opening the valve, he flooded the burner with white gas. With frozen thumb, addressed with appropriate epithets, he fumblingly lit a match and thrust it into the gasoline. Closing the valve again as the flames leaped from the burner, he dropped back into the sleeping bag, reminding all what miserable tasks befall him on this expedition, all the while rubbing his frozen thumb back into a state of sensation. As the flame gradually subsided, he reached up again and opened the valve. The roar of the flame resulting from the now heated and functioning stove carburetor buoyed the mood of all as they knew warmth would soon flood the tent.

"The frost, Ralph." Walt reminded them.

"I'll do it today," Art volunteered. "I had the middle spot in the bag all night."

While still in the sleeping bag he slipped his hand into the mitts he had taken to bed with him. Sitting upright he brushed the frost from the center of the bag. Then with wildly gesticulating arms, and with feet dancing frantically to keep from freezing to the icy floor, he beat the accumulated frost from the tent walls with all the demonic frenzy of a primitive medicine man. Brushing it quickly from the suspended clothing and sleeping bags before the stove's heat could melt it, he completed his chore as quickly as possible, and plunged back into the welcome warmth of the bag to await a more comfortable temperature before arising to dress.

Cold, miserable and shivering uncontrollably, he resolved to remind himself, were he ever tempted to consider the Arctic again after returning south, that there is nothing romantic about sleeping in an unheated tent at fifty below zero, Oh, God, how he hoped DeBlickey would be able to reach them today!

...

IT HAD BEEN A GOOD DAY, PLAISTED THOUGHT, although it had begun with little promise. Breakfast had been miserable—there was so little white gas available for fuel that none could be spared heating the tent. As soon as the food had been heated the stove was extinguished. With six in the tent there was little opportunity to move while eating and all had become thoroughly chilled. It was only the knowledge that the exercise would be warming which had enabled them to summon the self-discipline to drive themselves outside and load the sleds.

"Check with Eureka once more before we leave," Plaisted had asked Don. "At least I'd like to know what their weather is."

Powellek had unscrewed the generator's gas tank, dipped a pencil into it, withdrawn it and examined it closely. Without a word he had walked over to a sled, procured the catalytic heater and a funnel and returned to the tent. The serious state of their white gasoline supply had become obvious to all as they watched him drain the fuel from the tent heater into the radio's generator. The first of the choices forced upon them had been made.

Later Powellek had told them: "DeBlickey's in Resolute. Weather's okay there but it's still blowing at Eureka. Hans says if it clears at Eureka by noon Dick might get out of Resolute before the low pressure system hits there."

"Even if he does it'll be too late to get out here today. Forget it and let's go!" Plaisted had ordered gloomily.

And another cold night in the tent without heat, several others had thought.

It had been a hard day. There was still plenty of rough ice. Although the weather had remained bitterly cold all day, axes, chisels and shovels were still required, regularly enough to keep them warm. Neither did it escape Plaisted's notice that small floes were now being met with a frequency that

Belaying a sled down a steep slope

made their regular appearance predictable. The floes were still all small, rarely more than a few hundred feet wide, But all knew their presence gave promise of more and larger ones as they progressed.

It had been a long day too. With only the misery of a cold tent to beckon them, it had been easy for the men to be persuaded to work several hours longer than customary. Moving with meticulous care in the treacherously gray light of late afternoon, they had pushed their way over several more ridges and across a few more floes. When the darkening sky refused to tolerate further progress, Plaisted had noted with considerable satisfaction that the day had yielded a respectable traverse.

Pouring the second cup of that precious drinking water for each man in the tent, now Plaisted asked Pederson, "Did we make our ten miles today, Walt?"

"Odometer says about eighteen. With all our zigzagging through this rough ice we're traveling about twice as many miles on the surface as we actually progress north. I'll say we made somewhere between eight and nine miles north today," Walt answered.

"Turn up the stove, Ralph," Art requested. "It feels colder in here than outside."

"Can't waste it," Plaisted answered. "It's set so all the heat from the flame will go into melting the snow in that pot. Until we know when DeBlickey will get here we can't afford to waste any of the gas heating the air in the tent. As soon as we eat we'll turn off the stove altogether and crowd into the sleeping bags again,"

"By the way," Bombardier asked. "Can we use the bags tonight that were soaked with gasoline yesterday?"

"No," Art answered. "We unrolled and unzipped them, then tied them to the top of the sleds to air out all day. But they smell as bad tonight as last night. The air must be too cold for the gasoline to evaporate."

"What did you hear from Eureka, Don?" he added.

"It finally stopped blowing at Eureka this afternoon, but too late for DeBlickey to come in. He's still at Resolute and will try again tomorrow—if he can get out. Still no word from Ward Hunt either."

As each man was occupied with his own thoughts, the remainder of the meal passed without further conversation. The silence was broken only when Bombardier developed a cramp in his thigh and, because of the crowded conditions, asked if he could rest his foot in Ernst's lap to straighten the leg and relieve the tight muscle. No one needed to be reminded of how little white gasoline remained, nor what it meant when it was gone.

As they prepared to retire later, Plaisted handed them each a small foil-wrapped package and advised them:

"Take these and your clothes into the bag with you tonight."

"Why?" a surprised Pederson asked.

"Because you'll have to dress tomorrow without any heat. We can't afford the white gas, so we'll have dry vegetable bars for breakfast and then take off. You'll drink water in the evening only!"

...

"Still nothing from the ice party, Wes?" Dick DeBlickey asked in the radio room at Eureka.

"No, Dick," Wes Cook replied. "I usually hear from Don before 2000 every night but the last two nights he's come on just long enough to ask when you're coming and then he signs off fast—says they're so short of white gas. And tonight he hasn't come on at all,"

"Well, I'm glad you heard from base camp at Ward Hunt tonight. I'll want to know before I take off if I can land there tomorrow."

"Yes, Moriarty said the generator ran wild and blew out the fuses. Their supplies are in such a mess up there that it took him a day and a half just to find what he needed, even after he found out what had to be repaired. But they're back in operation now. I certainly wish, though, that we could give the ice party the good news you're here. When we talked to them last night we had to be pretty pessimistic about your chances of getting out of Resolute today."

"Well, I probably should not have taken off there today. It was blowing pretty hard, but I knew we needed to get out to the ice party pretty soon. When the Meteorology boys at Resolute told me it was a big low-pressure system moving in that looked as though it would hang around for four or five days, I figured this was the only chance we had. When you said it was clearing here I thought I'd try it."

"Well, they'll be glad you did. When will you leave tomorrow?"

"About 10:00, if Moriarty gives me the green light from Ward Hunt. I have two extra drums of aviation gasoline aboard and want to sit down at Ward Hunt to pour those into my tanks. We'll check with you by radio from there about noon. If you haven't heard from them by then, I'll just fly out over the pack ice in a blind search for them."

Pulling on his mitts he commented, "I'm going back up to the strip and spell off Weldy on the engine change job so he can get at least a couple hours sleep," then added facetiously: "You should take better care of him. You need him!"

...

WITH THE SNOWMOBILE TANK ALMOST DRY there was little stimulus to get up early the next morning. So it was after ten before they were all gathered in Plaisted's tent. No colder, more bedraggled, miserable group of men ever sat on the pack ice. With no opportunity to dry them for days now, they sat in their wet, chilly clothes, engaged in discussing the appropriate use of the remaining white gas.

Engine replacement at Eureka

"We've got enough for one more meal and about three radio transmissions or two more meals," Plaisted told them. "Which will it be?"

"We've got to call Eureka to find out about DeBlickey," Don declared emphatically. "We didn't check at all yesterday."

"And when we find out he's still weathered in at Resolute what have we got for our gasoline?" asked Bombardier bitterly. "If he did make it, let him find us out here."

"We've still got two or three hours of fuel left in the Skidoo tanks," Walt declared, "Let's eat, and then move until that's gone."

"If we bum up every drop of snowmobile fuel before we stop we might be in rough ice where DeBlickey would never spot us or drop us supplies if he did," Art answered. "Those few miles won't help either way. I vote to stay here."

"Can you get a position reading, Art?" Plaisted asked.

"Sure. The sky is clear and in about an hour I'll be able to see enough of the sun for a sextant shot."

Plaisted had dreaded the problem of exhausting snowmobile fuel supplies before DeBlickey's resupply run. Until now the men had been kept reasonably warm during the day through the sheer hard exercise of travel. It would be impossible to keep up their spirits if they were forced to sit in a cold tent in these temperatures twenty-four hours a day merely waiting. Yet it was obvious he could not render the group totally immobile by simply advancing until the machines stopped. He had denied Powellek the daily radio contact yesterday because he had felt it was so improbable that DeBlickey could come then. He knew Dick would take every reasonable risk to help them, but he recognized too, the frustrating restrictive limitations of Arctic air travel. He also realized it had been his decision to advance to this irretrievable point against the urging of some of the party, though he recognized now it had been a correct decision. Only one quart of white gas remained. He had already decided how to use this dribble of life, but felt the others would feel better about it if they had the opportunity to express their own feelings about it.

"Art," he ordered. "Go out and get your readings. Don, warm up the radio. When Art gets back and gives you our position, call Eureka. If we're lucky DeBlickey will be ready to come out and you can tell him where we are. If not, well, we've skipped breakfast."

As he approached the pressure ridge at the edge of the floe, Art wished he had been able to warm his hands well before he had left the tent. Even then he knew his fingers would have been white before he finished the task. Today it would be worse. Art was no navigator, and he knew it. Astronomy had always been confusing to him. With a mariner's help he had created a sequence of entries in a hook, by mechanically entering the sextant readings and other figures from navigation tables into the appropriate spaces, he had learned to calculate his position without understanding it. This had worked well on other Arctic trips, but he had never mastered the use of the artificial horizon. Last year, though, he had discovered that if he could mount a pressure ridge higher than any within several miles from him in the direction of the sun, he could accept the apparent horizon with only a minimum of error.

Mounting the top of the ridge, he was pleased that there was no other nearby ridge of significant size to the south, He opened the case, assembled the sextant, raised it to his eye and squinted through the eyepiece at the sun, Rocking it gently to be certain of its vertical position, he carefully advanced the lever until the upper edge of the sun's image was superimposed upon the horizon. He had been taught to use the lower edge but at this time of the year the sun was so low he frequently could not see its lower edge. Lowering

Art Aufderheide trys his hand with the sextant

the sextant quickly he glanced at his watch and immediately recorded the time. More leisurely now he read and recorded the sextant's reading. With pale, unfeeling fingers, he restored the device to its container and plunged his frozen hands under his belt, pressing them against his warming thighs. Minutes later, he repeated the process. And again. Sure now of the measurements' reliability he prepared to pack up his instruments.

Staring at the southern horizon, he could just make out the tip of Mt. Walker at the foot of which the base camp was located. So near it seemed. And so secure. Could they really get back if DeBlickey did not reach them? They would, of course, have to walk. Could they make it? It must be less than fifty miles. Two days' walk perhaps? Surely they could walk twenty-five miles a day. Back home he had walked more than forty once. But then the intruded reality of the terrain then had crossed itself into that dream. The pressure ridges, the many detours, the soft snow. The shore lead may have opened since they crossed it several days ago. Still, if they didn't stop, couldn't they make it? But then he remembered it was still fifty degrees below zero. And they couldn't carry anything. Their clothing was already too wet to be warm, But if they didn't stop? But no tent; no sleeping bag; no food; and no water. No water! That did it. The enormous water loss from the body these temperatures induced he recognized as limiting as the Sahara Desert clime. No, they had to stay now. They could only depend on DeBlickey to find them. They could not help themselves. He thought of his travels with Eskimos again and longed for dogs.

Mulling these thoughts, he turned to depart when the realization of the position of the sun struck him. He could still see the tip of Mt. Walker adjacent to base camp. His last reading a moment ago had been precisely at twelve noon, If they were directly north of Ward Hunt Island as intended, the sun at noon should be precisely south, or exactly behind Mt. Walker. Yet he could see it clearly to the right of it. He realized they must be west of Ward Hunt Island. This would help DeBlickey some. But how far west? Suddenly he realized his hand held the solution. Raising the sextant once more, he held it horizontally. Using the sun as a "horizon" Art superimposed the tip of Mr. Walker upon it. Gratified he recorded the ten-degree increment and returned to the tent.

Art was still working with his tables when Powellek came running over to his tent, reporting excitedly, "DeBlickey's at Ward Hunt right now, ready to come out. He got in to Eureka last night. Moriarty's got his radio back in business and I can talk directly to him. Where are we, Art?'

'Tell Dick to fly out thirty-seven miles on course ten degrees west of north from Ward Hunt and he'll fly right over us," Art answered, and Don galloped back to the radio in the other tent with this news. Art looked up at Plaisted's skeptical expression and added sheepishly, "I hope."

"Stay on the radio with DeBlickey and help guide him in," Ralph yelled at Don. Then to the rest he shouted, "Get out on the ice and tell Don if you hear or see him."

Art's own excitement was so great he did not even notice that in Plaisted's voice, but he smiled happily when Plaisted lit both burners on the stove and turned them up to their maximum. As the unfamiliar warmth billowed from the heating unit to fill the tent, Art grinned at his partner and said, "Know what, Ralph? Happiness is a surplus of white gas!"

The single-engine Otter drops a barrel of gas

7

THE BIG BLOW

"JUST THINK," DON COMMENTED GLEEFULLY, "as warm as we want it—all night!" He had already hung his damp underwear to dry inside the tent, and was now adding his shirt and a pair of mitten liners as well. "How much did he drop all together?"

"Thirty gallons of white gas, and thirty of mixed gas for the snowmobiles," answered Walt. "And not a cracked drum in the bunch! Did you notice how much he slowed down that plane when he came over for the drop?"

"Slow down!" exclaimed Jean-Luc. "He came in so slow a couple of times, I expected him to flap his wings to keep from stalling out. But," he added wistfully, "he sure did look sweet to me up there."

It was the first time they had been really warm in days, and they were reveling in it. Their catalytic heater had been started, and the cook stove now added its heat to the tent. They sat in their shirt sleeves, delightfully and even uncomfortably warm.

"Do you realize by the time he gets back, DeBlickey will have flown almost 3,000 miles just to drop us those few drums of gasoline?" Powellek suggested.

"And just in time, too," Art replied. "When I think of the many things that could have stopped him, it convinces me we need a more certain supply line than that if we expect to get to the pole. He snuck out of Resolute Bay just ahead of a blow; the guys at base camp flattened out a landing spot just barely acceptable for him there; gasoline supplies for his plane are pretty scarce up here; and an engine failure like Weldy's is catastrophic to a single engine plane."

But these sobering thoughts about the delicacy of their resupply line did not really depress their effervescent spirits. Their problems of the moment had been solved and they spent the remainder of the evening planning their progress of the next day in a mood of jubilant optimism.

...

"WES . . . WAKE UP, WES!"

Hans Michel shook the sleeping body once more before Wes Cook stirred and mumbled sleepily, "Ottawa's on the radio, Wes. They want to talk to you."

"Ottawa! What about?" inquired Wes, still not totally awake.

"They've got a medical emergency in Igloolik. A pregnant Inuit woman is bleeding."

"Igloolik! Where the hell is that?"

"About a thousand miles south from here. Fairly primitive, I'm told. They have a teacher and a government administrator, but no one that knows any medicine. Not even a nurse in the area, and it sounds bad!"

"Then why don't they fly her out, or bring in a doctor from the south?"

"They can't. Weather's bad down there. A big low pressure center has stopped everything in the southern Arctic. It looks like you're the only doctor north of the bad weather. They're asking you to make a mercy flight."

"How do I get there?" asked Cook.

"They'll authorize Dave DeBlickey to charter you over there. He came back to Eureka from the airdrop tonight and is on his way out in the morning anyway. And he brought Andy Horton out from Tanquary. Andy says he'll take over the expedition radio if you leave."

Wes Cook suddenly wasn't sleepy any more. He thought silently for a minute, analyzing the problem. The irony of the situation did not escape him. He was an orthopedic surgeon, a doctor who had spent his career setting fractures and operating on bones. He hadn't delivered a baby since his internship twenty years ago. An uneventful delivery would be simple, but a life-threatening hemorrhage in primitive conditions? When he had volunteered for base camp physician, he had tried to imagine every possible medical problem that could arise. He had used his colleagues' advice freely to refresh his memory on many conditions he had not encountered in his surgical practice. But the one thing he had never expected to face on a polar expedition was an obstetrical emergency.

He dressed hastily and hurried to the radio room where his contact with Ottawa confirmed what Hans had told him. Their request was impeccably courteous, but Wes realized clearly that there was no real alternative. A woman was in serious trouble and he was the only doctor who could reach her. Assuring Ottawa he would leave as soon as DeBlickey could fly, he signed off and turned from the VHF radio to his own ham radio that he had brought with him and set up in the radio shack at Eureka.

Cook, together with nearly a hundred other physicians who enjoyed amateur radio as a hobby, had formed "MARCO" (Medical Amateur Radio Council) just a few years previously. Through this amateur network they had been able to provide medical help in dozens of emergencies. A sailor at sea with suspected appendicitis, a bleeding highway accident victim, a possible diphtheritic infant at a remote mission station and many others had been guided through their crises by the skillful diagnoses and advice delivered via the radios of these physician "ham" operators. And now Cook needed them himself.

Even though it was nearly midnight in South Carolina, Wes found himself talking to an obstetrician friend within five minutes.

"Sounds like it could be a placenta previa to me, Wes," his friend told him.

"Okay, but what do I do?" Wes asked desperately.

"Can you operate there?"

"I brought a small belly surgery set along but from what they tell me about the place I'll probably have to do it on the teacher's desk in the school building," Wes replied.

"All right. If things look bad when you get there like they sound now, rupture her membranes. That ought to bring the baby's head down against the placenta, compressing it and stopping the bleeding. If that works, wait it out. If not, without blood transfusions, you'll have to do a cesarean section under spinal anesthesia fast, whatever the risk. There isn't any other choice."

Wes hesitated, then with the decisiveness of a surgeon, said, "Thanks, Bill. You've been a big help."

This was really what he had expected, but it was comforting to be reassured by a man who regarded as one of the best in the specialty. When he had joined the radio group he had expected to help others; never had he imagined he would so desperately need the advice himself some day.

"One other thing, Wes. I'll keep somebody on the radio here from now on. Call me when you get there and stay in touch."

When he and DeBlickey touched down in Igloolik the next afternoon, Wes no longer felt like the only doctor in the Arctic.

...

They moved much better today than at any time since they had started this year. It was a day when everything else seemed to go right for Plaisted. Whenever they hit an area of rough ice, there seemed to be a flat floe adjacent to it, permitting them to bypass the difficult areas with a minor detour. The floes were flat and plentiful, the ridges low and well-ramped with hard snow drifts. As the hours and the miles passed, Plaisted's optimism gradually returned. This was what he had waited for; this was what he had dreamed of so much during the days of slow advance and backbreaking effort through the near-shore rubble. A cold but quiet sunny day through "floe country." As they fashioned a path through a small ridge, Bombardier addressed Plaisted eagerly with the hope:

"Maybe this will be our fifty-mile day, Ralph!"

"Maybe," Plaisted admitted. He knew it wouldn't be, but he had been measuring their progress. The day was half over and they had covered an estimated fourteen miles north. It could be a thirty mile day!

"And, oh, how we could use it," he thought. It would bring them near their necessary ten mile daily average.

It was in the middle of the next floe that it happened. Powellek's engine stopped with an abruptness that belied simple carburetor icing as its cause. Plaisted saw it happen, but continued on unconcerned when he saw Walt stop to tinker with the engine.

It was at least forty-five minutes later when Plaisted reappeared on his sledless snowmobile, retracing his tracks to determine the cause of the delay. He met Art on the next floe, happily taking advantage of the pause and photographing every unusual ice formation in the area.

"What in hell is holding you guys up?" Plaisted demanded impatiently of Art, who was squinting through his camera's viewfinder at a wind-sculpted snowdrift.

"Don't know," Art replied without taking his eye from the camera. "Walt can't get our machine started again. The light is absolutely glorious for pictures today, Ralph," he added.

"It's absolutely glorious for snowmobiling too," Plaisted snorted, and roared off down the trail where Pederson was working on the incapacitated machine.

Even before he reached them Plaisted's heart sank, for he could see Pederson had disassembled much of the engine. Pederson turned towards him. Walt had obviously been working frantically. His right hand was bare and his fingers white. Small icicles dangled from his beard, and total frustration was written clearly over his frost bitten face. In spite of his hope for unusual progress that day it was clear to Plaisted that Walt had been punishing himself in this biter cold far beyond what could be expected of him, in his efforts to make the machine operational again.

"Problem's electrical," he told Plaisted in disgust. "I think the coil is burned out."

"Got a spare?" Plaisted asked quickly.

"No. If it is the coil it's a freak breakdown. And it's not something I can fix. We'll need a replacement part."

"Replacement part!" The ordeal of the recent air drop flashed through his mind. But he was also reluctant to abandon the machine.

"DeBlickey might still be in Eureka. Don, We'll set up a tent here, and try to get Eureka on the radio. Maybe we can get that coil out here this afternoon yet."

Art put away his photographic gear reluctantly when Plaisted and Powellek returned, but yielded when Plaisted asked him to select a good floe to pitch the tent since it might be their camp site for the night as well.

Within twenty minutes they had overtaken Bombardier whom they found working through a small ridge.

"Let's check that large ridge," Art suggested, pointing to an unusually high pressure ridge about a quarter mile to the east.

"Why that big one?" Bombardier asked in a surprised voice.

"We want an old, solid floe for a camp site and those usually have big pressure ridges around them," Art replied.

As expected, it was an old floe. Not huge but large enough—about a thousand feet in diameter. As they walked about to choose a specific location they passed an area that had been raked by winds. These had scoured the surface into a flat, hard area, large enough to set up two tents. Looking west they noted a low spot in the pressure ridge to the west that had apparently permitted the gales access to the floe.

"Here," Art declared. "We'll set up right here."

"Why?" Bombardier asked, somewhat puzzled. "Looks like a windy spot. Wouldn't that place over there in the shelter of the pressure ridge be better if the wind starts to blow?"

"Sounds sensible to me too," Art admitted, "but Arctic veterans have advised us against it. When we camp in the woods down south it makes sense to find a sheltered place, but up here they pointed out that the wind really moves an enormous amount of drifting snow. A tent pitched behind a ridge could be covered by snow within an hour or two."

"Well, I suppose," Bombardier said, though still eyeing the windswept surface dubiously.

"Besides," Plaisted pointed out, "if the ice moves, the most likely place this floe will crack loose is right at the edge. Better to bear the wind than to be crushed by a collapsing pole of ice or to fall into the water!"

Without further argument Don set up a tent, moved the stove into it and began warming the generator and radio.

Art could have added one other concern. While photographing, he had noticed a thin, black line along most of the northern horizon. At first he had assumed it represented the cloud of ice fog common over the water of open leads in these temperatures. But it was too long, and because he didn't understand it, he felt uneasy.

"We'll have to watch how we pack the tents on the sleds," Plaisted complained. "This one has rubbed up against a box and how has a three inch hole in the wall."

"I'll get the sewing kit and repair it while we wait," Art volunteered.

But it proved to be a miserable task.

The sun's brilliance was deceiving; the temperature was still fifty-four degrees below zero Fahrenheit. And it soon became apparent that a needle could not be manipulated by a mittened hand. Handling the tent material resulted in instant blanching of the fingers, rendering them useless after only three stitches. He began to alternate: three painful stitches, then five minutes of warming his hands against the bare thighs inside his trousers; then three more stitches, and five more minutes of hand warming. It was slow progress, but the chore was finished when Powellek emerged from the tent a half hour later shaking his head.

"DeBlickey left this morning," he reported. "He's on his way to Igloolik. Wes Cook went along on a mercy mission—some kind of medical emergency there. And, of course, Weldy needs at least a week or ten days before he can fly again. It'll be several days before DeBlickey can get back out here."

Plaisted's shoulders drooped. He had expected this but somehow hoped for something better. His dream of a thirty-mile day evaporated as he ordered:

"Then we'll have to stay here tonight. Put up the other tent while I go back with an empty sled to haul the broken machine up here. It might still be something Walt can fix and I sure hate to leave that machine behind already."

As he and Don were setting up the repaired tent after Plaisted left, Art eyed the northern horizon again. The dark line seemed more definite now than before, though shifting somewhat to the west. Since he had been deceived into unnecessary precautions by the unfamiliar grayout nearly every afternoon, he said nothing about his concern now. But he wished it weren't there.

As they were eating their evening meal that night Powellek tried to console a dejected Pederson. "You can't help it, Walt," he told him. "You can't carry a whole machine shop with you out here."

"A coil!" Pederson moaned. "Who ever heard of a coil shorting out on these machines? It's a fluke, I tell you. A freak accident. I can fix most anything else but how can you fix a burned out coil?"

"You can't Walt," Ralph declared, equally dejectedly. "But we need that machine. We'll have to tow it behind us tomorrow."

"The real problem is our supply line," Art commented. "Something like this will happen again and again. We won't get to the Pole unless we have Weldy standing by at Ward Hunt Island ready to bring us what we need anytime we call for it, weather permitting." Then, catching sight of Plaisted's

A typical camp

brooding face he added, "Sorry, Ralph, I know how much it hurt you to camp today. But if this kind of terrain and weather holds, we'll really move if we get the machine fixed."

Plaisted stared unseeingly at his boots, then wearily picked up a paper towel and began wiping a soiled spot. "Yeah," he said resignedly. "If!"

...

It was a sound Plaisted had not heard for nearly a whole year. Neither loud nor violent, it was still discomforting. Although he had slept well, he realized the flapping of the tent wall had recalled repressed memories of the previous year, which had penetrated his sleeping brain and awakened him prematurely. He listened first with unopened eyes and recognized the constant background hiss as the "ground drift" of blowing snow sifting around the base of the tent. The tent walls shuddered at irregular intervals as a gust tested its support poles.

He remembered last year's storm as he lay there. It had started this way, increasing until it had acquired the full proportions of an Arctic blizzard. For five days it had blown—and when it was over, it had broken the back of the expedition's first attempt to reach the North Pole. Was this another one?

At breakfast later, Don commented cheerfully, "Don't worry about it Ralph! After all, we've had perfect weather since we've been on the ice. You have to expect a little breeze now and then."

"Breeze, yeah. As long as it stays this way it won't stop us. But what we don't need right now is a blow. Art, you went out to take a look. What do you think?"

Art was silent. He had been out to check the weather. He had estimated the wind at only about fifteen knots. Long sinuous plumes of snow were drifting their serpentine course across the floe's surface. Their delicate structure was in constant change as each new gust shifted their direction and velocity. Enchanted, he had watched the kaleidoscope of motion, as beautiful as it was ominous.

It was only after the powdery snow had sifted through his zippered parka and wet his clothing as it melted that he began to evaluate its significance. The drift was still ground drift that would not prevent travel for it rose no more than six inches above the surface. But the dark gray line of the previous evening had risen to occupy at least one third of the sky. It had also shifted westward toward the source of the wind. He knew now the dark sky was weather, not the ice fog of an open lead. He wanted to believe it would be only an unpleasant nuisance, but he knew better. Still, it would serve no purpose to prognosticate gloom and so he merely replied:

"I don't know, Ralph. It's not bad now. Just be sure we all use our face masks today."

"It'll take a lot more than this to stop us," Bombardier declared as he finished his meal. "Let's pack up as soon as we can and move!"

It was nearly an hour, though, before they were all outside. Pederson had to dig out the snow that had packed under the hood of each machine, burying the engines. He grinned with pride, though, when he yanked on the rope no more than three times on any of the machines before the frigid engines submerged in snow came to life, shaking their blanket of snow from their shoulders.

"Jesus, Art, what do you mean—it ain't bad yet?" Plaisted asked apprehensively as he crawled out from the tent. "I can't even see the edge of the floe."

He was right. The wind had risen instead of subsiding. The drifting snow at times reached up to three or four feet above the surface, seriously obliterating distant visibility, though nearby areas were still no major problem.

"Come on, let's go," Bombardier pleaded. "We can see all right. All the machines are running!"

"What do you think, Art?" Plaisted asked again.

"I think it'll get even worse and pin us down completely within half an hour," Art predicted.

Plaisted wanted to go, very badly. Every hour camped was an hour they could have used advancing to the pole. But he remembered last year too. If it was going to blow hard he had no desire to be compelled to camp at whatever spot the worsening weather would force upon him.

"Turn off the machines, Walt," he ordered. "We'll wait in the tents for one more hour and then decide."

Pederson protested but Plaisted turn his back and re-entered his tent. He did not know then that he was not to emerge again until nearly a week later.

...

"HOLY CHRIST, ANDY, YOU WRITING A BOOK?" Weldy Phipps inquired.

"Cut it out, Weldy," Andy Horton replied good-naturedly. "You know it's just another letter to my wife."

"Another letter is right. You keep that up and you'll run the station out of paper here."

"If you had a wife like mine you'd write her every day too," Andy answered. "Makes it almost seem like she's here with me. Besides, even if no plane comes in to carry out the mail until we leave, the letters can serve as my diary."

"Okay, Andy. Just don't use my log books for stationery."

"How's the changeover coming?" Andy asked.

"Slow. We got both the new and the old engines on the A-frame. The company sent an 1,100-page instruction book along. We got about half the controls switched. The trouble is each time we add one more we have to readjust all the others. It'll take several more days before it's ready to put back on the plane. When will DeBlickey be able to get back here?"

"Don't know, Weldy. I had him on the radio this morning. Wes delivered that baby all right, but Dick said they had to go over to Pond Inlet on northern Baffin Island to take care of a man who cut his leg pretty seriously."

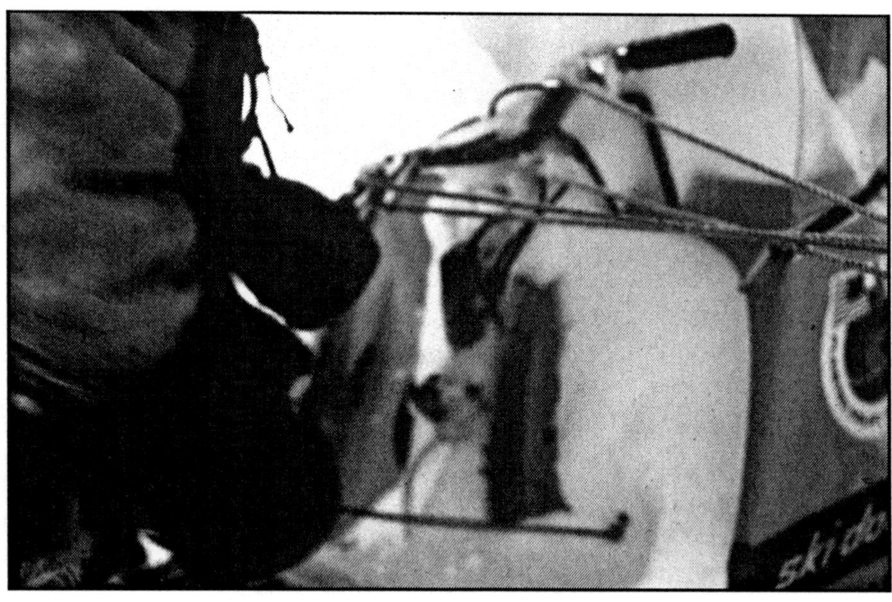

Morning routine: removing snow from the machines

"How'd that happen? Polar bear?"

"No. Believe it or not, he fell off his snowmobile against a sharp chunk of ice."

"The north is changing. Maybe they need traffic lights in Pond Inlet," Weldy chuckled. "Pretty soon they'll have gas stations all the way to the North Pole."

"We could use a gas station right about now. I could rig an automobile could to work on the snowmobile but what can I do with this mess?" Pederson asked morosely, staring at the burned out coil in his hand.

Plaisted did not answer. He was lost in his own thoughts. Shortly after they had returned to their tents the gray area to the northwest had moved in to darken the sky. The wind had risen to levels prohibiting any thought of movement. It was now mid-afternoon with conditions no better than in the morning. Clearly they would make no progress this day. He closed the book he had been trying to read and slammed it to the tent floor in a gesture of frustration.

"Don't fight it, Ralph," Art suggested. "It's too early in the season for a big one. She ought to blow herself out by tomorrow." But he couldn't forget the ominously dark sky.

"Delay! Delay! Delay!" Plaisted almost yelled. "You know every day we sit here we lose ten more miles? And you know what it takes to make up ten miles? A twenty-mile day, that's what it takes. And we haven't done that since we started. Every day we get farther behind. And every chance we get to catch up something happens. Don't give me that 'It'll be better tomorrow' stuff."

A vigorous gust rattled the tent poles. The lull that followed was heavy with silence inside the tent. They had learned to leave Plaisted alone when depression overwhelmed him. Pederson was generally more responsive, but it would be difficult to try cheering him with Plaisted in his present mood. So Art groped for his parka and left the tent.

"Welcome aboard, neighbor," Powellek sang out cheerfully. "You're just in time for the Don Powellek Show!"

Powellek was warming the radio over the gasoline heater. Bombardier was sprawled on the floor at the rear of the tent as tinny popular tunes recorded before departure emanated from his little tape recorder. Ernst sat in the other corner engrossed in recording his diary.

"I'm going to call Eureka in a few minutes," Don explained. "Before we left I told Andy if we had an emergency message we would transmit it some time during the first ten minutes of any hour. Andy is the most faithful radio operator I've ever seen. Some of his radio techniques may be a bit irregular, but if you've agreed on a schedule with Andy you can be certain he'll be there. With him absolutely nothing takes precedence over a schedule. If the radio shack caught fire during the first ten minutes of the hour Andy would simply burn up with it. When you're out in the field there's no substitute for that kind of reliability."

"Will the antenna be all right? The wind is really whipping it about."

"Don't worry about it," Don replied. "Just watch. I've been looking for a chance to see what this antenna will do in a storm."

The antenna outside resembled a flat metal measuring tape that could be wound up into the type of round container usually housing such tapes. In use the tape was merely pulled out to the length equal to the desire wavelength, the container mounded to the top of a ten-foot pole and the other end of the tape sloping gently downward to its anchor in the snow.

As Powellek started the generator and plugged in the radio, the dial lights lit up and the speaker crackled. When a wisp of apparent smoke oozed from the end of the radio, Art pointed at it in alarm, but was reassured by a calm Powellek. "That isn't smoke, Art. The condensed moisture on some of the hot tubes is being turned into steam. Listen now!"

Powellek's eyes glowed with pride at the operation of his system, as a weird howling, rising and falling in note and volume, emerged from the speaker.

"That's Andy tuning up on our frequency. Let's give him a surprise and break in on him as soon as he's done with it."

A moment later Don picked up the microphone and called, "CJU 942, this is Mobile One. Hello, Andy!"

The surprised voice of Andy Horton floated 200 miles across the mountains of Ellesmere Island out onto the pack ice and poured from the radio speaker. "Mobile One, this is CJU 942. Hello, Don. You caught me up short on that one. I just finished tuning the set when you came on. What's the matter—why are you on now? Trouble?"

As Powellek contacted Eureka, patiently explaining their situation and learning of the further need for Wes Cook's medical services, Art watched him operate the device. He noticed Powellek's instant change in personality as soon as he spoke into the microphone. No matter now agitated, threatened, alarmed or excited he was, the moment he spoke into the microphone his voice became subdued. In the steady, calm, and distinctly articulated speech they all later came to recognize as Powellek's "radio voice," he would transmit his messages with sufficient formality to be efficient without losing his natural friendliness. Above all, the compulsion with which he adhered to the regulations and broadcasting protocol reflected the awe with which he regarded the radio waves. Observing his hands he was amused to watch Powellek subconsciously fondle the microphone with an affection many men reserved for their sweethearts.

For more than two hours, Powellek stayed on the radio, relishing his first opportunity on this trip to transmit on the amateur band. He talked endlessly with amateur radio operators around the world; a bored American embassy employee in Oslo; a lonesome oil rig operator in Kuwait; an off-duty soldier in Korea; an Alaskan trapper; and a dozen others, carefully recording every contact. He even dashed outside and collapsed the antenna allowing it to be covered by drifting snow and was delighted when he could still reach Moriarty at Ward Hunt Island under those conditions. Four times the generator demanded refueling before he reluctantly turned off the set. When Art left several hours later Ernst and Jean-Luc were earnestly discussing the relative virtues of several Montreal restaurants.

"That's a happy tent," Art reflected. "Plaisted picked them well."

The wind continued unabated that night as he retired. Lying in darkness, enveloped by the sounds of the storm Plaisted suddenly sat upright and commanded: "Listen!"

Only the hiss of the drifting snow and the flap of the tent walls reached their ears.

"Listen to what?" Pederson asked finally.

"That thud. I bet a floe cracked," Plaisted declared.

They were silent a minute or two. Then Walt said simply, "You must have dreamed it. I didn't hear anything. Go back to sleep."

They arose the next morning. There was no need to arise early for the violence of the tent's agitations informed them clearly that the wind had reached gale proportions. It was not only a storm, but a big one. They didn't know how long it would last but it was obvious they were going nowhere that day, either.

Plaisted was unusually quiet all day. He grumbled a little about minor matters, but participated little in the dinner conversation that afternoon. He was obviously depressed but making a serious effort to avoid transmitting it to his men. Only once did his emotions slip from his control momentarily. Art had extracted a paperback book from his bag and when Plaisted saw *The Source* by James A. Michener, he wailed, "Oh, Christ, no. Did you have to bring that one along again?"

Pederson spent an hour meticulously recording the performance and defects of each machine, then repaired a switch on Bombardier's tape recorder, the pump handle on the stove's gas tank and the needle valve on a auxiliary gasoline heater. After fidgeting nervously for a while he launched into an hour-long recital of his wife's virtues, terminated finally by an irritated Plaisted who told him, "Oh, shut up, Walt, and let's go to bed."

The wasted day had been a strain on all of them and the vigor of the wind at bedtime was not promising.

...

IT WAS TWO O'CLOCK IN THE AFTERNOON on the third day of the storm. Plaisted had sent back enough food with the men from the other tent so they would not have to return for twenty-four hours. The violence of the storm had destroyed any illusion of an early termination.

Art lay on his back on the tent floor. He had given up reading. Or rather, trying to read. His eyes were attracted by the motion of the tent poles. These aluminum poles were sewed into a sleeve in each corner of the tent, meeting at the apex where they were joined together. Hurling itself upon the tent with the fullest fury the gale's gusts seemed to grasp the tent supports with invisible arms, threatening to tear them from their canvas envelopes. He watched their agonized writhing and wondered how long the tent would survive this punishment. He thrust the thought of a collapsing tent from his mind as another gust struck.

With every blast the windward tent wall was blown inward with a suddenness that made it snap like a rifle shot. Because of the snug interior the inwardly bending wall would compress the air inside the tent with an abruptness which, transmitted to the body, produced a decidedly unpleasant feeling of sudden pressure. It was a sound and sensation that simply could not be ignored.

No matter now hard he tried to direct his mind away from it by challenging it with thought-provoking concepts, Art found the storm barely beneath consciousness and constantly penetrating it with the more energetic attacks.

After a particularly violent blast he suddenly stood upright and struggled into his parka. Plaisted looked up without surprise. He and Art had shared a tent during the big blow the previous year and he had come to learn then that Art felt better if he went out periodically to face and feel the storm. He didn't understand this himself, for Plaisted did not wish to see the threatening elements; he had even invented an irrelevant record he was trying to set—the longest number of hours without leaving the tent. It was meaningless but it kept him inside. So the only thing he said now as he handed Art an empty pot was: "Fill this with snow when you come back in."

Art untied the inverted sleeve entrance carefully and thrust his body into it quickly before snow could sift inside. Wriggling through he stepped out—into a maelstrom. With the hardness of sand grains the snowflakes were being driven horizontally by the screaming gale, sandblasting his face. With eyes squeezed shut he turned his side to the wind, held the front of his parka shut with his hand, and waited until his eyes recovered.

Gingerly he opened them again and saw—nothing! Absolutely nothing! Not a feature of any kind could be distinguished in the gray-white swirl ahead of him. With his hand resting on his own tent lest he lose orientation completely he turned slowly toward the second tent. It was only ten feet away, yet was partly obscured during the more violent gusts. He moved slowly around both tents now, testing each support rope and making unnecessary adjustments. He inspected the hole in the other tent that had been sewn up the day before the storm and was gratified to see the repair still intact. Prowling through the sleds he checked that their contents remained secure under their protective tarpaulins. Eventually he found the box containing the weather instruments. Preparing himself carefully he opened the box, extracted the wind meter and closed it again quickly. Facing the wind and holding it above his head he squinted at his watch, then turned on the meter. The vanes spun instantly with a screaming whine as he held it there for thirty seconds, then turned off the switch. Reading the meter's gauge he waited for a lull, then shouted to Plaisted through the tent wall:

"Ralph, I just tested the wind. Write down 2,300 feet, will you? I'll figure it out when I get back in."

But even with only mental arithmetic Art knew that 2,300 feet in half a minute was a wind speed in excess of fifty miles per hour.

He was further dismayed when the thermometer indicated a mere twenty-six degrees below zero. It had been fifty-four below the day before the storm. He knew they could not expect the storm to abate until the temperature sank back down to near its previous level.

It was miserably uncomfortable outside but Art felt better. The impact of the wind was something tangible. Cringing in the tent might make him fearful but outside the threat had obvious and comforting limits. He turned his face into the wind to see how much the exposed skin could take. He studied the strain of the wind on the tent, and noted marked differences in the two tents, dependent on the height of attachment of the wall's support ropes. He turned the snowmobiles around with their back to the wind when he noticed the eddies behind the engine hood caused the snow to drift and pack in around the motor. He studied the snow action carefully on hands and knees and formulated a plausible survival plan in the event the tent would collapse.

Suddenly he stopped as, during a lull, his eye detected a dark shape. It was near the edge of the flow and it was huge—he guessed about the size of a house. But what could it be—a new, high drift? No, too dark. A fresh pressure ridge? Had Plaisted really heard the floe crack? Determined to find out he felt his way to a sled behind their tent, removed a coil of rope and tied one end to a snowmobile. Clutching the other end so as to be sure of finding the tent again he crawled cautiously out into the blinding gray whorl ahead. Only during the lulls could he advance for the shape disappeared during the gusts. As he approached it became clearer. And then abruptly and unexpectedly he was upon it. He picked it up in one hand—it was not a house or a pressure ridge but the upper half of a discarded food box projecting above the snow; and it was not at the edge of the floe, but a mere twenty-five feet from the tent. With no other objects visible for comparison Art's eyes had deceived him. Laughing at himself he followed the rope back to the tent.

He was surprised to find Pederson had come out too, allegedly to check the snowmobiles. They stood there, side by side in the midst of the storm, with the wind tearing at their parkas, the snow swirling about them as the more violent gusts occasionally hurled them to their knees. Pederson watched it all in awe, then shouted as reverently as possible in Art's ear:

"Thank the Lord for preserving this floe!"

Art had experienced the wind, the snow, the cold. It was real; it was here; he could feel it. It seemed sacrilegious to credit these things to some other ethereal element. But he understood Walt's faith and merely commented:

"Well, it's blowing just as hard on the next floe, Walt. And the drifts we saw before the storm prove there've been storms here before us. Are you sure He knows—or cares—we're here?"

"He's preserving us, Art, but punishing us for our sins. Lord have mercy!"

"Nobody can fight the Arctic, Walt," Art replied. "If we bend with her when she's angry and move when she smiles maybe we won't get hurt."

With frozen eyelids and snow-covered clothing, they re-entered their tent.

...

THEY CAME OVER FROM THE OTHER TENT shortly after noon on the fourth day of the storm. They engaged in small talk but strong opinions on such varied subjects as the practicability of using a hole in the snow under the caribou hide tent floor as a toilet; or the quality of Minneapolis and Montreal girls.

Desperate to keep his mind active, Art had brooded about the pack ice for several days, an interest not particularly shared by his tent mates. Anxious to test the logic of his theories he asked Powellek:

"Don, what do you think makes the pack ice move?"

He was delighted to find Powellek responsive. "I've been thinking about it. Do you suppose the expansion of the water when it freezes has something to do with it?

"Maybe," Art answered. "Maybe there are several different kinds of motion. If a solidly frozen surface cracks and separates it must mean the surface area is increased. Perhaps that's what happens at spring tides—the moon and sun pull a tidal wave along, raising and cracking the surface which then settles back with little separation after the tide passes. That could account for all the cracks we see just a foot or so wide."

"Great idea," Don replied. "But the large leads we've seen further out and in the summer must have a different explanation. The space between those floes is so great it could happen only if ice is lost from the ocean."

"Right," Art responded. "And we know ice is moving continuously from the Siberian side of the ocean across the North Pole and down the other side, all the way down the east coast of Greenland into the Atlantic, driven by ocean currents. More in summer than in winter, but always some. In fact it was some of this ice that sank the *Titanic*."

"Sure. In other words, we can expect a fairly sudden, major movement of ice when the warmer weather breaks up the ice down around Greenland, flushing out the ice there into the Atlantic, making more room up here on the Artic Ocean ice then?"

They felt free to speculate since they knew science had few of these answers available for them.

"After all," Bombardier mentioned at one point of the discussion, "there's been almost nobody out here moving around on this ice at this time of year like we have since Peary in 1909. How could anybody know what really happens here? There's only so much information you can get by flying over it."

For nearly an hour they speculated further and quit only when Plaisted finally entered the conversation. "I think it's all the wind. You have a wind like this blow, and it pushes against the ice hard enough to break it up. And it's like a bunch of billiard balls—if you push against the ice here, it can be felt a hundred miles away where there's no wind. This wind has been blowing four days now. I been listening and I been hearing it crack and break up. Believe me, we're drifting right now. When this wind is over we'll be awful close to Alert."

That broke up all further attempts at scientific discussion. Bombardier asked Plaisted:

"When do you think Weldy can supply us again?"

"How do I know?" Plaisted snorted. "If it's blowing like this at Eureka he sure isn't working on the engine out at the strip."

"Why can't he move to Ward Hunt after the engine is in?" Bombardier persisted.

"Lots of reasons but the biggest is we weren't able to move the aircraft fuel up there from Tanquary Fjord before we left."

"He can't set down at Ward Hunt fully loaded until he's got an air strip there either," Powellek volunteered. "And to do that Moriarty will have to fix the hydraulic line on the J-5 tractor there. He's never done that kind of thing before."

"Same thing is true at Tanquary. He needs a strip created there too. Besides, the gas is all in drums down on the beach where the boats dumped it, buried under tons of rock-hard snow. It will take several men days to dig those out and move them up to where a plane can land," Art chimed in.

"Ward Hunt needs to have that thirty foot radio tower erected too, before its communications are reliable," Don added. "And don't forget, Weldy needs to install the receiver so we can communicate directly with him in the airplane. And he has to install the navigation beacon receiver in the plane too. That needs a special antenna."

"Yes, and darn little of all that is getting done. The men back there will do anything for us, but I guess we can't expect Weldy to organize everything. At least not when he's so busy putting his plane back together."

The men were speechless then; only the contortions of the wind-buffeted tent broke the silence. They all recognized how fragile the supply line was; how the least of all these links in the chain could prevent the plane from delivering the needed supplies. Now it was a faulty engine, but they knew unless they solved the other problems and firmly established Ward Hunt Island as a functional base they would experience these delays over and over again. Days that should be spent traveling would be used waiting for a supply plane that could not fly. Finally Art spoke softly.

"Ralph."

"Yeah, Art."

"When Weldy gets the plane fixed and we get on to a floe big enough for him to set down, why don't you send me back?"

"Why, you backing out on us?"

"No, but somebody has to go back there and straighten out that supply line. We've got a willing crew back there that can do it—if they're organized. The main thing I can do for you here is shoot pictures. I've got enough for this early part of the trip. You need the skills of the others out here. A week or ten days back there and I ought to be ready to come back on the ice."

Plaisted stared at Aufderheide. He didn't dispute the logic, but did Art really mean it or was the storm just getting to him? Was he just bored and rationalizing, anxious to be active again, or was he really sacrificing himself?

In spite of the many other agreeing voices, Plaisted just answered:

"Hmm, we'll see."

...

On the fifth night of the storm, Walt unrolled his sleeping bag and was getting ready to disrobe when Plaisted stopped him.

"Keep your clothes on tonight, Walt," he told him. "And keep your mitts and boots handy."

Pederson stared in astonishment as Plaisted went on to explain, "This floe is moving. I've heard and felt the ice around us all day."

"But, Ralph," Pederson protested, "you know we sweat into our clothes if we sleep in them and the next day they're so damp they won't keep us warm."

"Better that than the other," Ralph replied. "I know this is a solid, old floe, but it's not that big. If the wind doesn't let up we could be in trouble."

And so they lay there fully clothed, their arguments and differences of the day behind them now, listening to the perpetual wind. They had learned to know it so well by now that they could not even deceive themselves into misinterpreting its behavior as an amelioration of its violence. The tent walls continued to convulse, the pole supports to writhe and the drifting snow to hiss as it sifted around their shelter.

"An envelope of air," Art told himself, "a thin, warm, envelope of air is all that's keeping us alive in here."

Then amid the roar of the wind and the tumult of the tent's contortions he added aloud, "But, Ralph, aren't you glad DeBlickey dropped us that white gas before the blow?"

...

They awoke a bit groggy on the sixth day of the storm. Art had passed out sleeping pills the night before. They had all had trouble sleeping, not only because every condition around them militated against it, but because there was no physical activity to tire them. As Pederson predicted, they were damp and uncomfortable.

Plaisted lay in his bag listening. The sickening sound of the tent's twisting and turning reached his ears as ge awoke; the sound depressed him.

"Six days now—that's sixty miles we're behind," he said to himself.

"With the fifteen before the storm that's a total of seventy-five miles we have to make up even if the storm stops now. We'll be a hundred miles down before we get going again."

He began to think. He might be depressed but he hadn't learned to give up. The goal could still be attained, but only if every unnecessary and avoidable delay hereafter were eliminated. He concentrated on his men and realized the time had come to reduce the party to four. But which four? Pederson's mechanical skills were essential; Bombardier similarly saved him so much time in breaking trail that his return to base camp would be self-defeating. Including himself this comprised three of the intended group of four. Who would be the others? Powellek? It was true that his machine trailed the group consistently and that others might swing an ice axe with greater accuracy. But he knew how desperately Powellek wanted to stay on the ice; he knew what he had given up to be there; and he remembered how they had lost radio contact without him on the ice at one point on the previous year's attempt. He did not want to send Powellek off. Ernst? His job was to get motion pictures. He had proved to be an excellent ice traveler but an expendable part of the final goal. He knew he needed motion pictures but he also knew the pictures had no value if they did not reach the Pole. Art? Whatever his motive for the suggestion, he would agree to it. After Ernst, Art was clearly the most expendable. He had many still pictures already, and Plaisted knew Art's previous experiences would enable him to establish Ward Hunt Island as an effective base camp. After that was accomplished he could re-evaluate and decide whether or not his return to the ice was justifiable. But if Art went he also lost a navigator. He would have to replace Art with Jerry Pitzl, for he simply dared not progress deep onto the pack ice without knowing where he was. Eventually, he realized, he would have to choose between Powellek and Pitzl. Perhaps, he hoped, circumstances at that time would help make the choice.

In the meantime he hoped he could continue to repress the agitation he felt at the frustrating delay imposed by the weather. He suffered all the strains the others did in addition to those his responsibility as a leader thrust upon him. At times he could scarcely restrain the demand for action which his whole being demanded, but he recognized that yielding would be fatal.

At mealtimes that day he no longer found amusing Powellek's daily greeting of, "But it's got to stop sometime, Ralph—I think."

Instead, Plaisted had reached his decision. He told them plainly, in his flat decisive tones, "Don, get Eureka on the radio as soon as the wind goes down and find out how Weldy's doing. Art, when this is over, you'll go back to build an effective supply line. Pitzl will replace you as soon as

Weldy can land. Ernst, shoot as much as you can as soon as you can, because you're going back too as soon as you can. The rest of you get all the stuff you don't need and send it back with Art. And remember, Art, as soon as you get Weldy stationed at Ward Hunt we'll cut our gear down to a three-day supply so we can really move. But that means you have to be able to send that plane out when we need it."

It seemed like a strange topic to be discussing with the gale blowing harder than ever, but it was therapeutic. They discussed every plan and possibility in exhaustive detail, then basked in self-satisfaction as though it were already accomplished.

When Ernst suggested to Art afterward that they go out to attempt storm pictures he found eager agreement. But something different struck Art outside. The snow in his face was not as painful and the neighboring tent was more clearly visible. Hardly daring to believe it he checked the thermometer. It read thirty-seven degrees below zero.

It required more than an hour to get the pictures they wanted and by that time they were sure of it. Just to be doubly certain Art checked the thermometer again. It had fallen four more degrees. They stared hard at the western sky and were rewarded with just the faintest glimpse of a hazy sun they had not seen for nearly a week.

Plaisted wouldn't believe it for the tent seemed to be buffeted as much as ever. But by four that afternoon they knew it was real. The violence had left the gusts and the lulls were longer. Powellek went outside to dig out and erect the antenna; shouting through the tent wall he told Plaisted there were times during a lull when he could see the pressure ridge at the edge of the floe.

Less than half an hour later they heard him start the generator. Shortly thereafter he turned it off and during the quiet of a lull he shouted joyfully, "They've had good weather at Eureka. Weldy's installing the new engine this afternoon. He plans to test fly it in the morning and if all is okay he'll be out in the afternoon!"

By six the tent walls were quiet. Stepping outside Art's eyes swept the pressure ridge surrounding the entire floe that they had last seen six days previously. He recognized several distinctive formations and realized the ridge was unchanged. The ice had remained immobile throughout the blow. The surface was scoured with new drifts and the snowmobiles were nearly buried. But their tents—and they—were intact and unharmed. Relieved he turned and was surprised to see Pederson had joined him outside. He was kneeling by the tent, and praying. Overhead the setting sun illuminated a broken sky.

It was over.

8

LOSING AND LOST

"I NEVER THOUGHT I'D LOOK FORWARD to seeing the temperature back down to forty-seven degrees below again, but it sure beats a blow," Bombardier remarked jovially at breakfast.

"Yeah, and what a relief not to hear those damnable tent walls flapping when you wake up," Powellek volunteered.

"Better to hear them than not to hear them during a blow," Pederson said seriously. "Sinners like us didn't deserve all the blessings the Lord's given us this past week."

"There's one of his blessing I could have done without, Walt," snorted Plaisted derisively. "And that's the storm itself."

Trying to direct the two, Art remarked: "When we get back, folks will never believe we didn't break down mentally and murder each other after a week under these conditions."

"You'll never know how close you came to getting it," Plaisted said dryly. "Did you ever spend a week in a tent with a guy who had to keep his mind active by inventing theories about every goddamn thing in nature he doesn't understand?" Then, changing the subject quickly, he asked Powellek, "How'd the weather look outside this morning?"

"Don't know, Ralph," Powellek answered. "Sun wasn't up yet. A bit hazy, maybe, but it shouldn't bother any for traveling—and it's dead calm."

"Well, get Andy on the radio at Eureka and see if Weldy's on his way here. It'll take us a while to dig out. If he's due soon we'll wait, otherwise we move. Walt, how's the snowmobile gas supply?"

"Nearly two days left but remember—the *Mary L* is still not fixed. We'll have to haul her and that'll slow us down some unless Weldy gets out here and drops us a new coil before we leave."

"It's been glorious not having to ration the white gas during the storm," Art added. "But we're down to less than five gallons now so don't forget to put that on the 'wanted' list."

Packing sleds at Ward Hunt

"I'll clean up in here while you fellows pack up outside," Plaisted indicated. "Oh, yes, Art, you better get a sextant fix for Weldy as soon as you can."

Viewing the camp outside Art felt a glow of pride over his selection of tents for the expedition. As proud and erect as two Buckingham Palace guards, they remained precisely as they had been placed a week previously before submitting to the violence of a six-day Arctic gale. An enormous drift had accumulated in their lee, confirming the advice they had been given to pitch arctic tents in open, unsheltered areas.

He watched Walt dig into a suspicious hump in this drift, uncovering a snowmobile. Digging down to the starter cord he saw Pederson pull it, and stared in disbelief when the third pull was followed by the roar of its engine. Smiling with self-satisfaction at this evidence of his skills, Walt helped the vibrating machine shed the remainder of its snow cover and then turned his attention to the next.

The previous year's experience with wind had been priceless. Each sled, chisel, box or other object had been placed side by side in a line at right angles to the wind. Each now stood in naked exposure, easily accessible. And each had caused a long, tapering snowdrift to form in its lee. Only the snowmobiles used to anchor the tents on the lee side were buried in snow.

An irregular high pressure ridge at the far end of the adjacent floe promised a panoramic view of the ice terrain ahead. Tempted by the photographic potential Art was crossing the center of the floe to reach the ridge. With lowered eyes he was picking his way carefully through an area of packed drifts. As he did so, the sun shone through a gap in the clouds, throwing the Arctic landscape into a moment of sharpened beauty that made him stop for a few moments and contemplate its unexpected radiance. The sight left him with rising spirits as he turned back to camp.

"We may as well go ahead," Art heard Pederson declare as he returned to the tent. "We got plenty of gas and the weather is great. We can drag the *Mary-L*."

"What happened?" Art inquired curiously.

"I just checked with Eureka again. Andy says the new engine flunked Weldy's test flight. Weldy isn't sure when it will be ready, but he's changing some adjustments now and will try it again in a few hours."

"A couple of hours work with the shovels on the floe next door would give Weldy a landing strip," Art commented.

"And if the engine still doesn't work after the next test it'll be too late to move and we've lost another day," Plaisted said gloomily. "No, we're nearly packed up now and Walt's got the machines ready. We'll haul the *Mary-L* with us but we'll go. If Weldy gets moving let him find us. We won't get to the Pole by waiting."

It was a day made for traveling on the pack ice. The storm had hardened the snow surface, which now bridged many of the smaller ridges.

They passed over a number of young floes and even an occasional old one. Peculiar areas ideal for machine traverse were also encountered which they did not understand. Large and flat, they lacked the discrete definition of floes outlined by pressure ridges. The only features seemed to consist of rather regularly spaced, upended small ice fragments and hummocks. When Art speculated the area might be a huge lead which trapped individual floating ice chunks when it froze, Plaisted only answered he didn't care a damn what it used to be but was just glad it was here now.

While the day and the terrain may have been ideal, their own arrangement wasn't. The incapacitation of Walt's snowmobile continued to plague them. Ingeniously he had reversed the skis of the broken snowmobile. With the rear of the machine resting on the back of his sled he tied it into position and attempted towing it backwards. It offered little resistance and he was proud of his solution, but it tore off the sled at the first pressure ridge crossing, upsetting the sled as well. He tried repacking the sled, as well as a dozen different attachments of the machines to the sled with the same in-variable result. He prided himself on solutions to such mechanical problems and became vexed by his failure with this one.

Finally Pederson gave up his reversed-ski solution and decided to try towing the snowmobile facing forward, behind a sled which was itself being towed by a working snowmobile. Since Pederson wanted to be able to watch in case the hitch failed, the *Mary-L* was tied behind the sled Plaisted's machine was pulling, like a train of three cars. Even on rather level surfaces this was unsatisfactory as minor irregularities often sent each of the two towed sleds caroming off in opposite directions, upsetting at least one. Threading a tortuous path through a pressure ridge became impossible as the second sled invariably became jammed between ice boulders at any sharp

Walt tries towing the broken machine

turn. Plaisted's patience began to wear thin as again and again he was compelled to stop and set an overturned sled upright again.

Thus, neither Walt nor Ralph was in a tolerant mood when they arrived at a small ridge and once again a red-faced Plaisted found himself wrestling with the overturned extra sled.

"Jesus Christ, Walt," he gasped between efforts, "can't you keep these machines running? We sit for a week going nowhere. Then the first nice day we get we spin our wheels because of that broken down machine."

Flushed with anger at the unjust criticism, Pederson opened his mouth to retort, but recognized the frustration written so plainly on Plaisted's face and contented himself with replying, "It isn't my fault the coil burned out, Ralph. If it could be fixed, I would. Maybe we should have waited for Weldy to bring out the coil first."

He didn't really mean it. He was merely trying to remind Plaisted that traveling, even slowly, was the only alternative to waiting. He had never urged any decision at any time other than immediate forward progress and so was stung when Plaisted, finally succeeding in setting the sled upright, lashed out at him again verbally, "If I'd listen to you guys we'd never leave base camp. But I know this—those guys at base camp have got to stop playing pool and do a little work too or I'll send 'em all home. We need Weldy out here when we ask for him—not the next day or the next week."

And, leaving Pederson standing there accused of being the cause of all his problems, Plaisted leaped aboard his machine, yanked the engine into life and roared off angrily, the two following sleds protesting the behavior by yawing wildly.

...

It was nearly noon when Weldy walked into the radio room at Eureka. Andy Horton could see that he was too obviously exhausted to be triumphant, yet he detected a sense of self-satisfaction in his voice when Weldy told him, "Got her, Andy. Engine works good now. Can you find out the weather at Ward Hunt? Maybe we can still get out to the ice party today. Call me—I'll be in the kitchen."

"Great, Weldy, congratulations!" Andy bubbled. "We all knew you'd do it, even if DeHavilland didn't. Yes, go ahead and grab a bite—I'll try to get John at Ward Hunt." And less than ten minutes later he dashed into the mess hall to announce, "John says it blew this morning, but it's bluebird weather there now. Says the air strip has some bad drifts on it though."

"Okay, ask him to get the J-5 tractor and level off the strip. I want to go to Tanquary to load up on fuel first, so I'll be coming in heavy at Ward Hunt."

"Fine. What's your ETA?"

"Tell 'em 16:00. Make sure Moriarty has the new coil packed in a box for an air drop."

Moriarty did have the coil packed in a box. Just to be sure, he had packed not only the coil but an entire electric assembly, removed from one of the snowmobiles at base camp.

"Weldy wants us to level the strip with the J-5," he told Pitzl. "Let's go."

It required nearly ten minutes just to get the tractor hut's door open and another ten minutes were spent shoveling snow to get at the tractor. Moriarty returned to the warm mess shack where he kept the battery and dragged it back in the sled behind the snowmobile. But when he installed it and turned the switch the engine barely growled briefly, then quit altogether. Further attempts proved useless.

"I'll take the battery back and warm it up," he told Pitzl. We've got a small spot welding torch; maybe we can use it to warm up the engine a bit."

But these efforts failed too, as another hour's work yielded only frozen fingers and feet.

"Better take the battery back in to warm up," Pitzl advised. "We'll have to tackle the strip with hand shovels."

They were still shoveling at 3:00 p.m. when the welcome sight of Weldy's Otter became apparent as he rounded Mt. Walker and approached the air strip. Running to get off the strip in time Moriarty gasped: "He's an hour early. Wonder why?"

It was a bumpy landing, for their hand efforts had flattened only the most serious ridges. Taxiing to a stop, Weldy informed them why he was early: "Blowing too hard at Tanquary. Couldn't get in there," he told them.

"But will you have enough gas now to go out to the party and still get back to Eureka?" Pitzl asked.

"Yes, but that will leave me no reserve so I'll stop back here on the way back. I'm sure there's some old automotive gas in some of those drums up there on the hill. While I'm gone bring one down here, will you?"

"Isn't that gas pretty dirty for your plane?" Jerry persisted.

"Much too dirty. Besides that gas puts a film on the turbines. But I might not have any choice. I saw a piece of chamois in the mess shack on a shelf. I know that drum will be heavy but filter the gas through that chamois into your new ten gallon drums, will you?" Weldy requested.

It would be a miserably cold chore but Moriarty and Pitzl assured him they would.

"I'll be back tomorrow," Weldy said. "I want to get into Tanquary and fly a load of good airplane fuel up here so we can get ahead of the game a bit. But to land here when loaded, that strip will have to be more level. Can you fix it up for me?" And after offering suggestions on starting the tractor and loading the supplies for the airdrop he climbed back into his plane.

"Oh, yes, one other thing," he called out as he started the engines. "We often have trouble hearing you in Eureka. Better get that antenna tower erected as soon as possible."

Dazed by the many additional tasks suddenly thrust upon them Pitzl and Moriarty watched Weldy disappear over the pack ice, then turned and trudged up to the gasoline cache to begin their most urgent chore. How, they wondered, could they ever prepare the base camp in time to be useful to the expedition when they couldn't even start a tractor in these temperatures.

...

"Sorry to have to say it, Weldy," Andy spoke into his radio microphone, "but it's closing in fast here at Eureka. The ceiling will be down on the strip before you can get back here. Better stay at Ward Hunt tonight."

"I can't, Andy," Weldy replied. "Can't risk not being able to start the engines in the morning without the engine heater that's at Tanquary Fjord."

"Going to Tanquary to get it then?" Andy asked him.

"No, Tanquary was socked in on my way over earlier."

"Where are you now?"

"Just left the ice party after the air drop. We had quite a bit of trouble finding them today. The storm had wiped out all of their previous tracks. I'm timing how long it takes to reach the shore at Ellesmere Island after leaving them and flying due south. When we resupply them tomorrow we'll come back to the point on shore we'll hit tonight, then fly due north from there that many minutes and we'll be back close to where they are now. Then we'll try to spot them by sight."

"Doesn't sound very scientific, Weldy," Andy remarked dubiously, "but all that counts is if it works. Where will you stay tonight then?"

"It isn't scientific, but until we get the beacon installed I've got to play it by ear. Alert says weather is good there. I've got a few extra drums of gas stashed by their ship, so I'll stay there tonight."

"Good. What are your plans for tomorrow?"

"If the weather at Tanquary opens up we'll make two runs out of there tomorrow—one to shuttle aviation fuel to Ward Hunt and the other to resupply the ice party with fuel," Weldy answered.

Even as he was advising Andy on the radio he was studying the details of Ellesmere's northern shore as it appeared on the horizon. For, as he had just informed Andy, the point at which he rejoined the coast now would have to be their point of departure again tomorrow on their way out to find the ice party. Deep in concentrated identification of landmarks, it was with a mixture of annoyance and amusement that he heard Andy's final plea:

"And Weldy, when you get to Alert tonight, find me a couple of pens. We're all out of them here and you know I like to write a letter home every night."

...

PLAISTED DIPPED A CUP INTO THE SOUP POT and passed it to Bombardier. His sullen mood oozed into his conversation as he muttered to no one in particular:

"First perfect day we've had for traveling and we make seven miles! Spend half our day hauling a dead machine and extra sled, then have to camp early because of the airdrop!"

Pederson quite obviously did not share his gloom. "It was worth it, Ralph, he declared. "With that new coil the *Mary-L* is back in operation. Tomorrow we should really be able to move!"

"Tomorrow, tomorrow, tomorrow!" Plaisted fumed. "It's always tomorrow we're supposed to go. Tomorrow it'll be something else. If Weldy doesn't get back out here we'll be out of gas by tomorrow night and then we'll have to wait for him again."

They finished their soup in morose silence. Plaisted was right. The satisfaction of having solved the problems of surface ice traverse was being eroded by the accumulating evidence that supply problems would create even longer delays.

"We're going to continue to have trouble until we can get Weldy stationed at Ward Hunt Island," Bombardier finally commented.

"I told you all last night I'd volunteer to go back for a while to get that done," Art reminded them, "but it's a big job. We have to get landing strips built and maintained at both Ward Hunt and Tanquary Fjord. Three hundred barrels of aviation gas have to be dug out from under the snow at Tanquary and moved up to the landing strip. Most of these have to be flown to Ward Hunt Island. The buildings at Ward Hunt Island have to be brought into usable condition. The remainder of the supplies at Eureka have to be moved up to Ward Hunt. And what has to be done with the radio, Don?"

"The big antenna tower has to be erected at Ward Hunt," Don replied. "Without that Ward Hunt won't be able to get through to the south consistently. The new crystal unit should be installed in Weldy's plane so we can talk to him directly from the ice. And of course the electronic navigation beacon receiver isn't installed in Weldy's plane yet either. He'll need that real soon now."

"How long will all that take you, Art?" Pederson asked.

"I don't know, Walt," Art replied, and after a little consideration added. "If the weather gives us a break, maybe ten days. I hope to be back out here within two weeks anyway."

And as they lay in their sleeping bags that night he added one more thought.

"Only one thing more really worries me, Walt," he said.

"What's that, Art?" Pederson asked him anxiously.

"How an I going to solve the terrible crisis of the fountain pen shortage?"

...

Art was again riding in the sled behind Powellek's machine the next day. Don's cautious concern for his sled passenger's safety had tried Pederson's patience beyond his limits of tolerance and Walt had long since passed them.

Powellek's machine gradually lagged farther behind, but Don refused to imperil his sled passenger by driving faster. Eventually the inevitable carburetor icing occurred and the snowmobile engine coughed itself to a halt. After several futile efforts to restart the machine Don sank back to lounge on the machine's seat. The other machines had advanced beyond sight and sound. As Art dismounted the sled and joined him Don held up his hand and softly suggested, "Listen to the Arctic, Art."

There was nothing but silence when Art threw back his hood, but he understood exactly what Don meant. Here on the ice, now that the other machines were out of earshot, was the pure silence of nature uninterrupted by any human or even animal sounds, a silence that only those who travel to the most remote places on earth ever experience. For Don, it was almost a religious moment. He took a stroll southward down their tracks, apparently feeling that even Art's silent presence was enough to break the magic spell of aloneness and utter silence. Art let him go, and waited until he was out of sight before attempting to restart the engine.

...

"WHERE IN HELL IS DON?" Plaisted demanded belligerently as Art drove up alone on the snowmobile.

"Out for a walk," Art replied nonchalantly as he reached over to turn off the engine.

"What do you mean, 'out for walk'? We've been here for ten minutes waiting for you two to catch up. Why are you always last?"

Art retrieved his camera from the sled as he answered:

"Carburetor iced up. Took me a while to thaw it out. Walt's got the wire in his toolbox so I had to soak my handkerchief in gasoline and hold the torch under the engine on a shovel. Don got tried of waiting and started walking. When I caught up with him he waved me on said it was so nice he'd walk a while."

Art was climbing the pressure ridge to photograph the parked group from above when Plaisted blazed at him in sudden fury:

"Walk! Nice day! Jesus Christ, you and Don must think we're on a picnic. Of course, it's a nice day—the first one we've had in a week. And we probably won't get many more. The first day we've had a chance to make up a little of our lost time and Don takes a walk! And you waste time with your damn camera! Take your pictures when we can't move, will you! And if Don wants to walk, let him walk all the way to the Pole. We can't wait for him. Now put that camera away and get back there to get him. Wait a minute, go ahead and take your pictures. Walt, he'll get here a lot faster if you go get him. And Walt—one other thing, if I catch you ahead of the others once more, I'm sending you back to camp. You've cost us another twenty minutes this time. It wouldn't have taken you two minutes to start that engine again. Now hurry up and bring Don back here!"

After a resentful Pederson turned his machine south to retrieve Powellek, Plaisted added, "The rest of us aren't waiting. Walt and Don will catch up fast enough now so let's go ahead."

...

JERRY PITZL STARED OUT OF THE AIRCRAFT at the ice pattern beneath them. From 5,000 feet the surface looked so deceptively smooth. The granular patterns reminded him more of a lacework doily than the thirty foot walls of jumbled ice he knew composed them. It was his first view of sea ice this year, and memories of last year's experiences flooded his mind. He relived the agonies of "the big wall " and "the rock quarry" in addition to many other obstacles on that trip. Chief among them were the unpredictability of the supply plane and their failure to work out an adequate electronic finding system. "Once again," he thought, "I'm going out here with neither of these problems resolved. And we had a whole year in which to solve them!"

It was already several hours past noon. An early morning ice fog had delayed Weldy's departure from Alert and wiped out plans for a separate fuel supply run from Tanquary Fjord to Ward Hunt. There had been time only for Weldy to stop at base camp, pick up the ice party's supplies and Pitzl himself, and fly to Tanquary to refuel the aircraft. They were on their way out to the ice party now. Reversing yesterday's experience they had flown out to near Cape Colombia about ten miles east of the base camp, which is where Weldy had encountered the coast by flying due south after leaving the ice party the previous afternoon. By flying straight north from this point for the same forty-seven minutes it had required yesterday, Weldy expected to be near enough to them so that visual contact could be made. Peeved by what he regarded as a primitive and haphazard method of finding the party, Pitzl recognized once again that the myriads of shadows cast by the low sun over this jumbled ice obscured any which might be produced by the diminutive ice party. Only motion would distinguish them.

"D'you think they might have made better time and be farther north?" Pitzl shouted into Weldy's ear, after they completed their first, fruitless ten-mile search circle.

Weldy shrugged, "Doubt it," he replied. "Never did that well yet. But we'll try the next circle ten miles farther north, Trouble is, once we start circling it's hard to be sure of where you are,"

The aircraft pointed north again and droned on. Superficially the scene below appeared singularly monotonous, but to the eye of one who had wrestled with the problems of traversing the surface there were outstanding differences. During the past ten minutes Pitzl had noticed the rapid appearance of large flows and particularly the paucity of jumbled ice areas between them. And even from their height the shadows outlined the long snowdrifts that ramped many of the pressure ridges. Such terrain could well support a rapid traverse, he estimated, and he began to search the ice ahead.

Within several minutes he was rewarded when his eye detected a faint suggestion of motion on a large floe in the northwest. Scanning it with his binoculars he recognized the yellow color of a snowmobile. Excitedly he shook Weldy's shoulder and pointed eagerly at the floe. The plane banked sharply, and overflew the spot a moment later to confirm Pitzl's observation. When the adjacent floes contained an invitingly flat surface at its eastern edge, Weldy circled to approach it.

...

PLAISTED WAS SHOUTING AT PEDERSON in furious rage. Once again his machine had stalled because of an iced-up carburetor and once again Pederson earlier had been unable to resist the temptation of good traveling conditions and abandoned his rear position to forge ahead behind Bombardier.

"Fifteen more minutes it cost us again waiting for you to get back here," Plaisted yelled.

"You know how to thaw out a carburetor," Pederson told him defensively as he began to work on the stalled machine.

"Of course I do, but you got the wires for the torch," Plaisted answered, "and besides, I got plenty other things to do."

"There's not that much to it, Ralph, and you know it," Pederson muttered.

"Keeping the machines running is your job, Walt, and you ain't doin' it. Now either do it or get off the ice."

They were all astonished to hear Plaisted say this to Pederson. For Walt had obviously carried out an almost incredible skillful service in keeping the machines operational with the available fuel under these extreme conditions. The cracked and bleeding skin covering his frequently frozen fingers certainly testified to his dedication. Plaisted's extreme outburst was quite obviously the product of all his frustrations with delays, and Walt's failure to maintain the rear position consistently hardly seemed to warrant such a harsh judgment.

Pederson reacted instantly. He laid down his tools and walked up to Plaisted. Looking up at the man who was a head taller and sixty pounds heavier he reach out to grasp his parka. Alarmed, Art began to run up to the pair, but they never finished it. At that moment the roar of the Twin Otter's engines obliterated everything as it passed overhead in its approach to a landing on the adjacent floe. Ignoring the others, Plaisted leaped on Pederson's machine and disappeared in the direction of the plane.

"One more minute and he'd have had his face punched in," Pederson mumbled angrily, bereft now of an opportunity to vent his righteous anger. "What's the matter with Ralph this year anyway, Art?"

"This is the last chance he gets at the Pole, Walt," Art told him. "He owes a lot to a lot of people, and everything's gone wrong so far. Try to think of it that way if you get to feeling like a football."

Jean-Luc was at the door of the plane even before it had stopped moving, anxious for a tobacco fix; he had run out of his last cigarette the previous day and now he felt the need acutely. When Pederson and Art arrived at the plane the others were already transferring the new gas supplies into the snowmobile tanks. Plaisted was obviously excited when Art asked to speak to him privately. Moving a distance away from the others, Art told him, "Ralph, you told me before we started you wanted me to tell you if it seemed to me you were going too far out. So before I leave today I've got to urge you to quit picking on Walt. You're driving him too hard when he doesn't deserve it."

Plaisted's eyes gleamed as he answered impatiently, "I'm gonna drive 'em all hard. Like they told me at National Geographic, I've gotta drive 'em till they hate my guts or we won't get noplace."

Art stared in disbelief. "That's the first time I heard you pay attention to anything they told you. And it's probably the only advice they gave you that's not right. These men'll give you everything they've got without that."

"Maybe," Plaisted declared, "but from now on they're going to work. They're not going to like it, but they're going to work!" And he turned to join the other group.

Pitzl moved over and asked, "How is it out here, Art?"

"Ralph's nervous and picking at the men," Art told him quietly, "especially Walt. Might be a good idea to try to get Walt into the other tent for a while." Then he added, "I've kept a detailed record of the ice so far, Jerry. If you'll keep it up we'll have a useful report when we're done. So far the ice doesn't look like it's moved much since last fall."

Bombardier shook hands with Art gravely, then, pointed to the sky and said laconically, "Keep it coming!"

"We'll try," Art promised, "but remember, you're the one who gets them started in the morning, Jean-Luc. If you pack up early and leave they'll have to follow you within a half hour or so."

...

The Twin Otter on the ice

The trials and terrors of the past three weeks streamed through Art's emotions as the ice terrain flowed beneath the aircraft on the way back to Eureka. Whatever its detractions, life with the ice party certainly was far more interesting than the unpleasant chore of molding the base camp members into an effective support group. He knew the momentary relief from concern for safety would be small compensation for the thankless duties he was about to undertake. But he knew too that their existing state of supply assured the ice party's failure.

"Oh, well," he reflected, "I never joined this bunch in order to get to the North Pole. What I wanted personally from this is experience out on the pack ice. And I've had three weeks of that which I can never lose. But I still want more experience with leads. A couple of weeks at base camp ought to be a small price to pay to get back out there!"

...

Art stared hard at the haggard, drawn features of the men around the mess hall table. Andy Horton was there, and George Cavouras; Weldy and Ken Lee, of course, and every member of the weather station group. Horton was obviously very tired and Cavouras looked as worn out as Weldy. These were not the visages of self-indulgent, irresponsible malingerers; instead these faces confirmed Plaisted's judgment of their selection. These men had obviously pushed themselves far beyond what should be expected of them. He was already proud of them, and only hoped now that coordination and direction of their efforts would yield a more effective flow of supplies.

"No, I mean it," he assured them. "We've got the ice beat. The machines have plenty of guts, and there's so much snow we're using the shovels more than the chisels this year."

"Then why didn't you move faster?" Horton asked dubiously.

"Tough luck in part," Art answered, and outlined the problems that had plagued them. "Sure, we could have foreseen and prevented some of them, but that doesn't change anything. Besides, they're behind us and most of them shouldn't bother us any more."

"You don't know how good it is to hear that," George told him.

"We've been breaking our backs back here but it's seemed as though it was all in vain—you just weren't getting anywhere out there. This is the first good news we've had since you left. Then we can expect the ice party really to move fast now?"

"Except for one thing," Art answered. "That's why they sent me back here. They can't move if they can't get gas and all the other things they need. And not just now and then. Time is tight now. They can't waste any more time waiting for the plane. It's our job now to move Weldy up to Ward Hunt fast, so that be can fly whenever they call for him."

With positive optimism infused into the group now the discussion grew more and more animated as they reviewed the otherwise appallingly long list of problems to be solved. And with rising spirits they rearranged them into a final list with appropriate priorities.

"So then," Art concluded, "Moriarty will move down from Ward Hunt and join Andy and George at Tanquary Fjord tomorrow. The three of you ought to be able to get the aviation gas drums dug out and moved up to the strip in about four days."

Finally, turning to Weldy, he promised, "We'll tell you how urgent the situation is, Weldy, but we'll never tell you whether or not you should fly. That's your judgment. And we'll teach everybody your plane chores so you can spend as much of your time in the air as possible."

"Great," Weldy yawned, "if it works! Let's go to bed."

"It will work," Horton replied grimly, "because we're going to make it work!"

Art studied Horton's adamant expression. Mentally he reviewed the base camp cadre: Andy Horton—a fifty-year-old military lawyer. George Cavouras—a forty-year-old insurance executive. Wes Cook—a fifty-two-year-old surgeon. John Moriarty—a twenty-nine-year-old food technician.

And, for a while at least, he could add himself, a forty-five year old doctor. Besides himself only Andy Horton had even seen the arctic before. And, he asked himself, you are expecting this improbable assembly of aging novices, under arctic conditions, to dig out and manhandle seventy-five tons of aviation gasoline, construct two landing strips, erect a radio tower, learn to service an aircraft, as well as start, operate and maintain such unfamiliar mechanical and electronic machinery as tractors, engine heaters, thermoelectric generators, electronic navigation beacons, sophisticated communications equipment and many others? And all within the next two weeks? And yet, if they didn't! Inwardly he moaned silently, *Oh, God, Andy, how I hope so.*

Home sweet home: base camp at Ward Hunt

But when he saw Horton's determination, aloud he could only echo Cavouras' emphatic affirmation: "You better believe it!

...

ART PUSHED OPEN THE MESS SHACK DOOR at Ward Hunt Island and led the way into its dark but warm interior. It was three days later and Weldy had just returned Wes Cook to base camp.

"Come on in and have a cup of coffee before you fly out to the ice party, Weldy," he urged. "Wes, you're a mighty welcome sight here. It isn't only that it's lonesome here, we need you badly."

"The past two weeks have been interesting, Art," Wes assured him. "That bad weather to the south held on so long DeBlickey and I made house calls all across the Arctic."

"I'm happy you had an opportunity to see a lot of the country up here, but for the sake of the Plaisted Polar Expedition I hope the locals stay healthy, because you're going to be too valuable to spare from now on." Turning to Weldy he asked, "How many supplies left at Eureka now?"

"About two more full loads, but there's nothing now that's critical. We'll throw the remainder on the plane on casual flights down there. We just dumped today's stuff out of the plane down on the strip."

"Okay, I finished that shed out front we'll use for unheated storage. The only lumber here is in a few wooden packing crates but I found an old cargo parachute and covered the roof with that. Had to steal the door off the outdoor toilet, but the shed's usable now."

"Is the toilet usable?" Wes asked apprehensively.

"If you don't dawdle," Art grinned. "Maybe we can nail a blanket up to keep the wind out."

"Here's a note for you from Andy down at Tanquary Fjord," Weldy said, extending a folded paper to Art. Unfolding it and laying it on the table he read aloud:

> Dear Art,
>
> John Moriarty, George Cavouras and I are doing well. We fixed up a landing strip for Weldy the first day. Also, found the gas cache. Dug out five barrels that day and moved them up to the strip. Snow is like cement. Moving them with the snowmobile is too slow. John figured out a way to start the J-5 tractor and so we moved up seventeen barrels the second day. Got thirteen out this morning already. Expect to get twenty-five or thirty out today. Any instructions?
>
> Andy

"Good," Art muttered, "but not good enough. There must be 300 drums there. That will take them nearly two weeks at that rate. How's their strip there, Weldy?"

"Good, but too short for a heavy takeoff."

"And you can't fly the fuel up here from Tanquary until the strip here at Ward Hunt is put into shape?"

"Right. And that has to be done with the J-5 tractor here."

"Then tomorrow Moriarty and I will switch places. He's got the tractor going down there at Tanquary Fjord and can show me how. I'll stay at Tanquary to help George and Andy while you bring Moriarty up here to Ward Hunt where he can get this tractor started and fix this strip. Then you can shuttle fuel up here so you can station yourself and the plane here at Ward Hunt. This afternoon Wes and I will start assembling the radio tower here after we move the stuff you brought today up into the cold storage shed."

Weldy drained his coffee cup, then rose and pulled on his parka. "Sounds good," he commented. "Just so you don't think we've been loafing, Ken fitted a plate for the navigation beam antenna into the plane's camera hatch and last night we installed the crystal for the ice party's radio frequency."

They were smugly pleased with themselves as they watched Weldy disappear over the pack ice out to the ice party. "Only three days and things are getting organized well," Art told himself. "First supply run on schedule. I'll be back on the ice within two weeks."

Ignorance must be a special gift from the gods for the protection of the naive mortal against the malevolence of the future.

...

AN UNUSUALLY LARGE, S-SHAPED PRESSURE RIDGE near the western horizon caught Weldy's eye through the plane's window. He checked his watch and nodded. From their height of 5,000 feet, Ken Lee was watching the ice below out of the other window.

"I don't know why Plaisted always wants us to fly ahead of the party before we leave them to tell them which way to go," he remarked. "It all looks bloody well alike to me."

"It does at first," Weldy agreed, "but there are differences that form a pattern. Flying out the same way from Ward Hunt Island every time is making me recognize certain formations that could serve as landmarks. As far as the ice party's gone, at least, the ice hasn't moved. I actually think if we had photographs of this ice we could use them like a road map. And so could Plaisted."

Ken Lee looked down again at the white jungle below. The disorder of shifting shadows affected an illusion of metamorphosis so confusing he was blind to Weldy's recognition of configuration in this apparent amorphia. He shook his head, then shrugged, but did not contradict the veteran arctic pilot. Instead, he asked, "How long do we fly out today before we start looking?"

"It took us sixty-three minutes to hit Ellesmere's northern coast by flying straight south after leaving them last time. Since then they've had two and a half days of travel. At ten north miles per day that would put them about twelve minutes farther out. We'll start looking at about seventy minutes after we left Ward Hunt—that's thirteen minutes from now."

"They're getting kind of far out for us to find them this way, Weldy," Ken commented.

"Yeah. They're going a little better than I expected. We better get busy and install that navigation beacon receiver before the next supply run," Weldy replied dourly. "Let's see if we can raise them on the radio direct on that new frequency we just installed."

But there was no response to his call from the ice party. Surprised, for he knew they were expecting his arrival, he tuned to Ward Hunt Island's frequency and called them. To Wes Cook's prompt answer he queried, "We don't raise the ice party, Wes. You had contact?"

"Roger, Weldy," Wes replied. "They've been trying to get you on their frequency too but no luck. I've talked to Don on that frequency so they're getting out all right. Your trouble must be in the crystal you put into your receiver."

"Roger," Weldy admitted reluctantly. "Tell Don to be ready to check it when we sit down out there. Can they hear us yet?"

"Negative, Weldy," Wes Cook told him, "but I'll switch back and forth between their frequency and yours so I can relay messages between you."

"Okay. Our ETA over there is in about seven minutes." And after a brief pause Wes replied:

"Roger. No sound contact to date."

Both Weldy and Ken were straining to view the terrain now. The transition had been gradual but the change was obvious to them now. Floes were everywhere—broad, flat-surfaced areas of relatively smooth ice separated by sharply defined, narrow pressure ridges. Some of the latter appeared of formidable size and there were also scattered areas of impassable crushed and jumbled ice separating some floes. But it seemed from the air that such troublesome regions could be avoided by the ice party. The minutes slipped by and as their estimated time of arrival approached Weldy picked up the microphone and asked again, only to have Cook reaffirm, "Negative, Weldy, Don says still no contact with you, either sound or sight, by the ice party."

"With this better-looking ice maybe they're moving faster than we figured," Weldy muttered to Ken Lee. "We'll fly on five more minutes, then start the search pattern."

Five quick minutes later with contact still unconfirmed, Weldy told Wes, "I expect they've drifted west again. Tell them to keep a sharp lookout. I'm starting a series of ten-minute east-west runs parallel with the coast, each about four miles farther south than the previous one. That ought to do it."

"Roger, Weldy. I'll stay in touch with both of you," Cook promised.

Weldy was uncomfortable. He knew they were not very likely to see the diminutive ice party from the air in that confusing mass of jumbled ice below. It was disquieting to have his success in anything dependent on someone else—in this case the ice party itself. He also knew it was much easier to describe the search maneuver than to carry it out. The first leg would be easy, but as he banked into the second he realized cross winds and absent landmarks would make it difficult to hold an imaginary course parallel with the first. By the third "run" accuracy would be down to little more than guesswork.

"Wouldn't a latitude-longitude fix from Jerry help?" Ken asked him as they continued to search the surface fruitlessly.

"Not much so far," Weldy answered with some irritation. "A reading with a little sextant from a small plane on a sun as low as that doesn't enable me to tell where I am much more accurately than the technique we've been using. Might help farther out."

"How much search time have we got gas for today?" Ken inquired.

"Less than forty-five minutes," Weldy told him.

Ken asked no more questions. More than half of that time was already gone. His eyes returned to the ice as he dutifully, but not hopefully, stared at the unraveling panorama below him, scouring its surface for a speck of life.

...

"Still nothing," Powellek answered Cook.

"But I hope he gets here pretty soon. Walt says we haven't got an hour's travel left in the machine gas tanks. By the way, is Art there with you? Ralph want to talk to him."

Expecting praise for launching the first supply run on schedule, Art answered: "Art here, Go ahead, Ralph."

"How's it coming at the base camp, Art?" Ralph inquired. "Got Weldy based at Ward Hunt yet?"

"No. We haven't got any fuel moved up there yet from Tanquary."

"None at all? What have you been doing, playing pool?"

"Of course not. We did get some moved up but had to use it all for today's run out to you. John, George and Andy are digging it out at Tanquary a little slow but it's coming. Have to improve the runway at both places first too."

"Well, hurry it up," Plaisted ordered, "We need gas when we ask for it. How come we can't talk to Weldy direct yet?"

Art apologized. "The crystal's in but I guess it doesn't work. Don will have to look at it when Weldy sits down."

"Okay. Why isn't the navigation beacon in yet?"

"That's a lot bigger job than I figured, Ralph. That should have been in and tested before we went out on the ice. Fittings have to be made for the antenna because that has to be installed in the camera hatch while operational. And I'm not sure that beacon antenna was made for these temperatures. It has to rotate in response to the signal and the center shaft sits in an oil bath. But we've started on it."

"I don't need excuses, Art. Just get it done. Have you got the radio tower up yet so you can reach the States and get our daily bulletin out?"

"No, but we've started on that too." Art answered weakly.

"Sorry to break in on you but it's time to check with Weldy again, Ralph," Wes Cook told him.

As Cook tuned back to Weldy's frequency, Art did not even hear them as he sank to the edge of the cot next to the radio and stared at the floor. His mittens slipped from his hands as he felt the fatigue of the several, nearly sleepless nights, spreading through his tired muscles. Suddenly their accomplishments of the past few days seemed decidedly less cosmic than they had a few moments earlier.

It was in this mood of total despair that the crushing reality of Wes Cook's message finally penetrated his consciousness as he heard him tell Powellek:

"That's right, Don. Weldy wants you to stay right there. Have Jerry get a sextant fix and call me on it at 12:00 noon together with your weather. He's used up his reserve fuel. He'll try again tomorrow at the same ETA, but he's given up the search today. He just simply can't find you."

9

Sacrifices Must Be Made

Through the near darkness Ken Lee could see a swirl of snow slithering across the Eureka airstrip toward him, driven by a puff of wind. A moment later he shrank deeper into his parka hood as the bitter breeze flung the needle-like flakes into his face with stinging fury. Arctic airstrips, he mused, must be among the most wretched of all the places on Earth. Always built atop a hill, such a landing field invariably seemed to generate or at least attract a perpetual wind. He recognized that drifting snow driven by the frequent arctic gales would quickly cover a field located in a more sheltered area, but that thought did not warm his chilling body.

It was past midnight when he and Weldy had completed installation of the electronic beacon receiver in the aircraft. Fatigued from the long day's activities he had wanted to retire but Weldy had insisted at upon a ground test. Taxiing to the center of the field he had explained the principle of the device. The receiving antenna was mounted on bearings. When the ice party's beacon was activated the antenna in the plane's receiving unit would rotate to align itself with the source of the beacon signal. The direction of alignment was indicated on a dial mounted on the cockpit instrument panel, informing the pilot of the position of the ice party. It looked simple, but Weldy didn't trust it; it appeared much too fragile to him and he hadn't used it before. Weldy liked to use things he had used before and he knew would work. Perhaps that's why he was still alive.

And so he had handed Ken a spare beacon, telling him: "Put it under your parka. Turn it on and walk around the airfield while I check to see if the receiving antenna in the plane here follows you around."

Twenty frigid minutes later Ken completed his circumnavigation of the landing field. In spite of his discomfort he was grateful for the opportunity of working with Weldy, for he knew that nowhere else could he learn so much about so many aspects of arctic aircraft operation than from this legendary pilot. Weldy was right so consistently that Ken was not surprised when as he reached wearily into his parka to silence the beeping beacon, he heard Weldy report:

"Seems to work okay Let's go to bed. With that thing we ought to be able to find the ice party tomorrow morning."

...

JOHN MORIARTY REPLACED THE CANVAS COVERING the tractor's engine. The catalytic heater he had placed under it two hours previously seemed to have been effective; the machine was ready to be started. Straightening up, his eye fell upon the mountains beyond, and their striking beauty arrested his attention.

The camp at Tanquary Fjord normally served as a summer base of operations for a Canadian group of scientists. It was at the very head of a fjord that slashed deeply towards the heart of Ellesmere's mountain range. On the opposite shore a towering cliff of ice announced the head of a glacier that must be the source of icebergs in the summer, John suspected.

Tearing his eye from the vista, Moriarty rejoined Cavouras and Horton. Together, after a warm and hearty breakfast, they had returned to their daily task of digging the heavy gasoline drums out from their tomb of cement-hard snow. While the heater was warming the tractor engine all toiled feverishly for several hours with chisel, bar and shovel, slowly and strenuously extracting these 450-pound barrels from the cache and laboriously rolling them up an incline to a site accessible to the tractor.

Moriarty watched for a moment as Cavouras inserted a heavy bar between two barrels and repeatedly threw the full weight of his body upon its end in an effort to pry the barrel from its frozen position. When it finally broke away did so with a suddenness that sent Cavouras sprawling in the snow. Without a murmur, George recovered his feet and, together with Horton, pulled the heavy barrel into position. Listening to their grunts as they forced the barrel up the plank Moriarty marveled. Less than a month previously he remembered how Cavouras had reprimanded a Montreal hotel bellboy for failing to carry his suitcase. "What," he wondered, "makes a metropolitan high-rise apartment dweller like George fling himself enthusiastically into a form of labor which a longshoreman would spurn?" But aloud he merely called out: "Coffee break!" and they returned eagerly to the mess shack.

"Twenty-three barrels in two hours beats yesterday by five," Moriarty declared proudly as he drained his cup.

"And we'll do better this afternoon," Cavouras insisted.

"Okay. Let's get the tractor started now so we can move these barrels up to the airstrip where Weldy can load them into his plane and fly them to Ward Hunt Island," Horton suggested.

They had worked out a routine for starting the tractor in these temperatures that incorporated all the elements for a successful comedy. After warming the engine by placing a catalytic heater under it for several hours while covered with a canvas tarpaulin, all three re-entered the mess shack. Here the battery had been warming and several quarts of oil heating on a shelf above the stove. When Moriarty gave the appropriate signal the comedy commenced. John himself dashed from the building and ran to the tractor. Seizing a shovel he worked feverishly to remove the gravel heaped all around the edge of the tarpaulin to weight it down against the wind. Simultaneously Horton seized the heavy battery, holding it awkwardly in front of him he followed John with an absurd, hurried, waddling gait. Cavouras carried the warm oil under his parka in a pot around which he had wrapped an old pair of discarded trousers to minimize cooling in transit. Moriarty, however, had no time to savor the humor of the situation for as soon as they arrived, he had to fling the canvas from the engine, remove the heater and open the oil-filling pipe. While Cavouras poured the warm oil into the pipe and Horton hurriedly attached the battery cables, Moriarty leaped into the cab, turned on the ignition and stepped on the starter. If no one stumbled or delayed in any other way, everything remained warm long enough so that the frigid engine would begin its agonized movements. It was always with enormous relief that they heard the engine roar into life. Once started the tractor could then be operated all day, transporting the barrels from the cache to the air strip.

"It may not be elegant," grinned Moriarty, "but it works."

"And we figured out how by ourselves," added Horton triumphantly.

Many times during the day one or the other of them would find themselves staring spellbound at the silent regal beauty surrounding them. And after the evening meal that night Moriarty sensed that Cavouras and Horton shared his feeling of peace and contentment. By the light of two kerosene lamps Horton was authoring a letter to his wife while Cavouras completed daily diary entries.

Digging barrels at Tanquary Fjord

Suddenly struck by a thought, John looked up from his writing and inquired of his companions, "Fellows, we work like dogs every day. Why do we like it here so much?"

Neither answered immediately. Then Cavouras suggested: "The scenery is spectacular. And it's quiet and peaceful."

"And we have nothing to worry about except getting those barrels out. Nothing else has any meaning here except those barrels and the mountains," Horton added.

"And the three of us; there's nobody else here," Moriarty commented, acknowledging the growing common bond between them.

They reflected in silent contemplation for several minutes more. Then Moriarty said, "Most of those things wouldn't be true if we had brought the radio along. I guess if you carry a radio, you've never really left home."

...

"OH, RALPH, LAY OFF THEM, They're doing everything they can," Pitzl told him.

"The hell they are. Does the base camp think I brought them along to enjoy the scenery up here? They are there so we can get supplies out here. And we aren't getting 'em. Wasted another day yesterday. I sent Art back and still don't get what we need when we need it."

"Well, he got the flight off and out here, Ralph," Pederson protested. "He can't help it if Weldy can't find us."

"Of course, he can. If he had installed the beacon receiver in Weldy's plane we would be thirty miles farther right now. Those thirty miles we missed are Art's fault no matter how you cut it," Plaisted declared. "He's got to quit that pool playing back there and get to work."

"We were weathered in at Eureka for five days before we started," Pitzl rejoined, "did you order its installation then? We had the receiver and tools there at the time."

"Oh, shut up. There wouldn't be any problem if they'd just get to work back there," Plaisted replied impatiently.

"It's no use blaming anyone," Bombardier volunteered. "I don't know whose fault it is and I don't care. I just hate to sit here when we could be traveling to the North Pole."

"Wes says the beacon receiver is installed now and we're to turn on our beacon at 10:45," Powellek informed them. "I'll go back on the air at 10:30. Jerry, what's our position?"

"It's 86° 21' N, 75° W," he answered, "That's about 140 miles north of Ward Hunt Island. Do you think the beacon will work, Don?"

"It should," Powellek answered. "It's been tested."

"In a plane?" Pitzl asked.

"No. Only on the bench. The day before we left," Pitzl shrugged.

"It had better work," Plaisted mumbled. Then, recovering his optimism he declared: "He'll fly right over us today, watch and see. How do you feel now, Don?"

"Much better. Headache's gone."

Don Powellek had brushed death so narrowly earlier that morning that all were still a little shaken by it. While Ernst and Bombardier joined Plaisted and the others for breakfast, Powellek had remained in the tent to carry out a radio schedule with base camp. The radio generator always required warming and would stop running if exposed to outside temperatures, so he had developed a technique of setting it just outside the tent opening partially wrapped in an aluminum blanket to retain some of its own heat. This morning the aluminum wrapper had become partly undone and through an unfortunate accident had directed part of the generator exhaust into the tent. He had, of course, smelled it, but had not accepted it as a serious threat until he had found himself fumbling with the radio dial. Alarmed, he had pawed at the generator, managing to stop it. Rising to leave the tent, he had felt his knees buckle, and fainted as he lunged for the tent opening. Hearing the generator stop, the men in the other tent had assumed he had completed his broadcast. When Plaisted received no answer to his call to breakfast, about ten minutes later he had sent Pederson out to get him. Walt had found Powellek unconscious, his head, shoulders and one arm projecting outside through the tent opening. Dragging him out and turning him over, Pederson had recognized the cherry-red lips instantly as a sign of that scourge of the Arctic, carbon monoxide poisoning. That final lunge had saved Powellek's life for the frigid, fresh, outside arctic air was already beginning to revive him. An hour later only the ache in his head remained to remind him of his carelessness.

At 10:30 the radio generator was started again, carefully arranged this time to prevent a recurrence of the problem. While calling base camp Powellek was pleasantly surprised to hear Weldy's voice replying, "Whiskey Whiskey Papa here, Don. Do you read me?"

"Loud and clear, Weldy," Powellek answered. "What happened? I thought the new crystal in your set wasn't working."

"Sloppy soldering job on a wire contact. Fixed it last night. What's your position?"

Powellek told him and asked for an ETA.

"We'll be over you about 1100 hours. Turn on your beacon at 10:45 and we'll zero in on you," Weldy instructed.

"Roger and since we can talk to each other directly now I'll stay on the air," Powellek promised.

Fifteen minutes later he handed the beacon to Pederson, telling him, "Keep it under your parka with the aerial sticking up out through the hood. Be sure to keep it vertical,. Walk, away about a hundred yards from the tent and turn it on. You can hear it "beep" if it's working. Stand quietly."

And when Pederson left, Powellek asked Bombardier, "I have to operate the radio inside the tent. Please stand just outside the tent and keep me informed of what's going on outside."

Powellek sacrificed his own shot at the Pole to make necessary repairs

Then to Weldy he announced:

"Beacon's on, Weldy. Do you receive a signal?"

Weldy didn't answer immediately. Powellek imagined him adjusting the receiver and playing with the dials. Anxiously he waited for his answer and was chagrined when Weldy reported laconically, "Negative, no signal."

"You sure Walt's got it turned on?" Powellek shouted to Bombardier. He could hear Bombardier depart on his snowmobile to return a minute later with reassurance that the unit was functioning audibly.

Calling Weldy again he asked, "What's your altitude?"

"Three thousand feet," Weldy answered.

"Try 5,000. Maybe the signal's going over you at that distance." But several minutes later Weldy reported, "Five thousand feet. No signal. We'll be over your approximate position in five minutes."

"Okay, Weldy," Powellek responded sadly. "We'll be outside and alert. How much search time have we got today?"

"Forty-five minutes," Weldy answered. "You're out so far now the spare available fuel gets less with every supply run."

Within five minutes the men had scattered themselves about the floe. Standing on top of the pressure ridge at the northern end of the floe Pitzl watched the others. The hoods of the men's parkas were directed skyward, swinging slowly back and forth like diminutive radar antennas.

As the minutes ticked by, Powellek's mind raced through the various possibilities. Was the antenna incapable of responding because of faulty mounting? Or perhaps its oil bath had become too viscous in the low temperatures? If so, Weldy should at least get an audio signal if he plugged in the headset. Ten minutes into search time he tried it again but Weldy answered once more, "Negative. No visual signal. No audio signal. Can you hear or see us yet?"

"Negative," Powellek replied, successfully managing to keep the discouragement out of his radio voice.

As the minutes of the search time sped by Powellek tried desperately to determine what could have gone wrong. Even though it was a moderately complex device, the wiring diagram seemed clear in his mind and he mentally began to trace the circuitry. A dozen times he had to admit the possibility of a failure in the various components. But he knew it could not be solved this way. In fact, even if Weldy arrived, he could do little without tools and instruments. Even back at Eureka all of the desirable testing instrumentation was not available.

And yet, it had to be fixed. They could not afford to waste still another day waiting for supplies, especially when the next day might offer no more assurance of success than today. If two or three attempts were necessary to make contact only 140 miles from shore with a given navigational fix, what would happen at 200? Or 300? Or at the pole?

Twenty-five minutes into search time and still no contact. His rising anxiety was becoming manifest in Powellek's voice as he shouted to Bombardier: "Doesn't anybody hear or see them yet?"

"Nobody out here says anything, Don," Jean-Luc replied quietly.

Except for the steady drone of the generator the floe was silent. The long wait in the frigid temperatures was making the men restless, and Pitzl could see most of them stamping their feet and beating their mittened hands together.

Powellek's thoughts turned back several months. He had not expected to be able to join the group on this second attempt, and when his circumstances changed to make it possible there was little time to prepare. He had worked desperately to complete the receiver, and when it became apparent there was not sufficient time, he had found it necessary to hire workers to complete it. Thus, he had been forced to accept an instrument on which both their success and even their lives were dependent without having the opportunity to field test it. If only he had had two more days.

At thirty-five minutes into the available forty-five minutes search time the generator stopped abruptly, shocking him out of his reverie.

"Out of gas! Refill it, will you please, Jean-Luc?" he shouted. "Quickly. The can is in the sled behind the tent."

Nervously he turned off the radio switch until the generator could be started again, when he heard Plaisted's voice shouting something from the ridge. Relayed by Pederson, Bombardier told Powellek:

"Ralph can hear him to the south; says for you to tell Weldy to fly north."

"My God, what a time for the generator to go out. Hurry up and fill it, Jean-Luc."

"I can't find the gas can," Bombardier complained.

"Not that sled, the one in the rear," Powellek shouted, his voice rising to a higher pitch as his anxiety increased still further.

Plaisted called again and Powellek would hear Pederson shout, "The sound is getting farther away in the southeast. Tell him to turn around and fly northwest, quick!

Powellek almost lost control of himself as he thrust his head from the tent. Relieved to see Bombardier replacing the generator gas tank cap after filling it he turned back to the radio and a moment later heard the generator cough itself back into life. Too hurriedly, he flipped the radio switches before the system could equilibrate and an unexpected surge of high voltage flowed into the radio. His trained ear could hear the fuse blow. Almost frantic now he tore the power cord from the generator, and whirled the radio about to expose the rear panel. It required but a moment to replace the dead fuse with one of the spares he kept taped there for just such a purpose, yet it seemed like an eternity to him. Just as he restored the radio to normal operation and picked up the microphone, Bombardier called through the tent wall, "Plaisted says he can't hear him anymore. The sound disappeared in the southeast."

With the turmoil of desperation seething inside him Powellek pressed the microphone switch. The effectiveness of the many years of training surprised even him as he heard his own voice talking into the microphone calmly, smoothly distinctly and quietly, "Whiskey, Whiskey Papa, we've got a sound track on you. You just passed south of us; we lost your sound southeast of us."

"Roger, Don," Weldy replied. "I'll fly northwest for five minutes. Break out a smoke bomb if you've got one. Still no signal on the beacon."

Pederson had reached the limits of his tolerance for inaction. Setting the beacon on the snow he leaped aboard his snowmobile. Anticipating the need for the smoke signal he was already extracting a smoke generator from a sled and a moment later a column of billowing, orange smoke was rising above the floe. That completed he raced his machine madly about the floe, hoping the movement would help attract attention. Remembering his luck with it last year, Bombardier fumbled for his reflective signal mirror.

Pitzl strained to listen but could hear nothing. Suddenly he saw Plaisted gesture again and a moment later heard Bombardier tell Powellek, "Plaisted can hear him again in the southeast."

Staring hard Pitzl made himself believe he could see a dark speck in the sky just over the pressure ridge at the southeastern edge of the floe. Wary of

Walt sets off a smoke bomb for Weldy

mirages low over the pack ice he said nothing but when the speck enlarged and moved to the right he shouted to Bombardier that Weldy was in sight now.

"We've got you in sight now," Powellek informed Weldy. "Keep coming northwest; you're heading right for us."

Bombardier was flashing his mirror at the speck in the sky constantly now. When Ernest saw him he remembered his camera equipment. Dashing to the tent he retrieved his battery—operated electronic flood light. Directing it to the southeast he turned it on and joined Bombardier in the wild signaling.

Pitzl stood on the ridge and watched the melee in disgust. Plaisted was waving a red handkerchief, Pederson was circling his snowmobile manically about the floe, Bombardier and Ernest were frenziedly flashing their mirror and light, and the plume of orange smoke surged higher and higher.

"This is the way they did it in 1928:" he muttered irritatedly, "but this is 1968!"

And he stared at the abandoned, forlorn little package of sophisticated electronics quietly continuing to keep its directional signal at an unhearing aircraft receiver.

A moment later the roar of Weldy's turbines passed directly overhead and he watched as the Otter backed and approached the floe for a landing.

When Bombardier shouted: "He's down!" Powellek sagged back in relief. Turning off the radio he checked his watch. The search had required forty-four minutes!

He heard Pederson's joyfully excited voice outside greeting Weldy, but Powellek did not go out to join them. Dejectedly he turned to pack his personal gear into his bag. For he knew what he must do.

...

It was nearly one in the morning when Art entered the shop at Eureka to find Powellek still bent over the counter, working on the beacon receiver antenna. He was concerned about Powellek for he had never seen him more despondent than upon his arrival from the ice that afternoon. To Art's surprised inquiry he had replied, "Beacon didn't work. Weldy never got a signal until he was less than two miles away—in fact he saw us before he got the beacon signal. But tell Wes not to put this into his daily report to the media in the south. I expect to fix it and be back on the ice in twenty-four hours."

But his disconsolate manner betrayed him. He had been working on the antenna ever since his return without finding the problem.

"How's it coming?" Art asked him.

"No good. I've completely disassembled it without finding anything. I'll have it back together in another half hour. Weldy find out anything?"

"I don't know," Art answered. "What was he trying to do?"

"He wanted to get in contact with an electronics man in Ottawa to arrange shipment of a complete low-frequency beacon system of the SARAH type."

"That's the kind we had last year and we never really got that one to a reliable state of operation either," Art objected.

"That's true but Weldy is partial to it because it's an old, tested system. This one is too new for him to trust," Don replied.

As Art entered the radio room in the adjacent building Weldy was obviously already in contact with his party.

"We'd need the whole business, Jim," he was explaining. "At least two beacons for the ice party, the special antenna units to be mounted on the wings and of course the entire receiving unit for inside the plane."

"Negative, Weldy," Jim's voice spilled from the speaker. "You know the USAF hasn't used them for a long time. We'd have to get them from England. They haven't made any new ones for years so we would have to scrounge for the different used parts. That would take months."

"Would appreciate it if you'd try, Jim," Weldy pleaded. "We might get lucky and pick up a complete system somewhere."

"I'll try," Jim promised, "but I'm not optimistic. Better figure out something else while you're waiting."

Disheartened by their repetitive failures, the base camp cadre was a gloomy group when it retired that night.

Both Powellek and Weldy looked even worse by the next night.

"For a while this afternoon I thought we had it licked," Powellek said. "Found a bad contact. Resoldered it but it didn't work any better afterward."

"Jim called in on the ham set this afternoon; said he'll keep trying, but I can just about forget about getting a SARAH set up here in time to help us," Weldy reported unhappily.

"Well," Art inquired, "let's lay it on the table. What are our choices? First, Weldy, can you find the party all the way to the Pole without an electronic beacon homing device of some kind?"

"Maybe. It won't be efficient. There'll be plenty of dry runs when we miss. The sun's high enough now too, so it's hard to take a sextant shot up front. We'll have to install my drift meter in the rear. Then, with a position shot from Jerry, we ought to be able to be more accurate in our navigation as they get farther out."

"Any problems installing that stuff?"

Without answering Weldy turned to Ken Lee and instructed him, "The drift meter's under my bunk. There's plywood in the shop, Cut a piece to fit the camera hatch and install the meter in it."

"Okay," Ken agreed. "How about the bubble for sextant shots?"

"There's a transparent globe light fixture over the bulb in front of the barracks building. Use that and install it in the top of the fuselage just above the drift meter so I can use both from the same position back there."

"What can we do about the beacon receiver, Don?" Art asked.

"I've been thinking. I still believe the rotating antenna is our problem. But maybe we could mount a loop antenna in the nose of Weldy's plane. If we shielded it so that I could receive signals only from straight ahead and if Weldy would wear the earphones continually perhaps he could locate the beacon signal by pointing the plane in different directions and listening for the loudness of the signal. The audio part seems to work much of the time."

"I've got a loop antenna in the airstrip shack. I'll get a roll of aluminum wrapping material we can use from the cook here and fix up the antenna this afternoon," Weldy promised. "But there's one other big problem."

They all turned to him as he continued, "The ice party's going to be at the limits of the Otter's fuel range very soon. We'll have to create our own refueling station out there on a big floe on the pack ice near about eighty-seven degrees. It won't be hard to find a floe we can use and dump a dozen barrels of fuel there but how do we find it again?"

"Yes," mused Powellek. "Our original plan was to put up a tent there and operate one of the electronic navigation beacons continuously, powered by a small thermoelectric generator using propane fuel. Now that we can't receive the beacon signal, how can we ever find our 'gas station' again out on that ice?"

"I've got an idea," Weldy told them. "A bit wild but I think it could work. Art keeps emphasizing the ice hasn't moved as far as the ice party's gone. It might hold for another month yet. Flying over it every day I'm beginning to recognize 'landmarks'. If I had photos of that ice right down the seventy-fifth-degree meridian out to about eighty-seven degrees I think I could use the pictures to find a gas cache again."

"You mean, use a series of pictures of the ice surface taken from the air—use it like a road map?" Art inquired incredulously.

"Yep," Weldy replied without further amplification. They all knew Weldy too well to take his ideas lightly, and yet, a 'road map' of the Arctic Ocean's pack ice? It had never been tried before, but that was true of a quite a few of Weldy's successful methods.

"I've got a complete set of aerial photography equipment," Weldy told them. "Often use it on jobs for oil exploration outfits or the government mapmakers. I could have it installed by tomorrow morning and we could 'fly the line' tomorrow if the weather's right."

"It ought to be real useful for the ice party too," commented Weldy further. "They could really pick their route with it."

"Maybe, but they're doing pretty well as it is. Our problem now is not to move them but to keep up with them. By the way, how do we process and print that film?"

"That's where you come in. I've got a set of chemicals and paper."

Art thought for a minute, and then looked at Powellek. Don nodded. Because it had not been done before, the element of minor adventure was alluring too.

"Okay, Weldy," he agreed. "Tomorrow you fly a photoline over the pack ice and I'll make you a road map. But Plaisted won't like it. He expects you to resupply him tomorrow."

"Can't anyway," Weldy said. "We assumed the beacon would be working. To save time he said he wouldn't even radio in to us—just turn on the beacon while on the go! Without the beacon I can't find him that way. He'll have to give me a position, sit and help guide me in by sight and sound."

The activity required to prepare for the various alternatives was at least a partial antidote for the dispirited state into which they had all fallen. Even though they labored at their tasks until nearly 3:00 a.m. the general mood was far less funereal than it had been the previous night.

But as they walked to the barracks building, Powellek still seemed unusually quiet.

"Forget it, Don," Art advised him. "I'm sure you'll get the beacon receiver operational soon."

"It isn't only that," Don muttered morosely. "Art, I don't think either one of us is ever going to get back on that ice!"

...

THEY COULD NOT HAVE CHOSEN A MORE PERFECT day for it. A windless, cloudless sky overlooked a sun-drenched ice surface, providing ideal photographing conditions. When they returned in late afternoon the darkroom was ready.

"How far out did you go?" Don asked him.

"Just about eighty-seven degrees," answered Weldy. "There are some big floes out there ideal for use as a 'gas station.' And the ice still looks tight all the way out."

"Good. I found several more bad contacts including the coaxial cable," Don told him wearily. "I'll install the whole system again tonight. I'll bet it works on your supply run tomorrow!"

Weldy's photo lab equipment had required considerable modification to be adapted to the primitive technical conditions at Eureka and these chores had taxed Art's ingenuity as well as his stamina. With some trepidation the ten-inch wide roll of film 100 feet long was immersed into the tank improvised from pails and plastic sheets. When they turned the light on again an hour later it was with relief they saw their day's labor had not been in vain. Weldy stayed long enough to see the roll of wet, crystal-sharp negatives mounted on a contrived drying rack, then nearly collapsed in a state of exhaustion into his bunk from which he did not emerge until fourteen hours later.

Since Powellek was still occupied with reinstallation of the beacon receiver, Art took advantage of the time required to dry the film before it was ready for printing. The ice party needed mixed fuel for the two-stroke snowmobile engines on the next day's supply flight. Cold oil does not mix with cold gasoline so he found himself out at the weather station's fuel cache a quarter mile from the camp. Selecting the desired barrel, he wrestled with a heavy steel bar until the pry wrenched the drum from its frozen fixed position and both he and the container rolled in the snow. Picking himself up and grasping the barrel's lip at each end he dug his toes into the snow, threw his weight behind the barrel and began the long burdensome task of rolling it all the way back into the warm garage. The frigid breeze assaulting his perspiring brow added to his misery and reminded him of his fatigue.

The matter had become obvious tonight, when Weldy had brought back a note from Andy Horton at Tanquary Fjord during their refueling stop there. With military precision Andy had reported the progress of the group and had added in part:

". . . probably have the last of them moved up in another day or two. While they haven't all been moved, we've uncovered and checked them all. Of the 300 barrels, all are aviation gasoline except six drums of fuel oil for the barracks stoves. There's not a single drum of oil here . . ."

Unless one knew Plaisted well it was difficult to believe. Every five gallons of gasoline consumed by the snowmobiles required one quart of oil for lubrication; without this the engines would grind themselves into useless metal in a matter of minutes. And yet it was now unmistakably clear; Plaisted had assembled an entire expedition and came to the Arctic to drive snowmobiles to the North Pole but had forgotten to bring oil! He had learned long ago that Plaisted was no planner. Instead he found the man simply hurled himself at an obstacle in whatever manner seemed most appropriate at the moment. Only if he failed did he pause to study the problem in detail. Since he usually succeeded, Plaisted ridiculed those who consume much effort and time evolving solutions he usually found unnecessary. But to forget a vital ingredient like oil? When the almost incredulous truth became evident Art had discovered no shortage of oil in the weather station's supply. Regulations did not permit the station's administrator to release the needed oil to the expedition, even though Art knew he would if asked. Not wishing to place him in this awkward position Art had simply "borrowed" several barrels without formally requesting them, but being carefully certain he was observed and that meticulous records were kept so that replacement from Weldy's cache at Alert could be carried out when more convenient.

Entering the radio building Art paused to examine the drying, processed film and found it nearly ready.

"It's going to be a long night," he commented wryly to Hans, the radio operator on duty, as he pictured the nearly 100 negatives that remained to the printed.

"They want you in the ham shack," Hans told him. "They're talking to the ice party."

A moment later Pitzl's voice from the ice greeted him. "Just a minute, Art. Ralph wants to talk to you."

Almost immediately Plaisted's voice, harsh with impatience, burst from the set without any greeting, demanding: "Why wasn't that plane out here today, Art?"

Art sank to a chair and replied weakly: "Beacon receiver still out, Ralph. Without that we can't find you unless you're camped and guiding Weldy in."

"Look, Art," the angry voice replied, "I want results, not excuses. I sent you back more than a week ago. You're still at Eureka. The plane still isn't here when we need it. What do I have to do to get some work out of you back there?"

It was below the belt—a clear foul. Propelled by his state of exhaustion, bitterness generated by the accusations injustice welled up in Art as he struggled for its control. Seizing the microphone he was about to shout his defense when he remembered an episode from the previous year.

At that time part of a chance remark, misunderstood and heard out of context, was passed on by an eavesdropping amateur and fanned into a major incident. Realizing there must be hundreds of amateur radio operators listening now, he hesitated, then replied simply: "It's too complicated, Ralph. I'll write you a note and have Weldy give it to you tomorrow."

After completing arrangements for the next day's supply flight Art signed off, returning to his room where he poured his hostility in a letter to Plaisted.

...

HORTON STRETCHED AND YAWNED. The evening's panorama of light in the mountains had been particularly spectacular and after the evening meal they had sat in silence for more than an hour, enraptured by the silent serenity immersing them.

"I hope," he said softly as though hesitating to disturb the thoughts of his partners, "that the others are enjoying their experiences as much as we are."

...

IT WAS STILL FORTY-TWO DEGREES BELOW ZERO the next morning when Art dragged the heavy gasoline heater from the shack on the airstrip. Ken and Weldy had been difficult to wake that morning and, to save time and their strength for flying, he was preparing to warm the aircraft's engines while they breakfasted. So tired himself he was performing mechanically, he managed to light the firepot, start the blower, attach the hose and direct the stream of hot air into one turbine's air intake.

It has been a trying night. Working feverishly to complete the task in time for this flight he had printed nearly 100 of the negatives, washed and dried them. Then, because of overlap of areas photographed, it had been necessary to cut each print differently, lay them end-to-end, and finally tape them together to provide a seventy-two-foot-long map providing a continuous sequence of pictures showing the appearance of the Arctic Ocean's ice surface from base camp northward over the pack ice nearly 250 miles to eighty-seven degrees north. It had been breakfast time before he completed it, rolled it all on a cardboard cylinder core and labeled it "Weldy Phipps' Highway map to the North Pole."

Weldy and Ken arrived shortly after both engines and the instrument panel had been heated. With the fuel and the other supplies aboard, Weldy climbed into the cabin.

"Turn on the spare beacon that's in the strip shack for about ten minutes after we leave, Art," Weldy requested. "I'd like to see whether the receiver works as Don hoped it would."

"Will do," Art promised, and handing him the letter asked, "give this to Plaisted, will you please?"

Weldy nodded, then added, "Better get some sleep while we're gone; you look sort of washed out."

"Tell Ralph I'd like to get back on the ice so I can get some rest," Art answered dryly.

When he returned to the radio room a half hour later, the operator called to him:

"Weldy reported in that he received your beacon signal loud and clear on his receiver."

Art heard him but was beyond caring. He fell onto his bunk fully clothed and did not move for the greater part of the day.

...

"TELL WALT TO STOP GASSING UP THE MACHINES and come in here so we can finish eating before we pack up and take off," Plaisted ordered Pitzl, as he ladled the indicated quantity of water into the dehydrated chicken noodle mixture.

A moment later Pederson climbed through the sleeve entrance into the tent, face aglow with anticipation of travel.

Ralph cooking, his self-proclaimed most important qualification

"They're all running like a clock," he told them with eminent self-satisfaction. "Ought to make twenty-five to thirty miles yet today."

"He didn't take too long to find us today," Bombardier remarked.

"No, but I'm concerned about that beacon receiver," Pitzl commented. "It worked when Weldy left Eureka, and he said he got our signal when still twenty miles out, but then it disappeared, came on again a few minutes later and then faded out for good. He still can't trust it; says it sounds like a bad contact to him. How will he find us when we get farther out?"

"Oh, quit worrying about it, Jerry," Plaisted advised impatiently. "Weldy will always find us. Besides, if he has to call out the Canadian Air Force for a 'search and rescue' operation the headlines will help us."

"Headlines won't help us get to the North Pole, Ralph," Jerry answered. "The best way to do that is have Weldy supply us when we need it with a minimum of fuss about it, and a reliable electronic navigation beacon system would do it best."

"Oh, all right but quit worrying about it. Don's back there and he'll get it going. I just wish Art would get on the ball and get things organized there, What's there to do except fly a few drums of gas to Ward Hunt? By the way, did you see that cute set of snapshots Weldy had of the ice? Said he used 'em like a road map all the way out here—that's why he found us so fast even without the beacon."

"Yeah," Walt answered. "By the way, here's a letter from Art that Weldy handed me to give you, Ralph."

"Have Pitzl read it out loud while I cook the chicken," Plaisted asked, discomforted by the knowledge his slow reading betrayed his lack of formal education. "I wonder what excuse he'll give us."

Unfolding the paper, Pitzl read aloud to the group:

> Dear Ralph,
>
> You're disappointed that we aren't established at base camp on Ward Hunt yet, but look at it this way; Because of inadequate arrangements to move aviation gas to Ward Hunt Island before the expedition was launched the plane cannot be based there until a minimum of at least twenty barrels have been moved there, because our supplies did not include oil we are spending flying time moving this up from Eureka—time we should be spending moving gasoline from Tanquary Fjord. The same thing is true of a gasoline heater for

the plane's engines and other aircraft maintenance equipment. But most of all the failure to field test the electronic navigation system has forced us to use all available time on its repair and on possible alternatives in the event of its complete failure.

What we *have* done these past nine days is dig out 250 barrels of snow-covered drums and move them to the air strip at Tanquary Fjord; create a serviceable landing strip at both Tanquary Fjord and Ward Hunt Island; built a storage shed at Ward Hunt and got those buildings into usable condition; worked almost continuously on the beacon receiver and prepared a photographic system to replace the beacon system. Add routine chores to that and you have a group of men so exhausted they've borrowed from tomorrow to give you today.

You'll remember the day I left the ice I told you that you were driving your men too drastically—that you were afraid they would regard the expedition too frivolously unless you did. That's not your usual attitude, Ralph. These men back here are already giving you everything they've got. They need and deserve your praise, not criticism. We know how great the pressure is on you, but trust your normal instincts with them; they trust you.

Good Luck,
Art

Pitzl finished and slowly refolded the letter. In the ensuing silence only the sough of the gasoline stove was audible.

Then Plaisted spoke quietly, "Let's hurry up and finish eating so we can take off. Let's at least do our share out here!"

...

BACK AT EUREKA, ART AUFDERHEIDE could only hope that the note would inspire a badly needed turnaround in Ralph's attitude. For the truth was, Art was hiding the worst of it. A few days earlier, Wes Cook had noticed blood in his urine. The two doctors had consulted privately before deciding that the symptom, bad as it was, was not yet acute enough for what would have to be a very difficult air evacuation. Wes would tough it out like the rest of them, although the stakes would be that much higher. He prayed that Ralph would get there soon.

10

The Big Lead

"You think you've got it fixed this time, Don?" Weldy inquired as he raced the right engine prior to take-off.

From deep within a visage lined with fatigue and disappointment, Powellek's dark-brown eyes flashed with the excitement of anticipation.

"I'm sure of it," he asserted. "It'll respond like a compass."

The plane moved rapidly down the runway as Weldy pushed the throttle lever forward. Freed of cargo it leaped from the ground like a thing alive. It was already a hundred feet high and climbing steeply as it passed over the end of the landing strip where Art stood with the activated beacon under his parka.

As the plane gained altitude Powellek hovered over the receiving unit like a mother bird over her nest, snapping a switch, twisting a dial or checking a connection. Mostly, though, he kept watching the directional indicator needle on the control panel and then glancing out the window to verify the position of the landing strip.

"Three thousand feet. Shall we check it?" Weldy inquired and as Don nodded. The plane banked and began a long circle centered on the weather station.

Powellek first smiled, then grinned broadly as he heard the antenna rotate to retain its alignment with the beacon on the ground. No matter how Weldy twisted or turned the plane, the indicator needle persistently pointed toward the beacon.

"Okay," Powellek exulted. "Now take her straight out and see how far we can go before we lose it. Don't let any hills get between us and the beacon, though."

Weldy obeyed and nearly twenty minutes later announced; "Still coming in strong at nearly thirty miles. Got to turn behind that range now so we can't test it any further out, but that's more than enough. With a position report I can be within twenty miles of the ice party by celestial navigation without any problem. The beacon will take me in the rest of the way now. What was the problem with it?"

"No one problem," Don replied. "And no complicated ones either. Just a whole series of bad contacts and broken solder joints."

"Why have you got that blanket under it?" Weldy asked.

"We had it bolted to the floor of the fuselage. But it's apparently too delicate for the kind of beating this plane takes when you land it on rough ice, so I had to cushion it to prevent further damage."

"That still sounds like a makeshift arrangement to me. You better stick around for a few days to be sure it works," Weldy commented dubiously.

"It'll work," Powellek guaranteed him. "Just get me back on that ice and to the ice party and their radio as soon as you can."

...

Plaisted was lashing the tent into position on his sled when Pederson walked over to check his machine before the morning departure.

"How did you sleep last night, Walt?" he asked.

"Better than I expected," Walt replied. "Plenty warm."

"If all four of us can sleep in the two zipped-together bags every night we won't have to replace those two bags we sent back with Ernst yesterday. There's fifty pounds we gain."

For Plaisted it was just as well Ernst had left. There were four of them now with four machines, each with a sled. Each sled carried only five days of food, one tent, two sleeping bags, navigation instruments and about 100 pounds of odds and ends. All the rest of the weight was for snowmobile fuel now, enough for three long days of travel. Stripped down like this he hoped to be able to make time.

"Yes," Pitzl agreed, "and the ice is getting better all the time now. The floes are bigger and the pressure ridges older and more easily crossed. But with only three days of fuel and five days of food it means the plane has to be sure to be here every few days when we need it."

"Don and Art will be wanting to come back out on the ice soon too," Bombardier reminded them.

"Don hasn't got the beacon working yet and Art hasn't moved the whole base camp to Ward Hunt Island yet," Plaisted said flatly. "We'll worry about that when they're ready. In the meantime, let's find out how fast four men and four machines without passengers can travel on this pack ice." And then he added, "If you're ready, Jean Luc, let's go!"

Plaisted's machine was second in line behind Bombardier. As they crossed the floe, he saw Bombardier scour the pressure ridge ahead, then head for a snow-ramped depression. The lead machine climbed the irregular incline, aiming directly at a huge ice boulder. Just before reaching it he saw Bombardier throw his body to the right, skillfully guiding machine and sled around it and down the other side. Freed of its usual top-heavy passenger, Jean-Luc's sled slalomed through the turn without the least hint of wanting to overturn. Without hesitation Plaisted followed, and from the level surface of the floe beyond he turned to watch first Pitzl and then Pederson execute the difficult maneuver successfully.

"That's it! That's the combination we needed," he told himself with great satisfaction, as they roared by him, Pederson waving an elated greeting. For the first time he was beginning to dare to hope they might succeed. "This is a no-nonsense group; I just hope I can keep it down to these four for a long time."

...

Moving gasoline at Tanquary Fjord

WITH ALL THE BARRELS DUG OUT AND WAITING at Tanquary Fjord, Andy, John, and George discussed plans for a well-earned day of rest. Every detail of their various proposals was savored through repetition and elaboration. While submerged in this reverie, John Moriarty suddenly started, raised his hand and commanded, "Listen!"

The perpetual silence of the fjord was disturbed as a faint but familiar crescendo reached their ear—the sound of the Otter's engines. That sound grated their ears with all the raucousness of a waterfront saloon. Hurriedly they donned their parkas and arrived at the landing strip just as the engines were turned off. They were unpleasantly surprised to see Art and Powellek emerge from the plane, though their greeting was cordial.

"Beacon receiver's installed and working so we're moving everything up to base camp at Ward Hunt Island today," Art informed them, and when he learned they would finish their work that afternoon he added. "Good. Weldy will make two more runs in here today to haul fuel up to base camp. He'll bring you out on the second run."

Their dismay was so obvious it was unmistakable.

"What's the matter?" Art asked puzzled.

"Well, ah,—you see," Horton stammered, "we were sort of planning a day off here tomorrow. If Weldy's hauling fuel tomorrow too, couldn't he take us out then?"

Art stared. He didn't understand their reluctance, but sensed it had some meaning to them. Nevertheless, he felt he had little alternative and answered: "It would be nice, Andy, but the Otter isn't really as predictable as a taxi. The weather could turn sour and you could get hung up here for a week. And we need you at base camp."

They didn't answer at first. The logic was obvious, but they accepted it reluctantly. The spell was broken, their Shangri-La invaded.

On the flight back, Andy Horton stared in spellbound silence at all beauty so seldom viewed by man, not really understanding what had created nor what destroyed the fantasy in which they had been suspended this past week.

...

THEY SAW IT LONG BEFORE THEY GOT THERE. It was Pitzl who detected it while taking his noon sextant shot. It was merely a thin dark line all along the northern horizon then. Plaisted's eye followed Pitzl's pointing finger with dismay. Yesterday had been their first full day with only four men on the ice and their performance had justified all of Plaisted's expectations. Forty-two surface miles were registered on their snowmobile odometers when they camped and Pitzl declared twenty-six of them were north miles:

"We'll cross eighty-seven degrees tomorrow for sure," Pederson had exulted. "Maybe by noon!"

But there it lay, ominous on the horizon. Plaisted knew it was no mirage.

"It looks just like it did the night before the big blow," he muttered disgruntedly. "We might as well go as hard as we can before it hits us. I wonder how long it will be this time!"

But that this one was different was soon obvious. They had crossed only a few more floes before the gray cloud seemed to rise higher very rapidly.

Pitzl stopped the group, studied it intently, then turned to Plaisted and said: "I don't think that's a blow, Ralph. See how sharp the upper limit of the cloud is? It looks like Lake Superior did last December when I visited Art in Duluth. Ralph, that's a lead!"

A knot tightened in Plaisted's belly. He stared at the cloud in the distance a long time, without saying anything, a hundred thoughts and a thousand emotions racing through his mind. But aloud he said only: "Maybe you're right, Jerry. But if that's a lead, it's a big one!"

They hadn't long to wait. Three more pressure ridge crossings brought them onto a huge floe—the largest they had seen this year. The usual pressure ridge also marked the far end of the floe, but there it was low and incomplete. Bombardier, leading the group, stopped several hundred feet short of it and waited for the others. Together they dismounted their machines, shut off the engines and gingerly approached the floe's edge.

An eerie spectacle unfolded before them. The floe had not split, but become detached from its neighbor. Part of the pressure ridge had remained on their floe, the other part apparently drifting away on the other.

The ominously black, exposed ocean water stretched from the floe's edge— a liquid chasm. Although near freezing temperature, this water was many degrees warmer than the bitter air above it. As heat flowed from the water into the frigid air, its moisture quickly condensed into a foggy vapor. From countless vaguely defined areas this "steam" seemed to emerge from a quiescent pool. As though wafted by a thousand wands, it swirled slowly in a myriad of rising spirals, gradually blending into a bank of fog hovering a thousand feet above the water. The vapor's oscillations, revolving in utter silence, imparted a phantom quality of surrealism that evoked the terror of the unknown.

The sun danced merrily among the foggy plumes nearest them, brightening them with all the cheer it could muster, but it was a feeble effort. The merging masses of nebulous forms fused into a collective density which absorbed the penetrating sun until the whites faded into gray and the grays into a dusky opacity, shielding the secrets of its deeper recesses from their anxious vision. Like a giant witch's cauldron the vapor oozed perpetually from the ocean, whirling slowly upward in a symphony of motion to feed the ever blackening cloud above it.

"Dante's inferno!" murmured an awestruck Pitzl, half-expecting a Stygian boatman to emerge from the murky mists.

Plaisted stared in silence. The revulsion that the very sight of the black water generated in him had no basis in logic, a phobia unrelated to any other quality of courage in the man. Unhesitatingly he had led them into unknown hazards of the pack ice; he had jeered at temperatures that unnerved the most stable of the group. Even a charging musk ox had given way to his unyielding stance. Each had his phobia; for Art, it was beacon failure and abandonment; for Walt it was a polar bear. For Plaisted, his irrational terror of plunging into the icy waters of the Arctic Ocean revived a hundred nightmares. Tearing his eyes from the evil lure of the inky deep he turned to Pitzl and asked simply, "How wide is it, Jerry?"

"No way of knowing, Ralph. Until it freezes over and stops steaming we won't be able to see the other side."

"Maybe we can get around it," Pederson suggested eagerly. "Maybe it's just a short, narrow crack that comes to a point."

Plaisted looked at Pitzl inquiringly, who merely shrugged and opined, "Maybe, but I doubt it."

"This floe safe, Jerry?" Plaisted inquired.

"Yes. It's an old one. The floe's surface is at least one and a-half feet above the water which means it's plenty thick. Besides, if it were weak it would have cracked instead of separating at the pressure ridge. Just don't camp near the edge."

"Walt, you and Jean-Luc take your machines along the edge of the lead and check it; you go east and Jean-Luc go west," Plaisted ordered. "Jerry and I will set up camp. Both of you be back here in an hour."

Another lead to cross

Pederson crossed a dozen ridges, finding the lead twisting and turning as it followed the irregular periphery of the floes. On and on he traveled for a full hour, hoping desperately to arrive at its terminus, but his final futile effort yielded nothing but a continuation of the same limitless, billowing apparition of ethereal vapor. The unworldly vision before him ultimately overwhelmed his resolve. He sank to his knees begged forgiveness for whichever of his iniquities had offended so seriously as to warrant this punishment.

Bombardier returned a half hour before Pederson with no better experience.

"There's nothing we can do except wait here for it to freeze," said Plaisted in frustration.

"We can pray," suggested Walt.

"Pray!" retorted Plaisted. "Go ahead and pray—pray for bitter cold."

...

"THE ICE PARTY'S HALF WAY TO THE POLE, but we've finally got base camp established at Ward Hunt Island," Art sighed with relief. "That's what I came off the ice to do. What remains to be done before we can return to the ice, Don?"

"Establish a gas cache on the ice, and prove the beacon works," Powellek replied.

"And raise the radio tower," added Wes Cook. "I still can't get through these mountains all the way to Minneapolis consistently without it."

"The beacon receiver worked on the last run. If it works on the next we can forget about it. But the ice party is near eighty-seven degrees and Weldy says that's about the limit of the Otter's range. We've got to create a refueling station at about that latitude out there on the pack ice if we expect him to continue supplying the ice party as they move beyond it."

"What are your plans for it, Don?" Cavouras asked him.

"We have two choices: a manned or an unmanned refueling station. We have an extra tent, stove, sleeping bags, food, radio and spare beacon. We could fly out to about eighty-seven degrees, select a large, old floe, land, store a half dozen fuel barrels there and leave two men on the floe. With the radio for communication they could turn on the beacon when Weldy approaches during the next supply flight. Guided in by the beacon Weldy could find that gas cache again, refuel and have plenty of range to supply the ice party all the way to the Pole."

"Wouldn't that be dangerous for the two men on the floe? After all, if the beacon failed could you ever find them again?"

"Probably not, but isn't the same true of the ice party?" Don queried.

"Not really, " Art answered. "They've got a sextant and Jerry can always supply them with a latitude and longitude position. The gas cache floe will drift too but the men on it won't know where they are, and in the event of beacon failure they'll be lost."

"Doesn't sound likely," Horton interposed. "I'll volunteer for the job and run the radio."

"And I'll go along to run the generator," Moriarty added.

"What's the other alternative?" Art inquired, proud of the men's reaction.

"We brought along a thermoelectric generator. That's simply a propane gas tank and a device to turn its heat to electricity. The generator is designed to put out fifteen watts. If I remove its battery the beacon could be hooked up to this generator and put out a continuous signal. We could set this up in the tent on the gas cache floe. Then whenever the floe would drift, we could always find it again simply by following the beacon signal. Nobody would have to stay on the floe to turn the beacon on."

"Sounds great," Cavouras commented. "Why not do it that way?"

"It hasn't been tested," Powellek admitted. "One other problem: if there's the slightest leak in the couplings the propane gas could concentrate inside the tent and finally blow up the whole tent and apparatus."

"All we'd lose is the equipment and the fuel," Art replied. "That's better than risking the men."

"Right," agreed Powellek. "I'll make the wiring changes now. Weldy says he'll be ready to leave in an hour."

"We'll work on your antenna tower in the meantime, Wes," Art promised. "But the ground's frozen. How do we anchor the cables?"

"I hope you figure it out," Wes Cook said. "I've got to keep my schedule with the ice party now," and he left for the radio room set up in the barracks hut.

Several hours later Horton came back in briefly to recruit help in raising the tower. To anchor the cables they had frozen old, used gasoline drums into position by pouring water around their base. In answer to Cook's query about the source of the barrels he grinned, "We used the ones stashed behind the outdoor toilet. We'll have the only radio tower in North America held up by frozen outhouse contents!"

...

PITZL'S EYE SCOURED THE SURFACE. The open lead had held them up here about twenty-four hours now. A crust of ice had formed on the water's surface, thin enough so that the ebony water shone through it, but thick enough to prevent the lead from steaming. Its mist dissipated, the lead's naked anatomy lay before them. Pitzl could not remember a more disheartening sight. The pressure ridge marking the other side of the lead was barely visible more than a mile away—perhaps two. What had been open water yesterday was now almost entirely a flat, dark, foreboding surface of skim ice, only an occasional wisp of escaping ice fog betraying scattered cracks. Even though it was their first real lead, Pitzl knew they had encountered a colossus, for he could not remember seeing one this large on any of the photographs of the oceanographic survey flights taken at this time of year. And he knew of its enormous length, from Pederson and Bombardier's reconnaissance.

The ominous appearance of the new ice did not deter Pitzl's eye from its habitual attention to detail. He knew how thin the ice was by its dark color. Scattered indiscriminately in the lead were random fragments of floating ice chunks, residual debris from the fragmented edges when the floes separated. He noticed the ice was a bit lighter, and, therefore, thicker, for several inches around each one of these, and when this led him to inspect the ice at the main floe's edge he noted the same process there.

"So freezing extends out from the edge of any floating object," he reminded himself. "That means not only that the ice will be thinnest at the middle of the lead, but one could strengthen the ice in a more narrow lead deliberately by throwing ice chunks into it to create a 'bridge,' since each of the pieces will serve as a nucleus to initiate freezing."

He picked up a piece of ice about the size of his head near the floe's edge and heaved it into the lead. It plunged through the surface film, revealing the ice's thickness as less than an inch.

"How thick does it have to get before we can cross it, do you think?" Pederson asked him.

"Because one this size will be thinner farther out, I'd hate to try it until we have a good four inches near the edge here," Pitzl answered.

"But at less than an inch per day we'll be here nearly a week at that rate," Walt complained.

"Once the surface acquires a film of ice, it freezes faster," Jerry promised. "While it's open it gives off heat. The cooler water is denser and sinks, bringing warmer water to the surface which, in turn, cools off. Not until all the water several feet down from the surface has been cooled and turned over does it freeze on top. It's still nearly fifty below so I'd expect better than a couple of inches of new ice tonight."

"Maybe we can cross it in the morning," Pederson hoped. "Why does the water look so black?"

"The ice cover on the surrounding floe is thick enough to block out most of the sunlight," Pitzl explained. "It's deep enough of course so the small amount that does penetrate the surface does not reflect off the bottom, nor is there any significant silt or other suspended matter in the water to reflect light."

When Pitzl returned to the tent he found Pederson in deep discussion with Plaisted.

"The ice is still so thin it would break away with no problem, Ralph," he was assuring him, and turning to Pitzl he asked:

"Don't you think so, Jerry?"

"Don't I think what?"

"If we took those sleds of ours we could use them like a rowboat. One man could paddle, in the lead sled, while the other broke the ice in front of it. The second and third sled could each carry one man and a snowmobile. After several crossings we'd have all the equipment ferried over."

"Forget it, Walt," Plaisted snorted. "At these temperatures ice would build up in those sleds every time they rocked the least bit in the water. Before you'd gone a hundred yards you'd be on your way straight down instead of forward."

"Then how about laying the antenna poles sideways across two sleds side by side?" Pederson persisted. "We could create a platform on the poles like a catamaran and ferry things over that way. That would be even safer."

"Forget it, I said," Plaisted persisted. "Nobody's going to float anything on anything. The only way we're going to cross a lead is on ice thick enough to walk on. Jerry says that's four inches so when we get four inches of ice, we'll walk over, and not before."

"How deep is the bottom here?" Bombardier inquired.

"Over 10,000 feet," Pitzl told him.

After a minute of silence Bombardier said, "Maybe we should wait for six inches!"

...

"I've been up since four melting the ice out of the stove and getting breakfast ready. Weldy, I wish you'd go so I can get back to bed," Cavouras teased him. "When do I have to have your chow ready upon your return?"

"Don't know, George," Weldy grumbled sleepily. "If the position Jerry reported last night is right they must be within thirty miles or so from where we set up the gas cache yesterday."

"I'd feel more secure if we could take you along today, Don," he added, "but with all that gas we're overloaded now."

Powellek did not answer immediately. Yesterday's flight was to have proved the beacon system so reliable that he could return to the ice party certain his electronic services would be needed no longer. The unmanned beacon, powered by the propane gas tank, had operated efficiently from the floe on which they had stored four barrels of aviation fuel. Its signal had been detected by the plane's receiver easily as far away as thirty-eight miles. Yet, when they radioed base camp as they approached it upon their return, activation of the base camp beacon produced no signal again in the plane's receiver.

"I spent all afternoon and evening on that receiver again, Weldy," Powellek moaned. "I can't find a thing wrong. This time I'll stay here and check the base camp's beacon itself."

Art watched him as Powellek manipulated the diminutive transmitter after Weldy reported shortly following takeoff that its signal faded about two miles from camp. His skill and knowledge were obvious as he deftly tested the device's circuitry while Weldy radioed effects of the various adjustments. He was relieved, too, by Powellek's smile of elation when first detection, and the correction of a flaw produced a joyful report from the Otter that its signal was now registering forcefully in the plane's receiver.

Powellek, Art reminded himself, had not smiled much since he had come off the ice. He had returned with the greatest reluctance, determined to rejoin the ice party again the next day. But the succession of technical problems with the capricious system had thwarted his desires. Accepting his obvious duty to keep the system operational it was nevertheless a disheartening experience for him to be relegated to base camp activities. As the days progressed he began to voice his concern about returning to the ice party more frequently. Particularly he referred commonly to the expected interpolar radio transmission at the completion of the traverse. His normally cheerful and positive disposition, drained by the chronic fatigue into which he drove himself with his repair efforts, was being eroded, gradually replaced by an unfamiliar, morose, introspective manner. Only when he spoke into the microphone did his customary, smoothly professional voice return, temporarily erasing, or at least masking, his personal frustrations.

"It wasn't the receiver," he gloated. "This beacon's been dropped; one of the resistors was cracked and leaking. No problem now!" And his diagnosis of a normally functioning receiver in the plane was confirmed an hour later when Weldy reported receiving a strong signal from the fuel cache.

Pleased by Powellek's temporary optimism Art joined Moriarty and Cavouras outside to complete erection of the radio tower. Engrossed in their efforts they were surprised when they saw the Otter suddenly reappear at camp more than an hour early. Completing their chore they entered the mess shack to find Weldy and Powellek in deep discussion, each wearing a mournful face more befitting a basset hound than Arctic explorers.

"The receiver's okay, Don," Weldy assured him. "I picked up the gas cache beacon on it more than thirty miles away and it stayed strong all the while I searched."

"Then it's got to be a conflict between the two," Don muttered agonizedly, and in answer Moriarty's inquiry he replied: "Weldy got out to the fuel cache and beacon worked fine. He didn't land, but flew on to try to find the ice party. Even though he was in radio communication with them he never received their beacon signal, nor could they find each other by sight or sound."

"What's the problem—receiver out again?" Moriarty asked.

"Can't be," Don replied. "The gas cache beacon came in strong on the receiver. I think what's happened is the ice party is camped near enough to the gas cache floe so that the receiver can't recognize both signals. They're both on the emergency frequency so the stronger would predominate and drown out the weaker one. Evidently the propane-powered beacon at the gas cache is obliterating the ice party's weaker, battery-powered signal."

"So why didn't Weldy simply land and turn off the gas cache beacon so he could pick up the signal from the ice party?" Moriarty persisted.

"And after I leave the ice party how do I find the gas cache again?" Weldy asked sardonically.

"Oh, yeah," muttered John, embarrassed by his oversight.

The thoughts of each were occupied with the problem in the silence that followed, until Powellek finally turned to Weldy and sighed, "Even after crossing that lead the ice party will not have enough fuel to advance far enough to get beyond the gas cache's beacon range. That beacon has to be turned off. Let's take a couple hundred pounds of fuel out of your tanks, take me along instead and drop me at the gas cache. While I stay there and deactivate the beacon you take off again. Then you ought to be able to receive the ice party's beacon and find them. One hour later I'll turn on the gas cache beacon again and you pick me up on your way back to camp."

Weldy nodded. He had known this was the only alternative but he would not ask any man to take the risk. Powellek would have no radio, and if the beacon failed . . . he didn't want to complete that thought.

"We've got no fuel left here at Ward Hunt now so Ken and I will fly to Tanquary to refuel. We'll be back here to pick you up by 15:00. Give the ice party an ETA of 18:00 for our arrival," he answered.

Powellek had assembled an emergency kit containing food, a small stove and similar articles when the Otter returned. As he climbed aboard Weldy commented, "Take the spare, battery operated beacon along as a safety measure. But hurry. From 5,000 feet we could see a cloud cover moving in from the west."

And a few minutes later Powellek could see it too—a low, dusky layer with a sharply-defined front suggesting a thick cover. He watched it nervously as they flew north, the sun now gradually beginning to descend behind it. But as they approached eighty-seven degrees north his attention was diverted to the detector, when he heard the antenna changing position in response to the signal. Hesitant initially, the signal soon became distinct and pleased Powellek with its precision. Only minutes later the Otter descended to the surface of the floe on which they had erected the tent with its continually operating beacon just two days previously. Without ado Powellek jumped from the plane, grabbed his hurriedly assembled emergency kit and waved to the immediately departing aircraft. He entered the tent and moments later the signal disappeared from the plane's receiver.

Climbing as quickly as his load permitted Weldy contacted Pitzl operating the ice party radio, requesting him to activate their beacon.

As they approached 3,000 feet he nudged Ken Lee, grinned and pointed at the dial. A strong signal was again registering.

"Don was right," he commented. "That's the ice party's signal because it's coming from northwest of us and the gas cache is the opposite direction. That gas cache beacon simply overwhelmed their weaker beacon before."

"Let's get out there and get back to the cache to pick up Don as fast we can," Lee answered evenly, his eye scanning the approaching front.

"Yeah, I'll feel better when Don's back in the plane," Weldy agreed.

Nor was he surprised when they appeared directly over the ice party in less than fifteen minutes. But before landing he flew across the lead.

It was huge and impressed even Weldy, who had seen good number of large leads in his life. More than two miles wide it followed an east-west direction as far as he could see and climbing to 8,000 feet did not yield a view of its ultimate limit. From the air its dark, ominous surface appeared less regular than from the lead's edge, for the otherwise monotonous structure was speckled with the irregularities of floating ice debris and escaping vapor in occasional open spots. While the edges were twisted and contorted, the opposite side of the lead presented a mirror image of the distortion. Weldy was always impressed by how precisely the two sides of a fresh lead could be juxtaposed mentally even though separated by several miles of open water. Only later did lateral movement usually occur, these very irregularities serving as a guide to the extent of such movement. Sometimes after initial formation of such a lead the water acquired an ice cover of six or eight inches after which the forces of separation might recur. The newly frozen ice would then split in the middle, exposing water again, which would freeze subsequently. Thus the initially formed ice might be a foot thick at the edge of the lead but the more recently refrozen area in the center might not support a man. Weldy had seen leads with up to five "generations" of ice formed in this manner. He also knew that currents sometimes forced the ice of the two sides of the lead in opposite directions. Because of the zig-zag nature of such leads it was common for the two then to come into crushing contact with each other at occasional points. Making a mental note to warn Plaisted of these hazards he prepared to land on the ice party's floe, deliver their supplies and give them his discouraging reconnaissance report.

...

After silencing the beeping beacon in the tent Powellek emerged from the tent to inspect the floe. It was large, perhaps a mile in diameter, and had been chosen by Weldy because of its unusually smooth surface. They had piled the fuel drums two barrels high to prevent them from becoming buried in subsequent snowdrifts. Although the sun was still shining brightly just above the horizon, the dark edge of the cloud bank approaching from the southwest was uncomfortably close. He had about forty-five minutes to wait and strolled about the floe looking for animal tracks. His failure to find any did not prevent his imagining an encounter with a polar bear.

The cloud mass had hidden the sun now, casting a dull, gray gloom over the area. It was advancing rapidly. If Weldy did not return within ten minutes his floe would be enveloped by the foggy mass. Certain it was already too late, he nevertheless re-entered the tent and activated the beacon. Resumption of the steady beep emanating from the diminutive unit was a source of both pride and relief. It required several minutes to complete the restoration of the unit after which he left the tent once more for a final view of the floe. The nebulous mass had reached the edge of the adjacent floe, obliterating the view beyond it when he was astonished to hear a faint hum penetrate the silence of the floe. Whirling he saw the Otter approaching low from the northeast. Without circling it touched down at the edge of the floe and roared up to the tent at nearly take-off speed. The fuselage door was opened before the craft came to a complete stop. Without hesitation Powellek accepted Ken Lee's proffered hand, vaulted into the interior and pulled the door shut behind him. Without taxiing to the end of the floe, Weldy applied full power. As the plane's skis cleared the pressure ridge at the edge of the floe the aircraft plunged into the haze of the approaching foggy mass, rose and headed for base camp.

...

JERRY PITZL LOWERED HIS SEXTANT and glanced at his watch quickly. Recording the time in his notebook he turned back to his instrument, carefully reading its vernier. Even before plotting the new position he knew it would extend the line initiated by the readings of the past two days. Their floe was drifting now—nearly three miles every day. And southeast at that. The three days they had been here had carried them about eight miles that would have to be retraced. How much longer, he wondered?

Replacing the instrument in its container he strolled to the lead edge. The ice was less black—more a dirty gray now, exhibiting a surface speckled with myriads of small white crystals. Kneeling down to study them more intently he heard Bombardier's voice behind him ask: "What are they, Jerry?"

"Salt," Pitzl answered laconically, but with an inflection betraying his interest in and admiration for the ways of nature.

For each of the small white structures was an exquisite sculpture of crystal. As the seawater froze, the resulting ice actually was made up only of crystallized water. The salt, now dissolved in less water than initially, thus gradually became concentrated. With the removal of still more water this saline solution ultimately thickened into a viscous brine. That near the surface was then expelled from the ice where subsequent evaporation deposited the salt in a striking array of delicate crystal forms. With the noon sun reflected and refracted from a thousand sparkling surfaces it was obvious how they had acquired their popular designation of "salt flowers."

"How thick is it today?" Bombardier wondered.

"Ought to be adequate at the edge," Pitzl opined. "Let's find out."

Armed with an ice chisel Bombardier held it vertically and dropped it from a height of about three feet after first looping its cord around his wrist. When it did not penetrate the ice he stepped from the floe onto the gray ice of the lead. Repeating the process he gradually worked out about thirty feet, but then called back:

"Ice is darker out here. Can't go much further." The past few steps had caused the ice to sag beneath his feet, and Jerry's breath caught in his throat as he watched his Canadian companion. But Jean-Luc seemed unconcerned by that peculiar flexibility of young, thin ocean ice so disturbing to the novice.

As if in verification of Bombardier's opinion the incision in the ice, cleft by the chisel, slowly filled with water and when he repeated the test, lifting the chisel still higher before its release, it dropped swiftly and without hesitation through the surface. But for the cord around his wrist it would have plunged to the bottom.

Carefully he backed up, sliding his feet along the surface to avoid putting all his weight on one foot. The thin ice under him bent as though it were stretched fabric, until he reached the safety of the lead's edge.

"It'll be another day before it's strong enough farther out," he estimated.

"We've got plenty of gas now," Pederson exclaimed irritatedly as he walked up in time to hear Bombardier's last comment. "I'm going to scout the lead edge again with my machine." And without waiting for an answer he flung his restless body onto the snowmobile and soon disappeared beyond the pressure ridge.

They were just finishing their lunch in the tent when they heard him return. The unvarying roar of his engine betrayed his excitement as he plunged indiscriminately forward over hummocks and cracks in the urgency of his mission. Skidding to a lurching halt in front of the tent he shouted even before the engine noise subsided: "Let's go! We're moving! The lead is closing! Hurry!"

Ralph ponders his options

And he babbled on so nearly incoherently that Plaisted had to shake him and ask him directly: "What's moving, Walt?"

"The floe on the other side—and us too," he answered excitedly. "Our floe is moving to the right and the other side to the left. We're going in opposite directions."

"So what?" Plaisted inquired.

"About two miles down the lead has a big zig-zag in it, Ralph," Walt panted, trying to regain his breath. "I think a part of the floe from the other side is going to scrape against the one on this side if they keep moving the way they are now. If they do, we can sneak across there."

Pitzl had walked to a sled, retrieved a pair of binoculars and, leaning his elbows on a snowmobile hood, was studying the coveted, distant shore of the lead. Plaisted left Pederson and asked Pitzl: "How about it, Jerry?"

Lowering the glasses Pitzl told him, "He's right, Ralph. Take a look for yourself. There's a crack in the new ice of the lead near the other side. And we're drifting in opposite directions. You can see some of the thin ice fracturing and piling up along the edge of the new crack."

Plaisted peered through the glasses, then asked: "What's this about the two sides coming together?"

"I haven't been down there but he's probably right about that too," Pitzl answered. "These leads are usually quite angular and, as the two sides move in opposite directions, projecting 'points' of ice from the two sides will scrape against each other."

"For how long?" Plaisted demanded.

"Depends on their size and speed. From a few minutes to an hour or two, I suppose."

"And Walt wants us to cross on that moving, scraping ice? He's crazy. We'll just sit here and wait for it to freeze until it's thick enough walk across," Plaisted declared emphatically.

Turning, to walk away he paused when Pitzl said quietly: "It might be a long time, Ralph. There'll be open water in the middle again even after this movement stops. We'll have to start our wait all over again."

Plaisted hesitated. He peered at the thin ice he hated so vehemently, then muttered: "All right, we'll go down to look at it."

"Let's pack up and be ready to cross," Pederson urged. "We can knock this camp down in fifteen minutes."

Led by Bombardier, the small caravan reached the area less than half an hour later. Although the lead was very wide, they were standing at a point where it bent sharply to their right. As Walt had described, a nearly mile-long peninsula of ice jutted from the other side. Both the sound and the motion of the floes was obvious here—too obvious for Plaisted. Their own floe appeared motionless while that on the other side was moving. Not fast, but relentlessly. And as it moved toward their left, the steady crush of the ice at the edges of the irregular crack in the center testified to the unyielding power of the unseen forces driving the pack.

Walt had also been correct predicting collision between the two sides. The tip of the ice peninsula projecting from the other side reached out so far that it was obvious its continued course would bring it at least transiently into contact with their floe. The thin ice preceding it was already piling up at the floe's edge.

Plaisted stared and shuddered, then looked at Pitzl.

"I think we'll have plenty of time," Pitzl said. "That piece is nearly a hundred feet wide and it's not moving real fast."

Once again the command weighed on Plaisted's mind. Walt was eager, and he knew Bombardier would be game to try any risk if it advanced them toward their goal. But for Plaisted the safety of the party was paramount. Turning to face the others Plaisted announced reluctantly but firmly, "I'm not going to order any man across here. If there's just one of us that doesn't want to we'll all stay here and wait it out to cross after it freezes thick enough. How about it?"

Bombardier's and Pederson's instant chorus of "Let's go!" was expected, and when Pitzl also nodded his assent it settled the issue. They arranged their machines, Bombardier in the lead as usual, followed by Plaisted, Pitzl, and Pederson.

They had not long to wait. Steadily the distance separating them narrowed, only the crunch of the crumbling lead ice breaking the silence. With scarcely twenty-five feet remaining Walt ordered: "Start your machines now and keep them running."

The engine din drowned out all other sounds, but the floe's contact was announced by a tremor which rolled beneath their feet, betraying any illusion of stability. For an initial, indecisive moment the two floes clawed at each other, crushing and pulverizing their peripheries. But the enormous power of the driving forces rendered their forward progress invincible. In the resulting struggle the opposite floe yielded and began to slide slowly and irregularly beneath theirs.

"Now!" Pederson screamed above the clamor, and Bombardier's thumb closed forcefully on the throttle. Leaping forward his machine accelerated to its maximum. Nearing the edge he guided it off their floe across a slowly rising mass of rubble ice, gaining the surface of the other floe deceptively easily. He advanced nearly a half-mile before halting, safely across and secure on the old ice of the other side. Looking back now he was relieved to see Plaisted halted a short distance behind him, watching Pitzl begin the traverse.

Just as with the others, his machine and following sled passed effortlessly across the junction onto their side.

That was when it happened. It wasn't really a sharp report—more a loud, crushing reverberation sending a quiver of reaction through the ice. The relentless pressure had fractured the impacting finger of ice.

"My God, now look what you've done," Plaisted shouted helplessly to no one in particular. "We're over here, Walt's on the other side and Pitzl's on an island in the middle."

But Pitzl wasn't really on an island. Or at least it wasn't stationary. Compressed between the two floes it was slowly being rotated like a colossal gear wheel. Recognizing his only chance lay in crossing at a point of contact he directed his machine sharply to his right, anticipating the floe's rotary movement. The grinding and fragmentation at the points of contact were frightening, but he did not hesitate, hoping frantically that overriding edges would not obstruct his transfer to the main floe. Fortunately the movement was sluggish and he selected a rising area of pulverized fragments. Approaching it with maximum acceleration his machine hurled itself upon the mushy surface, its track clawing in search of a firmer grip.

Whether it would have yielded or succumbed to the crushing motion of the floes he would never know for as he leapt from the machine to add his own strength to the effort, the four hands of his companions grasped the rope behind his snowmobile, pulling the loaded sled onto the floe. A moment later they lay, breathless with exertion, safely on the snow before turning their attention back to Pederson.

Walt had watched Pitzl's progress and realized how important it was to cross quickly now. Riding along the floe edge he headed for an area of smoother transfer. Pushing the machine to capacity he was approaching the edge when, to his horror, a narrow zone of water opened between his floe and the island of ice that the fracturing had produced. The pressures were relenting and separation had again begun. Fully aware of the appalling hazard, the desperation of necessity drove him on. Upon reaching the point, the area was wider than he expected—more than three feet of black ocean water forming an ominous gulf between the floes. With total abandon his machine leaped from the surface, the skis striking the water, but propelled by momentum skidded forward, traversed the foot of loose ice at the edge and then climbed smoothly to the surface of the main ice beyond. Only the sled hesitated momentarily, then lurched forward and followed the machine to its point of temporary safety.

He did not even turn around to look, recognizing from the operation of the machines that the sled also had negotiated that part of the crossing successfully. His eyes were occupied with the action of his ice island and that of the main part of the floe on the far side where his companions were awaiting him. With release of the pressure, rotation of the flow had decreased and slow separation was also occurring there. He recognized he would not have the opportunity to duplicate Pitzl's direct approach and sought out other alternative quickly. On the far side his attention was arrested by a roughly linear group of ice fragments floating on a sea covered by the intact, dark, newly-formed lead ice. The ridge led to the desired floe and he directed his machine to that area. If he could maintain adequate speed he felt the thin lead ice between the floating chunks would probably support him. He left his ice island reluctantly but was relieved when his assumption proved correct. The thin ice sagged, but held, as he reached the first of the series of the floating larger ice fragments that led to the floe on the far side where is companions were waiting. Almost immediately, however, he felt the sled begin to drag and one glance proved enough to detect the problem. The machine's track was cracking through the thin ice periodically, the sea water welling up through these cracks and slowing the following sled. As he directed the snowmobile across the first of the chunks of ice debris he felt the machine's track bite eagerly into its surface and gain momentum briefly, only to lose it again gradually as it traversed the thin ice beyond. Again and again this happened but Walt realized it was not often enough. Slowly but detectably his forward speed began to decline. His eyes anxiously measured the remaining distance and the intervals between the lifesaving heavier fragments. The final one was obviously the worst—a distance of over 200 feet separated by only the dark, thin lead ice. But he had no choice now and prayed only that the engine would not fail him. On he forced the machine on its race with death, as the dragging sled diminished his speed alarmingly. For a fleeting moment he even considered pulling the pin which would disconnect and abandon his sled. He might have been tempted in spite of its vital contents, had he been able to do so without stopping. The friction of the slush accumulating on the sled now was dragging the rear of the snowmobile downward. The flexible, thin lead ice yielded to the pressure, forcing the snowmobile into an uphill incline, further straining its capacity. There was less than fifty feet remaining but he knew now he would never make it.

But Plaisted knew it too. He had been watching every move Walt had made, and was at the floe's edge, mentally straining to aid the struggling machine. He too realized Walt's plight and his impending fate. It had to be done quickly and he could certainly ask no one else to do it. With sinking heart he slid his feet from the safety of the thick floe onto the dark, precarious lead ice. Feeling the ice bend and depress beneath each foot he glided forward before it could give way. Gingerly but rapidly he arrived at the last fragment of ice Walt was trying to reach just as the snowmobile bogged down altogether. With its track now spinning ineffectively he saw it begin to chew through the ice and slowly begin to subside. Keeping his feet on the larger piece of ice debris he reached forward, seized the handles on the tips of the skis and pulled with the despair of futility. For a moment the device hesitated while Plaisted could feel the entire area sag beneath the pressure. Then slowly it moved forward—at first a little, then more and then, as it reached the small piece on which Plaisted was standing it used its rough surface to gain just enough momentum to reach the main floe where willing hands completed the rescue.

"And if any of you think we're going to try anything like that again, you can forget it right now," Plaisted declared in the tent that night. "I've had enough thrills today to last me a lifetime."

Again the fates mercifully concealed the terrors of the future from them.

Plaisted on the trail

11

Promises Made and Broken

"Here, Don, add your autograph to this, will you?" Art asked, thrusting a peculiar white object at him. Powellek studied it briefly before recognizing it as a sun-bleached musk ox vertebra which Moriarty had found near camp several days ago. One of its faces was now emblazoned with the greeting "Happy 50th Birthday, Andy" while the signatures of the other members covered the remaining surface.

An attempt at frivolity was precisely what the base camp group needed badly. They had been driving themselves to the utmost, perpetually fatigued, continuously wrestling with every new problem that seemed to present itself just after some other crisis had been overcome. The strain on all of them was becoming serious. When Art learned Andy Horton would be fifty years old today he announced a party would be held in Andy's honor and a bottle of Scotch would be sacrificed from the supply reserved for the final victory party.

But the conviviality had not prevented Horton from returning to the radio room to monitor the ice party's frequency for the first ten minutes of the hour as had been agreed.

"Any word from the ice party?" Powellek asked.

"No, but Ottawa complained about the gas cache beacon again," Horton replied.

"They were really upset about it last night," Wes Cook commented. "That beacon signal must really be strong."

"Stronger than I expected," Powellek said. "It's 243 megacycles, to be used only for emergency distress signals. It was the only frequency crystal we had so I thought we could use it as a navigating signal to mark the gas cache out there on the ice. I didn't think any one else would be around to receive it."

"Well, they were," Wes Cook replied. "The first night you hooked it up SAS airlines reported they picked up a distress signal on their transpolar flight from Scandinavia to North America and the next night a KLM flight said they had received a signal from a plane down in the Arctic Ocean. It didn't take Ottawa long to figure out we were the only ones in the area. They told us in no uncertain terms that frequency was illegal for navigating purposes and to get out there and turn it off."

"If we did that we'd never find the gas cache floe again and without it Weldy can't reach the ice party," Horton replied.

"We'll fix it tomorrow," Powellek promised. "There's an explorer by the name of Humphries over at Alert, planning a pack ice trip with dogs but held up by equipment problems right now. He's got a beacon like ours, but at a legal 245-megacycle frequency. Weldy flew over this afternoon to borrow it."

It was past midnight when Horton was coaxed away from the radio where he was vainly attempting to reach Weldy at Alert to request he remember their desperate need for a fountain pen.

Tightening the two screws attaching the wires from the gas cache's thermoelectric generator to the new beacon, Powellek was pleased to hear the monotonous beeping of the signal resume.

"There," he commented to Weldy, placing the one he had disconnected in his pocket. "Ottawa ought to be happy now. It's putting out a signal on 245 megacycles."

"Now let's see if we can pick it up as well on the plane's receiver," Weldy commented skeptically as they returned to the aircraft.

But fifteen minutes later his skepticism vanished when reception of the potent signal at a distance of twenty miles testified to Powellek's skill.

A few moments later they passed over the big lead near eighty-seven degrees. But it was now not the tidy, orderly structure Weldy had found there just a few days previously. The paradoxical motion of the floes had shattered the freshly frozen lead ice near the center where large pools of open water now vented their smoky vapor. Fragmented ice lined the edges with huge new pressure ridges and large masses of amputated floe segments drifted like islands in a black sea.

Immediately beyond, the terrain altered dramatically. Here was a region almost entirely of floes of titanic magnitude, an agglomerated mass of juxtaposed, flat, massive pans of ice rendered tenaciously cohesive through fusion of their shared peripheral pressure ridges. Both the floes and the ridges were largely old and weathered. This was the ice of which Powellek had dreamed so often while fighting the contorted ice surface early in the trip. Floes of three or four miles long were common, and there seemed to be occasional ones twice that size. Leads appeared more frequently but were largely small and presented less obstruction to traverse (though admittedly more hazard) than did the pressure ridges of the nearer ice. The transition was so abrupt he turned to glance back quickly again at the ice on the south side of the lead to reassure himself of the smaller, rougher floes there.

Bending forward he yelled in Weldy's ear, "Sure looks like that big lead at eighty-seven degrees marks the edge of a different kind of ice motion."

"Yep, and Plaisted ought to like it. They'll be making good time over this stuff!"

Less than five minutes later the plane's skis touched the surface of the floe where the ice party was waiting. Jumping out of the aircraft Powellek was greeted by a cheerful grin and a laconic salutation from Bombardier, who promptly opened the delivered fuel can and began filling the machines' gas tanks. Pederson, diligently reassembling one of the engines, called out to him, waved, and continued his repair efforts. Pitzl was on the distant side of the floe recording a sextant reading, too far away to seek out. Plaisted strode over to him and Weldy, speaking rapidly and enthusiastically. He described their precarious crossing of the big lead, then lauded their own progress in this new type of ice.

"Honest to God, Weldy," he exclaimed, "we must have made twenty miles already today and we got six or seven travel hours left yet. If this ice keeps up we can cover half a degree north every day. But we'll probably get blocked by leads again soon. See any ahead of us?"

"Only little ones," Weldy answered.

"How's the navigating beacon working, Don?" Plaisted demanded. "Good," Powellek replied eagerly. "Completely reliable now. I'd like to get b—"

"Fine," interrupted Plaisted, "Then, we'll send back more stuff with you. Some of these leads have a pretty thin ice cover and we want to be as light as possible."

"When do you want me to refuel you again?" Weldy inquired.

"Day after tomorrow," Plaisted replied. "If the weather stays good; we really burn up the gas in this kind of territory."

"All set, let's go," Walt sang out as he put his tools away and started his machine.

Turning to leave, Plaisted waved to them excitedly and urged, "Keep 'em coming!"

The caravan had crossed the floe and disappeared behind the ridge before the Twin Otter began to taxi for take-off. All the way back Powellek sat slouched in the seat, his unseeing eyes staring out the window.

...

JERRY PITZL DREW THE SECOND LINE CAREFULLY, circled the point where it crossed the first and recorded the latitude. "Twenty-eight north miles today—just short of half a degree!" he announced with pride.

"That ought to put us beyond eighty-eight degrees tomorrow," declared Pederson confidently. "The Lord's with us now!"

"Just think, only 150 miles to the North Pole," Bombardier added, "and the best ice we've had yet."

"Yeah," Plaisted agreed, then hesitated and became silent.

"What's the matter, Ralph?" Pederson inquired. "You don't sound happy about it."

"I am, but there are two fellas at base camp that aren't."

They all fell silent. They knew their experience had demonstrated the efficiency of traveling in a group of four men and four machines. Especially *these* four men.

"I don't think we'd have crossed the big lead with six men," Bombardier ventured.

"Of course not," Plaisted answered, and all fell silent again.

Powellek and Aufderheide had been with them from the very first day the expedition had been conceived. They were all deeply and sincerely attached to them. Yet they could not deny their ice experience. Until they had reduced the party to four the expedition had wallowed in ineffective traverse. Still, it did not seem right these men should sit at base camp while the others carried out what they had all planned.

"By tomorrow night we'll be 120 miles from the pole. Even if we travel slower after that with six men we ought to make it," Pitzl suggested.

Plaisted had waited for them to say it. He felt the full responsibility of success weighing on his shoulders now. Obviously returning these men to the ice would impede their progress. If he did it and the group failed how could he justify the decision to the other three of the ice party as well as to the dozens of men who had sponsored this expedition and trusted his judgment? But if he left them at base camp and *did* succeed in reaching the pole easily, how could he justify it to these two men? He wanted Pederson, Pitzl, and Bombardier to share the decision, for they would share the possible expedition failure.

They discussed it for an hour. Then Plaisted wrote the note.

It was suppertime when Weldy returned from the supply flight to the ice party the next night and handed Art the note. Unfolding it he read it rapidly, the reread it aloud, nearly shouting .". . . and on the next supply flight we want you and Don to come back on the ice. And, oh, yes, bring Andy out here too. We're all going to the pole together."

If they had had a bottle that night they would have drained it.

...

"But we've got to have somebody prove we're there," Powellek insisted into the microphone. "Are you sure about that?"

"Who's he talking to?" Cavouras asked as he entered the radio room. "Jim, our contact man in Chicago," Horton replied. "He just told Don that Thule airport over in Greenland is closed down."

"So what?" Cavouras inquired.

"Well, we want somebody not associated with us to verify our position when we reach the pole."

"So what's that got to do with Thule?" Cavouras persisted.

"Every spring, the Oceanography Department in Washington, D.C., flies from Thule to the North Pole and back—up one longitude and down another, doing ice research and ice surveillance to predict iceberg hazards in Atlantic shipping lanes later. The exact dates of their flights are somewhat flexible, and Ralph had arranged to coordinate one of their flights with our arrival at the Pole."

"What happened at Thule?"

"They've had an aircraft accident and spilled radioactive material over the area. The place is closed to air traffic, The Oceanography Department's North Pole flights have been scratched indefinitely."

"We can't afford that, Jim," Powellek was saying. "Contact the U.S. Air Force. Contact the Canadian Air Force, contact the President. Anybody. But arrange a confirmation flight to prove we made it when we get there. Just be sure it's a public service group of some kind with no attachment to our expedition and with complete public integrity. Keep in touch with us. Good luck." And he signed off, unhappy with the latest threat to their success.

"Well, this is one Jim will have to solve for us," Art commented. "Right now our aviation fuel supply is down to nothing again, and Weldy says it looked cloudy toward the south in the direction of Tanquary Fjord. If we could only even get about ten drums ahead here all the pressure would be off. This way the margin is so narrow every flight becomes an adventure." And he ambled off to discuss the next day's possible flights with a weary arctic bush pilot.

...

If Bombardier had not already disappeared into its interior Pitzl would have stopped him from entering the area. For more than a day they had been traversing only ice displaying every symptom of old age. Now this ridge before them was new, composed of blue ice with clearly fractured edges, bare of snow cover. It was anomalous and since Pitzl could detect a gradual northward curve several miles to his left he would have deviated westward to bypass it. Reluctantly he followed the torturous tracks of Bombardier's snowmobile through the ridge.

Almost immediately he felt his concern deepening. Not fifteen feet beyond lay another pressure ridge—just as fresh. He could not remember encountering two such parallel ridges so close together before, and his suspicion of the new and the different increased. He turned off his machine but could hear the engine of Bombardier's still operating ahead of him so he moved on.

Cresting the second ridge his alarm rose precipitously. Before him lay a third, lower ridge, and beyond that others. All were separated by only twenty to thirty feet and all were parallel. And from his vantage point, he recognized the oval slope of the area. As his eyes followed Bombardier's trail he was horrified to find a slowly widening crack split the tracks left by the leading machine and expose the ocean water at its depth.

The true nature of the area's ice activity lay before him now, clearly confirming his premonition. Some gargantuan force was thrusting waters upward at the central point of the area, shattering the ice in successive, concentric circles, forcing it outward and compressing it into a series of parallel pressure ridges alternating with narrow leads. With the entire area in slow-motion turmoil, the vulnerability of their position was obvious. He did not understand the geophysics of the process, but no clairvoyance was necessary to recognize their personal peril.

Signaling frantically to the trailing Plaisted and Pederson to remain where they were, he abandoned his machine and clambered quickly over the next small ridge. Bombardier was parked at its foot, chiseling a path through the next ridge when Pitzl rushed up to him. Grasping him by the shoulder he shouted, "We've got to get out of here, Jean-Luc. Fast. This is a trap!"

And even as he began to explain to the surprised Canadian, a startling quiver beneath their feet was followed by a new, slowly widening crack.

Within an hour they had fought their way back out of this unpredictable ice. Safe again on the broad, stable ice of the adjacent old floe, Pitzl stopped. Although still shaken by the experience he climbed to a high point on the outer ridge. While Pederson stood with head bowed in silent prayer, Pitzl pulled a notebook from his pocket and quickly sketched the outlines of this unique phenomenon.

It was less than an hour later when they found Bombardier halted at the edge of a new lead. In contrast to most of the others they had seen, this one had split down the middle of a floe. A thin, dark gray layer of new ice speckled with occasional 'salt flowers' covered the surface. Averaging a hundred feet wide, the lead contained several constricted areas to somewhat less than half this width.

Bombardier had unpacked his axe and now walked back to the edge of the lead. Swinging it gently he watched the axe's point bang into the ice without penetrating it. Stepping confidently down into the lead ice he repeated the procedure with the same results. But about fifteen feet from the edge, water spurted from the axe's blow, revealing a thickness of less than two inches. Gingerly he slid forward and repeated the process with similar findings. Returning to the floe, he told Plaisted, "It looks like about one and a half inches all the way across."

"Doesn't sound thick enough to me," Plaisted replied. "Now where in hell do they think they're going again?"

Pederson and Pitzl had both disconnected the sleds from their machine and were darting fitfully about the lead's edge. Plaisted had watched this reaction develop and increase over the past few days, beginning with their hazardous crossing of the big lead at eighty-seven degrees. Since that time each encounter with another lead seemed to galvanize the other three men into a frenzy of activity, driven by some nameless compulsion to accomplish the crossing without delay. Even when the ice was quiescent with no indication of motion the men appeared gripped by this obsessive impetuosity. Had they talked too much about the hazard of being thwarted by leads, he wondered? Or did the nearly disastrous initial lead crossing install a deep-rooted anxiety applicable to all leads? Or was it something else? He didn't really understand it, but knew this irrational monomania impelled them to unnecessary risks.

"It's thick enough for the machine, but probably not with the heavy sled behind it," Bombardier remarked as Pederson and Pitzl returned.

In the ensuing silence each man obviously struggled with alternative plans and just as Plaisted was about to declare his intention of making camp and waiting for thicker ice, Pederson announced excitedly, "I've got it. There's a spot a half-mile to the west where the lead's only about fifty feet wide. If we use all the rope we have we can make a tow line long enough to reach across the lead!"

New ice overnight, and newly cracked this morning

Their whoops of eager affirmation indicated the others needed no further explanation and they followed him quickly to the indicated area. Here Pederson fashioned a sixty-foot towline. Attaching one end to the back of his snowmobile, he carefully coiled the remainder and laid it on the ice in an orderly manner, fastening the other end to his sled.

"Wish me luck," he called cheerfully as he guided the machine onto the lead ice and accelerated quickly. As Bombardier had predicted, the ice bent and rippled as he crossed but it remained intact. The pile of rope unwound smoothly and only two coils remained when Pederson's snowmobile reached the opposite floe and climbed upon it. As the rope straightened and then became taut, the snowmobile's tracks bit firmly into the underlying snow. The loaded sled shot forward and slid smoothly across the lead. A moment later both had safely traversed the lead.

A silent Plaisted watched the exultant Pederson detach the rope, weight one end with a chunk of ice, swing it above him and hurl it back across the lead. Retrieving it he witnessed first Bombardier, then Pitzl use the technique to cross and then he followed them himself. He was not even really annoyed with Pederson when he found the man had been so confident he had not even waited for the others, and was now barely visible several miles distant, heading north.

"How," he wondered, "would we have gotten Aufderheide and Powellek over that one if they'd been along too?"

But he was soon to learn more about leads—much more. As the frequency of pressure ridges declined the number of leads increased. Again and again they found themselves facing still another one, each presenting its own unique problem. Most of them stretched themselves toward the east or west across their path but an occasional one was directed northward and, if covered with a sufficiently thick ice surface, could be used as a highway toward the Pole.

On one occasion, Plaisted looked around to find himself literally in the midst of a sea of leads with neither floe nor pressure ridge in sight. As he watched in disbelief, Jean-Luc yielded to that constraining drive which compelled him to fling himself across almost any treacherous surface. A lead ahead was in the process of freezing, with a gap of perhaps three feet of open water left in the middle. Gunning his engine to top speed, Jean-Luc flung himself and his Ski-Doo across the gap, water splashing up from his skis as he found himself safely across to the other side, his ten-foot sled following easily behind. Walt Pederson quickly grasped the idea and followed, also making it across as Ralph stared dumbfounded. The enormity of their folly finally penetrated to his judgment.

"You guys are crazy," he yelled at Pitzl who had just joined him at that spot. "Just plain nuts. I'm not going any further. We're staying right here."

"Then you'll be awful lonesome, Ralph," Pitzl replied. "Look around you. If this stuff moves it will all be crushed into ice cubes. Don't lose your cool now!"

"Lose my cool!" expostulated Plaisted. "It's you that's lost your sense. One wrong guess here and we've all had it."

But as Pitzl gunned his engine to follow Jean-Luc and Walt, making the jump easily, Ralph had to acknowledge their commitment to finish what they had begun. He swore at himself, then gunned his own engine to follow. Just a few weeks ago, Ralph thought, he was worried about driving the men too hard. Now, the men were driving him. They moved together from one menacing lead to another, now the perpetual omniscience of disaster never completely dulling their sensitivity to danger. They learned a hundred subskills of the art with ever rising proficiency reflected in northward progress. The increasing proximity of their goal seemed to spur them to even greater abandon.

It was a thoughtful quartet in the tent the next night, April 15, 1968. "Eighty-eight degrees, forty-six minutes," Pitzl said gratifiedly as he restored his instruments to their container. "Less than seventy-five miles to the pole."

"How much gas do we need to get there, Walt?" Plaisted inquired.

"About a hundred gallons," Pederson replied. "We're completely dry now.

"One more supply flight after tomorrow's."

No one spoke for several minutes. Then Plaisted probed: "If we sent the extra tent back, all slept in one sleeping bag and cut back to minimal rations, we might be able to get there in three days."

Visions of the dozens of leads they had crossed raced through their minds. Thin leads. Thick leads. Old leads and fresh leads. Closed leads and open leads and narrow leads and wide leads.

And then followed visions of trying to cross them again with seven men instead of four, together with all the additional baggage necessary to sustain them. They all knew that with seven men they would still all be back near eighty-seven degrees waiting for a lead to freeze.

"If we only knew what's ahead," mused Bombardier.

"Peary had a lot of trouble with leads in this area," Pitzl reminded them, but then went on to admit, "and, while fewer, there were enough to bother him all the way to the Pole. And you've forgotten one other thing, Ralph."

"What's that?"

"Ernst. We need motion pictures of us at the Pole, especially when the Oceanography Department's plane flies over us to confirm our position. I've been able to take some footage for him of lead crossings since he left the ice, but the pole pictures are too important to be done by an amateur."

"We need that film; without it we'll never pay our bills," Pederson muttered.

Plaisted agonized over the decision. "We trust your judgment, Ralph," his chief supporter had told him just before he left this second time. "With your experience we know you'll make it this time." And again he remembered too the taunting challenge that the snob at National Geographic had thrown at him: "You can't get to the North Pole with a bunch of your Minnesota cronies."

Yet he also recalled the eager anticipation in Art's expression the very first night they planned the adventure together, the total dedication to the group's effort Powellek had rendered and the blindly and optimistically faithful service Horton had yielded on both expeditions. But then the recent impressions of the ominous, black water in the leads submerged all other thoughts. Again and again he recalled all the considerations. Again and again he wanted to yield to his impulse simply to bring the men out on the supply flight in the morning and to deal directly at that time with whatever problem that would create. Then he would remember the leads again.

It was fully an hour later before he sighed, turned to Pitzl and ordered, "Get base camp on the radio. Have Weldy out here tomorrow with ninety gallons of mixed snowmobile gasoline, ten gallons of white gas, two new sleds and whatever parts Walt wants. We'll send back about 500 pounds of reserve and emergency gear."

Ironically, while they had dominated the thoughts of each man, no one had spoken the names of Horton, Powellek, or Aufderheide aloud. And no one spoke of them now. None wanted this decision, yet each knew it was inevitable. Now it was done.

Powellek looked over Moriarty's shoulder as the latter carefully recorded the items being requested by the ice party as Wes Cook repeated them. When Pitzl had initiated the radio contact by announcing their position they had all cheered and Cavouras had leaped to the map on the barracks door to plot the new position. But as the supply list lengthened Powellek's face began to display signs of concern. Pederson wanted to exchange a new snowmobile from base camp for a battered one with the ice party. Two sleds, food and other requested items were swelling the available aircraft space. A dawning suspicion was reflected in the expression which suddenly leaped to full conviction when Pitzl concluded the list by asking for ninety gallons of snowmobile fuel.

"Ninety gallons!" Powellek nearly shouted. "That's enough to take them all the way to the Pole." Whirling to face Aufderheide he challenged: "And there certainly isn't room or available weight for us in that plane with all those things they asked for!"

Recognizing the implications Art too had been dismayed by the growing list of requested supplies. "Maybe," he suggested hopefully, "they expect two supply flights—one for goods and one for people." And after a brief pause

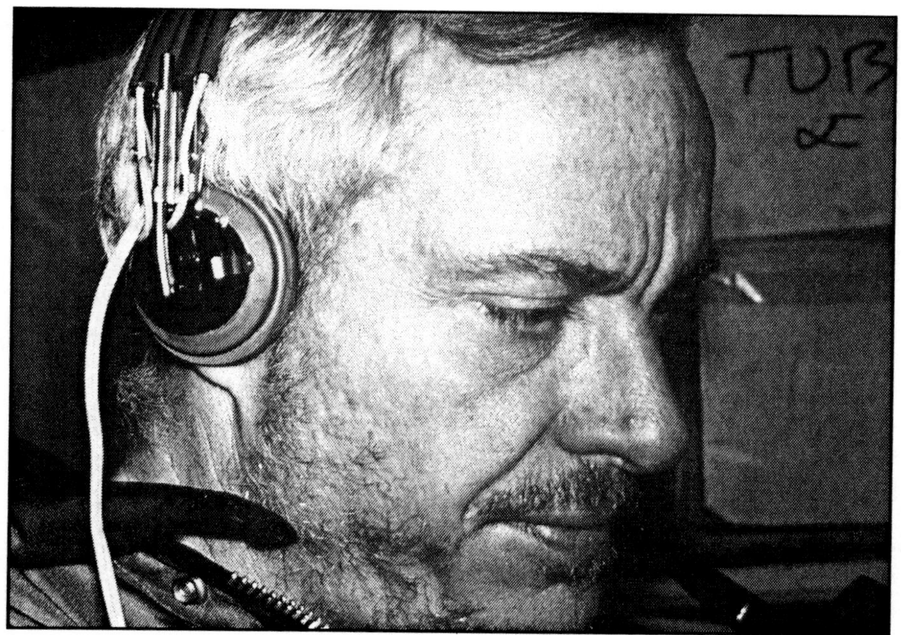

Andy at the radio

he added, "But if so we can't do it. There's no aircraft fuel left here at base camp and they're out so far now that to fly down to Tanquary, out to the gas cache, then to the party and back here is one big day's effort. Two flights is out of the question."

Just then Pitzl's voice floated out of the radio speaker again, ". . . and send Ernst out. Ralph wants him to film the overflight at the North Pole."

This time Powellek didn't even shout. He just stared in disbelief. He didn't even hear Pitzl reply to Wes Cook's query about the next radio schedule or he would have recognized there was no intent of the ice party to return to radio communication before they reached the North Pole. Finally he stuttered the question, "But . . . but . . . don't they . . . don't they want us out there too?"

And when Wes Cook relayed the inquiry they all heard Pitzl say, "I have no orders for other personnel change."

With an indefinable grimace Powellek spun around and strode from the barracks, only the violence of the door slam testifying to his mood.

It was fully half an hour before the preparation of the requested items was assured and Art could follow him. He found him in the mess shack, alone, staring at the wall. His face was suffused with a dark expression reflecting the mixture of hurt and loyalty buffeting his mind. Art knew his mood without being told. He recognized the thousands of hours Powellek had dedicated to this expedition, the major sacrifice his voluntary self-removal from the ice had been in order to repair the navigational beacon, the vital role he had played in creating and maintaining all expedition communication, the enormous importance which Powellek attached to the planned North Pole-South Pole radio transmission, and the sense of total betrayal he felt at the hands of the men to whom he had committed his dedication.

"Why did they do it to us, Art?" he asked mournfully. "Why?"

Art knew how he felt simply because he was tormented by the same emotional upheaval. Although achievement of the North Pole had never been any more than an interest distinctly secondary to his desire for experience on the pack ice itself, and although he had openly declared this repeatedly, the sense of rejection by the ice party which he experienced now led him to yield to an orgy of self-pity. He had acknowledged the importance to Plaisted and the others of the success of their goal, and had committed himself to it as completely as they themselves. To be discarded now, he felt, was to have his loyalty exploited and he felt it as keenly as Powellek.

"Just think, the film means more to them than we do," Powellek pointed out dejectedly, and he picked up a glass and smashed it against a wall in frustration.

It was 4:00 a.m. before their mutual commiseration had exhausted them both and they fell asleep in their chairs.

12

Sprint to the Finish

"WAKE UP, DON," HORTON WAS SAYING, shaking his shoulder vigorously, "Jim wants you on the radio."

Sleepily Powellek awoke and rubbed his eyes. Yawning he asked, "What time is it?"

"Nearly noon," Horton answered. "Weldy's been to the ice party and is on his way back. Jim is on now from Chicago. Says he has a message for you."

A minute later Horton was again astonished to view the metamorphosis Powellek underwent when he accepted a radio microphone. Regardless of inner emotional turmoil he heard Powellek's voice emerge evenly, distinctly, without passion, polished and professional, totally independent of his own feelings.

"The United States Air Force has a weather jet scheduled to fly between England and Alaska several times during the next few days," Jim was telling Powellek. "Since they'll be passing over the Pole anyway, they'll drop down low enough to confirm your presence at the Pole."

"Many thanks, Jim. That's an enormous relief for us. Without that kind of independent confirmation we could be in a Peary-Cook type of controversy. What's their arrival time there?"

"About 5:00 p.m. your time tomorrow. Have the ice party turn on their beacon a half hour before that."

"Can't do, Jim," Powellek replied. "We won't have radio contact with them again until at least tomorrow night."

"Well," chuckled Jim, "if the plane finds them, won't they be surprised?"

...

JERRY PITZL SAT DOWN ATOP THE PRESSURE RIDGE and rested his elbows on his knees. Thus stabilized he raised the sextant to his eyes, carefully aligned the sun's image and recorded both time and instrument readings. This was the third measurement he had made at hourly intervals since they had made camp, and he knew from the results that this measurement would confirm his previous determination that they were located at eighty-nine degrees twenty-six minutes north and fifty-five degrees west.

He had become even more laconic than usual these past few days. Until now he had had little more direct responsibility than to keep the party oriented northward, determine a rough position daily and operate the radio. But each hour now the party was becoming increasingly dependent upon him.

He knew the North Pole was merely a theoretical point in the ocean, covered with constantly drifting ice indistinguishable from that covering the rest of the Arctic Ocean. They would know they were at the North Pole only when Pitzl would tell them so. And Pitzl knew only what his marine sextant readings indicated. This was really why he was here. He wondered whether his many hours of practice had rewarded him with sufficient skill for the task. He expected a military plane of some type to be checking with him all the sophisticated navigational gear available to them, and he wanted desperately to be at the North Pole when they were.

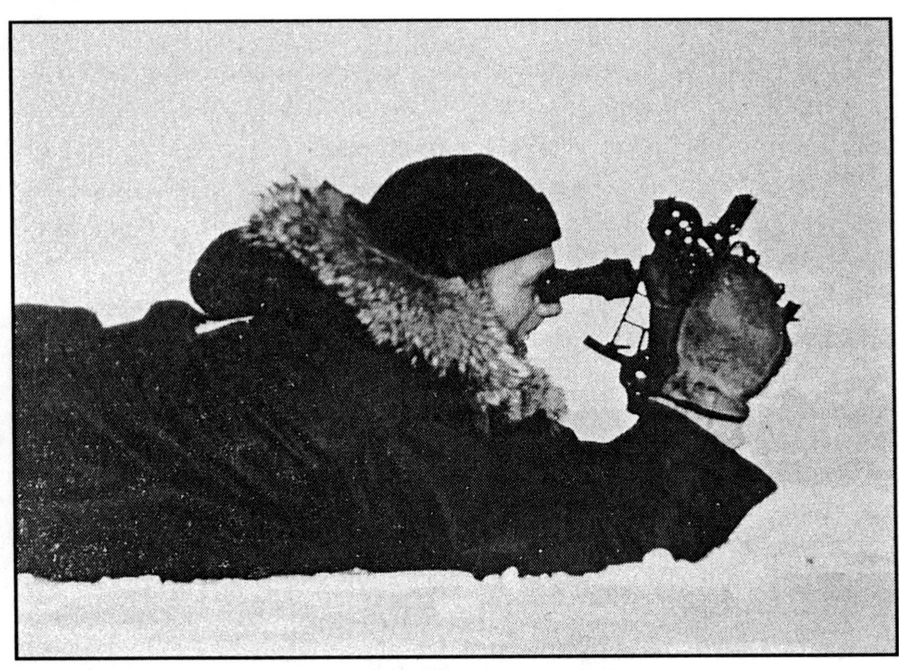

Jerry Pitzl takes a sextant shot

Replacing the sextant in its case he was astonished to detect an aircraft low on the northwestern horizon. Weldy had supplied them the previous morning and was not to return until requested. Instinctively he reached into his pocket and extracted the signal mirror he carried there. Even as he raised it to his eye and began flashing it, he recognized from its speed it could not be Weldy. Yet no aircraft capable of such speeds had any reason to be flying only 1,000 feet above the ice.

Almost immediately he saw the plane turn and as it approached he recognized the shape of a Boeing 707 four-engine jet. But the markings on the fuselage betrayed its military nature and his heart pounded wildly as it passed over their floe fifty feet above the ice with a thunderous roar.

Plaisted, Pederson, and Bombardier had been preparing the meal inside the tent when it happened. Unprepared for this reality they interpreted the deafening roar as some type of unexpected ice catastrophe and ejected from the tent in instant alarm. When one glance skyward revealed the truth Pederson reacted instinctively. Leaping aboard his snowmobile he roared off to dash conspicuously about the floe. Unfortunately he had forgotten that he had used the machine to anchor one corner of the tent, and as the tent rope tied to the machines tightened, the abrupt deceleration of the snowmobile not only catapulted Pederson sprawling onto the snow, but it also brought the tent crashing down behind him. In the midst of the pandemonium, with Bombardier quickly extinguishing the stove, Plaisted strode over to retrieve a box dropped by the aircraft. Inside he found a note requesting he activate the button on his battery operated beacon and a minute later learned the nature and purpose of the flight.

"Our navigator says you're at eighty-nine degrees, twenty-five minutes, thirty seconds north and fifty-five degrees west," the plane's pilot told him.

"Roger, we've got that," Plaisted answered after recording it. "Are you coming back again?"

"Tonight," promised the pilot. "ETA near midnight. Activate your beacon about 11:00 p.m. so we can find you more easily."

"Okay. We'll shove off again. We had camped early because we traveled much of last night but we'll be ready for you again later."

"You were only a half-mile off in your position, Jerry," Plaisted told him when he arrived at the tent. "Congratulations."

Flushed with pleasure, Pitzl grinned and asked facetiously, "What do you mean, *I* was? *They* were!"

Abandoning their plans to sleep, they ate hastily and resumed their travels.

And then, after their many adversities, nature shared her benevolence with them. The leads, which previously had retarded their progress, in this area included several directed northward. With a smooth, thick ice cover these permitted rapid progress, leading ultimately to a complex area of jumbled ice from which they finally emerged onto a large floe about 10:00 p.m.

"We're not there, but we're close enough," Pitzl advised. "Let's camp here and I'll fix our position. We can make our final approach in the morning then."

He had been unusually diligent in marking deviations from northward progress these past hours so that he knew they were within a dozen miles of their goal. Careful plotting of these records, the snowmobile odometer readings and a final sextant reading gave him a position of eighty-nine degrees fifty minutes north.

"We're ten miles from the North Pole," he announced with glee.

"Let's go now before the plane gets here," Walt urged eagerly. "If we can find one more of. those 'freeway' leads we'll be there in an hour."

"And if we don't we won't be ready for the overflight," Plaisted declared. "No, we'll stay right here like Jerry says. From here on we do exactly what he tells us to because he's the only one who knows where it is, understand?"

With the beacon activated they were surprised to hear the sudden appearance of the aircraft an hour earlier than expected, but happily pressed the audio button and received their greeting.

"Ask them our position," Jerry requested anxiously.

"Eighty-nine degrees thirty-five minutes north and 125 degrees east," the plane's pilot answered. Pitzl's jaw sagged as he received the incredible news.

"Ask him to repeat that," he finally stammered, and when the same figures were resubmitted he asked the pilot to request their navigator to recheck the readings.

"Same thing," the pilot affirmed a few minutes later. "We have to go on now, but the final flight will come back over the Pole at 1100 April 20, about thirty-six hours from now. See you at the Pole. By the way, it looks the same over there as over here—just a lot more floating ice."

It was shortly after 1:00 a.m. when Pitzl returned to the tent after yet another sextant reading and plotted it on his charts.

"I've plotted it both ways—the conventional assumed position technique and also the system using the North Pole as the assumed position. Either way it comes out the same: eighty-nine degrees fifty minutes and fifty-five degrees west. I just don't understand it," he complained.

"Well, you both agreed where we were just a few hours ago," Plaisted reminded him.

"Yes, and if they're right we've passed over the North Pole and gone twenty-five miles down the other side," Pitzl pointed out.

"That's silly," Pederson emphasized. "We would have been out of gas three hours ago if we'd gone that far. Forget it, Jerry. We've got confidence in you."

It was silly, Pitzl thought. All his readings at least had been consistent with each other and roughly with the snowmobile odometer. And his most recent prior position had been precisely confirmed on the previous overflight. He could not possibly suddenly have introduced a thirty-five-mile error. And yet this was his adopted family, the military, the very group whose respect he sought, that had offered the challenging report. In spite of the reassurances of his comrades, emotionally he did not wish to defy the Air Force, yet his logic and his science suggested their error.

"I don't even know which way to tell you to go if we accept their position," Pitzl advised as he checked his figures once again.

Sleepily he picked up the straightedge and began to draw the line on the chart when he realized his fatigue was so great he was inadvertently plotting the line backwards. Reaching for the eraser his eye suddenly noted the erroneous position and studied it intently. A moment later he announced joyously: "I've got it. I know what happened. The plane's navigator plotted the position backwards. See?" he pointed, "it comes out to where they said it was."

"We're glad you found out why," Plaisted said, "but you were the only one really worried about it. We knew you were right all along. Now go to bed."

"I will except for one thing: I want to get a sextant reading every hour through the night. I think this floe is drifting and I need to prove it to know exactly where, when and how far to make our final move so that we'll be exactly at the Pole for the overflight," Pitzl replied as he wearily crawled into the sleeping bag, placing his instruments conveniently accessible for frequent use.

...

"WELDY REFUSED TO TAKE ERNST ALONG on the last flight out to the ice party as Ralph requested because he was already overloaded with the gear they needed," Art was telling Powellek. "Now he doesn't want to take more than one man along out to evacuate them from the Pole because he still doesn't trust the beacon. If he takes more he can't bring them all out in one flight and he won't leave any one out there in case the beacon goes out on him again."

"Who cares?" Powellek asked. "Let the photographer go if you don't want to fly out there yourself, because I certainly don't. If they didn't want me out there before, why should I go now? Fly to the Pole? Big deal! No thanks," and he stalked away angrily.

Art was vexed with himself for, while the necessity and inevitability of the events were beginning to make their impression, he still found himself reacting like a spurned suitor.

He found Weldy in front of the barracks, using a small hand torch to weld a crack in a tubular metal structure.

"Thought you were going to Tanquary Fjord for fuel today," he commented.

"Can't. Broken exhaust. Have to weld it or it could start the engine on fire," Weldy replied.

"We need to get film of the Air Force overflight at the Pole, Weldy. Ernst will go along with you to do the photography. Don and I will stay here."

"Don't you two want to fly to the pole?' Weldy asked surprised.

"No. Just be sure you get Ernst out there in time to film the plane flying over our tent at the North Pole."

"What time will that be?"

"About 11:00 a.m.' Art answered. "I'll get you up at four."

"Can't do it," Weldy replied laconically.

"Why not?' Art asked, alarmed.

"Got to go to Tanquary fjord first for fuel. Won't be enough time to do both that and still get out to the North Pole by 1100."

"But we've got to," Art persisted. "Without that scene the film's a flop. That's the whole climax of the film."

"Sorry, Art, can't get to Tanquary today and there just won't be enough time in the morning."

Art paused, then turned and facing Weldy told him frankly: "Weldy, when I came off the ice I told you I'd never tell you when to fly. So far I never have. And I still won't tell you. But now I'm going to ask you. I know that old automotive gas and kerosene at the camp here is so bad you've always refused to put it in your plane. But we need that film sequence tomorrow, Weldy. If you can't get to Tanquary today to refuel I'm asking you to use that old gasoline and kerosene so you can leave directly from here in the morning and get Ernst there on time."

Weldy stopped and stared. Art had never talked to him like that before. He knew Art hadn't come along to be at base camp. He knew Art didn't enjoy manipulating the variety of personalities there to keep an effective crew operational while the ice party was enjoying the adventures he had expected himself. And he had watched the doctor learn the unique skills needed to maintain and operate machinery and aircraft at fifty below zero. He empathized with his reaction to being forced to remain at base camp.

Turning to Ken Lee he ordered gruffly: "Fill it up with the stuff, but be sure you filter it at least twice through a chamois!"

"Thanks, Weldy," Art smiled his gratitude and entered the barracks.

"CBS was just on the air. They want to interview Ralph by radio while he's at the North Pole," Horton advised. "And WCCO in Minneapolis is completing arrangements for a North Pole-South Pole transmission. Several other newspapers and TV stations want interviews too and CBC wants one with Bombardier."

Art glanced at Powellek upon mention of the interpolar transmission and watched him wince and turn away silently. Cavouras was pointedly ignoring the photographer, convinced that the photographic priorities were the source of the problems. The tension was so tangible he found it intolerable.

"Going out for a walk. Back in a few hours," he announced and left the barracks before the surprised Horton could inquire further.

Several hours later he reached the summit of Mt. Walker. It was another quiet, sunny afternoon, and the tranquility of the diminutive dome was mesmerizing. He sat down on a rock and stared down at the tiny buildings before him. "This isn't the way it was supposed to happen," he mused. He understood the discontent of each man, yet had done all he could. What he needed now himself was merely several hours of isolation.

"The Plaisted Polar Expedition should have its own cairn," he told himself and began accumulating boulders at the summit in an orderly pile. Four hours later he returned.

"Art, where have you been? There's been excitement here all afternoon. Right after you left Ralph came on the air and announced they'd reached the North Pole. When we relayed the message south all hell broke loose. CBS interviewed Ralph, CBC got a French language interview from Jean-Luc, congratulatory messages are pouring in from every politician in North America and every ham in the world is trying to jam into the frequency!"

"How about the interpolar radio transmission?" Art asked apprehensively.

"That went off smooth as silk. Jerry sounded kind of bored though. All he did was ask them how the weather was down there."

Art found Powellek in the mess shack, alone, staring out the window. They said nothing to each other for several minutes. Then Powellek turned and said: "Art, if even here the system is more important than the man, then why are we here?" Art didn't answer. There was nothing to say. He left.

...

"Now listen carefully," Pitzl instructed Plaisted and Bombardier. "According to my sextant readings our floe has been drifting steadily eastward—toward the Pole—at the rate of about three miles a day. That's why we haven't moved our camp. But we're still about four miles from the North Pole. Take your machines and sleds, watch the odometer and proceed exactly east precisely four miles, stop and set up the tent. At ten minutes before 1100 fire the smoke bomb and turn on your beacon. Got that?"

"Roger," grinned Bombardier and the two disappeared.

The route was easily traversed, but they encountered a lead near their goal. Checking the odometer, Plaisted declared: "Now isn't that handy? We won't have to cross it. This is just four miles."

After setting up their tent they waited. At 10:50 a.m., they ignited the smoke bomb and a billowing plume of orange smoke rose skyward. Plaisted had expected to be excited, but was surprised to find himself composed. A few minutes later Bombardier pointed to the west at a rapidly enlarging dot in the sky and in a moment the plane roared over them.

Pitzl was agitated. He was absolutely certain he was right; he had been all along but when the Air Force's corrected reading confirming his position had been radioed this morning he had felt some relief. Nevertheless today was the ultimate measure and his final opportunity. Desperately he hoped Plaisted and

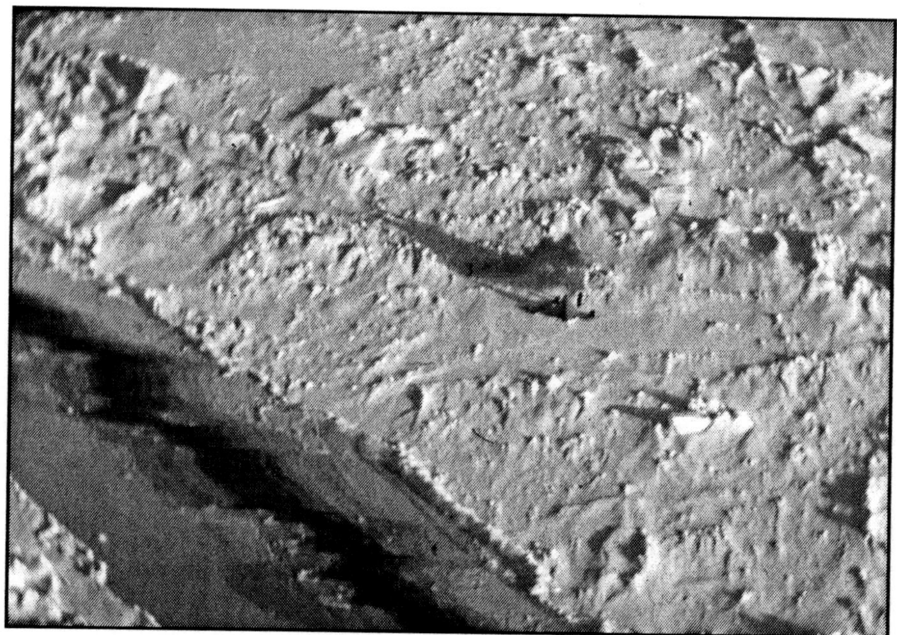

North Pole camp of the Plaisted expedition, taken from Lark 47

Bombardier had followed instructions precisely. He was tempted to rush outside for a final sextant reading but immediately recognized the folly of the impulse.

At ten minutes before the hour the radio burst into life with the report: "This is Lark 47 on approach to the North Pole."

And when Pitzl explained their arrangements—a permanent camp four miles from the Pole with Plaisted and Bombardier at the temporary camp exactly at the North Pole, the pilot promised to fly directly over the Pole, counting out the last ten seconds before arrival there aloud over the radio.

Pitzl could feel himself clutching the microphone as the minutes passed. No lead crossing had ever caused him so much anxiety, no blizzard such concern. When he heard the pilot begin with: "Ten seconds, nine seconds, eight, seven" he fought off a wave of nausea. "six, five . . . I see them dead ahead . . . four, three, two, one, NORTH POLE—dead on!"

He almost fainted with relief as he heard the pilot tell Plaisted over the audio beacon unit. "Every direction from where you fellows are is south!"

...

USAF C-135 Lark 47 overflies the North Pole camp

"I WAS WORRIED THEY WOULDN'T GET THERE IN TIME," Cavouras bubbled. "Weldy didn't leave here until 5:45 this morning."

"We're lucky they didn't leave earlier. When Plaisted's beacon battery failed from his overuse of the audio unit, Weldy would never have been able to find them by himself if the Air Force plane hadn't been there to turn on its own beacon which Weldy could then use to be guided in to them."

"Jerry told us on the radio it worked out just perfectly. The Air Force plane had just about used up its reserve fuel when Weldy arrived. Ernst got a chance to film the overflight both from the air and also from the surface after Weldy landed. The plane made two passes for him before it left," Horton said animatedly.

Powellek added: "He also said they went out to a lead at the North Pole to take some pictures there, but Pitzl refused to cross it. Said it was too dangerous to cross leads if you don't have to!"

Moriarty completed lettering a towel with "Ralph's Big Campout Wins" and suggested: "They're due in five minutes. Let's go down to the strip."

At 7:00 p.m. the Otter touched down at Ward Hunt Island and taxied to a stop. The base camp cadre stood there, unsure of themselves. The fuselage door opened and Bombardier jumped out. He faced them and grinned. They hesitated, then howled a greeting and rushed forward to shake his hand. Pederson, Pitzl, and Plaisted emerged and were similarly greeted. Art, too, greeted them, then turned to Plaisted. They stared at each other for a moment, then Plaisted opened his arms, Art rushed into them and they embraced briefly while Plaisted nearly sobbed: "Art, I never intended for it to end like this!" Abashed by their transient but spontaneous displays of emotion they turned quickly and helped unload the plane.

The party began slowly. The two groups were quite self-conscious of their different roles in the expedition, and of first kept muttering amenities to each other. Cavouras brought out the refreshments and their tensions disappeared slowly. Art had prepared two copies of a summary of the expedition and had every one sign it. The mood thawed slowly as they exchanged tales of experiences when suddenly Powellek arose, confronted Plaisted and demanded: "Why didn't you bring us back out there, Ralph?"

The room suddenly became silent. Conversation ceased as all eyes turned to Ralph Plaisted. Ruefully Plaisted stared at his friend, then answered as gently as possible: "Because we'd never have made it, Don. It isn't the way I wanted it, but it's the way it had to be. I never had a choice. I'm sorry, Don."

The silence persisted a few moments longer. Then Powellek extended his hand and replied: "I'm sorry too, Ralph, but I wanted to hear you say you really wanted us out there."

"Listen, everybody," Art pleaded. "We've had several years of great fun and wonderful friendships out of this. That's all we ever wanted from it, remember? When we get back lots of people will want a slice out of each of us, because everybody wants to be part of a winner. Let's not let anyone cut us apart after we return."

Cheers destroyed the tension. With the expedition once more an integral unit the party proceeded as such celebrations should, and it was 3:00 a.m. before the last man retired. Before extinguishing the lights Weldy announced: "Tomorrow morning we'll all fly over to visit Admiral Robert Peary's cairn which he built at Cape Columbia in 1909."

"What for?" Plaisted demanded. "Let's get an early start home."

"But, Ralph, that's where Peary started from on his trip to the Pole. His record must still be there. That's a very historic place," Pitzl protested.

"Oh, all right," Plaisted relented. "Sounds like it might be good for some newspaper publicity anyway."

...

WITH THE CAMP QUIET ONCE MORE, Art found a plastic bottle and sealed one copy of the expedition record in it. In front of the mess shack fluttered s tattered flag bearing the expedition's title. Carrying these items Art began his last, lone ascent of Mt. Walker. Reaching the summit he partly disassembled the cairn he had built the previous day. Placing the bottle containing the record within it he replaced the rocks, mounted the flag on the cairn and photographed it. Returning his gaze to the pack ice he watched the ominously dark gray fog bank drifting toward the camp. "I'd better get down off the mountain before that mist traps me up here," he muttered reluctantly. Turning his back on the cairn he had constructed he began the long descent down to the camp and to the other men to whom he belonged.

...

REACHING THE CREST OF THE 2,000-FOOT RIDGE, Walt Pederson turned to view the group below. Struggling up the steep snow-covered incline were a dozen men in a dozen different, brilliantly-colored parkas in a line leading back from the twin engined Otter aircraft which had brought them and was

1968 expedition members at Peary's cairn. Left to right: top row: Wes Cook, Don Powellek, Andy Horton, Ralph Plaisted, John Moriarty, Weldy Phipps, Ken Lee; bottom row: Art Aufderheide, Jean-Luc Bombardier, Jerry Pitzl, Walt Pederson, George Cavouras. Actually shot in 1968 but used old flag.

now parked at the foot of the rocky hill. Retrieving the microphone of a small tape recorder carried inside his parka he flipped the switch and, still panting breathlessly, announced: "Beat the others to the top of Cape Columbia. It's a steep climb up. Only about thirty below but a strong wind makes it chilly at the top. Admiral Robert Peary's cairn is here. It's a pile of rocks about five feet high that he built in 1906. He failed to reach the North Pole that year and came back, leaving from here in 1909, the year he says he made it all the way. Ralph is going to put the record of the Plaisted Polar Expedition into the can that Peary left in this cairn."

When Art Aufderheide arrived, the other expedition members were already crowded around the cairn, pawing at the rocks in ribald joviality. Their irreverence was disturbingly offensive to him, for he viewed Cape Columbia as a historic temple and the cairn as its altar, to be acknowledged with the veneration appropriate to a shrine.

"Here it is," Weldy Phipps called out.

It was a small metal can of rectangular shape about four inches high. The thin layer of orange lichen growth accumulated on the outside almost obscured its presence among the red rocks. Weldy pried open the press-top lid, clearly revealing the words "Breakfast Cocoa" imprinted upon its inner surface. Reaching into the can's interior he extracted several pieces of paper, and handed one to Ralph Plaisted.

"Here's the note I left," he said. "Nobody had been to this cairn since Peary built it in 1906 when I first visited it about ten years ago."

"And here's Hattersley-Smith's note. His glaciologist party stopped here a few years later. They removed Peary's original note for the National Museum of Canada and left a copy, together with their own note. They also left here the piece of the U.S. Flag that Peary carried, made for him by his wife, and that he cut out and put into the container here in 1906. Here's the flag fragment," he told him as he handed Plaisted a thin, faded blue scrap of cotton about four inches in diameter.

"Here, Andy," Plaisted told Horton, "read Peary's note out loud."

"May 7, 1906," Horton began as Pederson shoved the microphone in front of his mouth. "Killed three musk-ox south from here. One February 28 we . . ."

Art never heard the remainder. He was watching Plaisted who had opened his knife and was now half cutting and half tearing the piece of Peary's flag into smaller segments. Before he could object the piece had been subdivided into four tattered fragments. Looking up, Plaisted saw him and thrust one at him. He accepted it speechlessly and gingerly placed it securely inside a camera filter container.

When Horton finished, Plaisted unfolded a paper from his pocket and read it aloud, then quickly stuffed the paper into the can together with the others they found there. "All right, Art," he called out. "Take some shots of everybody standing around the cairn. It'll make good newspaper copy when we get back. It's damned cold up here, so if you'll hurry up we can get back down into the plane and get out of here."

Ten minutes later only Pitzl, Weldy Phipps, and Art still remained on top. The rocks they had removed had been hurriedly and casually replaced, so they rearranged them until the cairn's original structure was restored. One of the rocks had fallen and broken into smaller fragments. Art stooped, picked up several of these and reverently secreted them in his pocket. Straightening up again he looked around him for the last time. Far below, the pack ice pressed against the foot of the precipitous north face, stretching northward to the pole. Reluctantly he picked up his camera and began the slow descent to rejoin his companions. The crush of civilization awaited.

The awesome beauty of the Arctic

Epilogue

After his return, Ralph Plaisted laughed when *National Geographic* wanted to buy the rights to the expedition's story. Remembering how uncooperative they had been when he first asked them for help, he happily sold the story to *Life* magazine instead. But Plaisted's ten minutes of fame were closer to five. He had the misfortune to choose a year, 1968, that was full of earthshaking news: assassinations, Vietnam, men orbiting the Moon, riots, and a presidential election. There was a nice parade in St. Paul on their return, but the world barely noticed. When *Life* published their forty-year retrospective on that momentous year of 1968, Plaisted's achievement was not mentioned.

The men of the Plaisted expedition who visited Peary's cairn believed they were honoring the memory of one who had stood on the Earth's axis some six decades previously. In 1968 no one questioned Peary's claim except a few diehard supporters of the charlatan Dr. Frederick Cook. Today, few historians accept Peary's story at face value, and Jerry Pitzl's careful navigation shows why. When approaching the Pole, Pitzl took sextant shots every clear day, increasing to hourly shots near the Pole, to enable the team to zero in on their goal while moving over the constantly shifting Arctic ice. In 1911, Amundsen had employed the same meticulous method to arrive at the South Pole.

Peary's navigation, if you can call it that, was altogether different. He had ordered the last navigator (other than himself) to turn back when they were 135 miles from the Pole. From there, Peary marched six days *without taking a single sextant shot*. After pitching his tents, Peary left camp to take his sextant sightings alone, and returned with a morose look on his face. He then retired to his tent for twelve hours without saying a word. When he finally emerged, he called for the flags and camera to be broken out, and photographed the scene for posterity. After six days marching, Peary had determined (or more correctly, *decided*) that not one more foot of travel in any direction was needed to reach the Pole. At least that was the story.

TO WHOM IT MAY CONCERN

In 1968 while I was owner operator of Atlas Aviation Ltd. at Resolute Bay, Northwest Terriories, Canada, I contracted with Ralph Plaisted of St. Paul, Minn. to provide air support for his North Geographic pole Expedition. The Plaisted Expedition successfully reached the Pole on April 19th of that year.

It has been brought to my attention that someone has started a rumor that the Plaisted party was airlifted over obstacles such as open water during his trek to the Pole. With my co-pilot Ken Lee I personally flew the air support for the Plaisted Expedition and guarantee that no such operations took place. Furthermore it was not even remotely suggested by Mr. Plaisted or any member of his party that such a fraud be perpetrated.

Witness

A [illegible]

Date 3 April 89

W.W. Phipps

April 3/89.

Date

In the face of mounting skepticism, Peary's family opened the explorer's personal archives to inspection in the late 1980s. Explorer Wally Herbert (whom Plaisted's team had aided in 1967) examined them carefully and found them wanting; his brutally honest book *The Noose of Laurels* remains the best biography of Peary available.

No other person, before or since, has duplicated Peary's claim of traveling 135 miles over the Arctic ice in six days; and no other person, before or since, has duplicated Peary's claim of traveling such a distance to arrive

6 April 1989

655 Richmond Road
Unit 31
Ottawa, Ontario

TO WHOM IT MAY CONCERN:

The following statement is in regard to the "Plaisted Polar Expedition" of 1968.

In my capacity as crewman and mechanic for Atlas Aviation, I was on board any time support was flown to expedition members on the ice.

At no time were any team members and equipment, which reached the pole, flown across open water, obstacles or in a northerly direction.

Yours very truly,

Kenneth C. Lee.

I, RICHARD BEN SORENSEN, certify that KENNETH C. LEE appeared before me on the 10th day of April, 1989, and signed the above document and he produced for my inspection his Driver's Licence.

Richard Ben Sorensen, Q.C., a Notary Public in and for the Province of Ontario. My commission expires at the pleasure of the Lieutenant Governor.

at a precise destination without making navigational fixes. Historian Dennis Rawlins has derided the navigational claim as a "pole in one," but the actual situation is even worse than that. Taken together, Peary's dual claims of distance and navigation are roughly the equivalent to an unwitnessed hole in one on a par five: in other words, flatly unbelievable.

It was only years later that Plaisted began to realize what they had really accomplished in 1968. Given that Peary's claim was false, then the first team to arrive at the North Pole "the hard way"—over the surface of the Arctic

Ocean ice—was none other than Ralph Plaisted and his unlikely group of friends. From an abundance of caution, Plaisted got back in touch with Weldy Phipps and Ken Lee, their pilots, and asked them to sign affidavits confirming that the 1968 expedition had been accomplished from Ward Hunt Island to the North Pole entirely over the surface, without air movement. Their affidavits appear in this book.

Every year on April 19 the surviving members of the Plaisted expedition, at least those within striking distance of Minnesota, gather to reminisce. These days, the group is quite a bit smaller that it used to be.

John Moriarty, the "Mayor of Ward Hunt Island," had to give up his job as a food scientist at Pillsbury to go north with Plaisted. After returning, he went back to school and got a degree in mechanical engineering, a field in which he worked successfully until his retirement in the 1990s.

Shortly after his return south, Dr. Weston Cook had surgery for bladder cancer and recovered well. He returned to his medical practice in Columbia, South Carolina, and made hunting trips to Alaska in the 1970s. He was one of the few who lost touch with the other expedition members afterward.

George Cavouras, who pulled his weight digging fuel at Tanquary Fjord and as base camp cook, returned to his insurance business. He lives today in Phoenix, Arizona.

Weldy Phipps retired in 1972 after an unequaled career in aviation. He was inducted into the Canadian Aviation Hall of Fame and was awarded the Order of Polaris and the Canadian Order of Flight, and twice won the Trans Canada McKee Trophy for outstanding achievement in aviation. He died in 1996 and is buried in his hometown of Ottawa.

Jerry Pitzl, the expedition's navigator who guided them to the Pole with pinpoint accuracy, returned to St. Paul where he taught geography at Macalester College for more than thirty years. He and his wife moved to Santa Fe, New Mexico, in 2000, but Jerry couldn't stay retired for long. He now works at the New Mexico Public Education Department as a program manager in the Rural Education Bureau.

Don Powellek, who sacrificed his own chance at the Pole in order to fix the SARAH beacon, and then to man the fuel cache, returned to his insurance job in Minnesota and remained friends with Ralph. He hid his disappointment at not reaching the Pole from everyone, including his wife. Don died of a heart attack in 1992 while shoveling snow.

Fortieth reunion, 2008: (back row) John Moriarty, Ralph Plaisted, Walt Pederson, Art Aufderheide; (front row) Noelle Bombardier, LaVaughn Powellek

Walt Pederson returned his Honda dealership as the only expedition member who never signed away his book rights. He published his ice diary privately in 1988, and then a very sweet children's book, *Little Lady*, that told the story of his (anthropomorphized) snowmobile going to the North Pole. He still lives in St. Cloud, Minnesota, and is the last survivor of the three who went all the way from Ward Hunt to the Pole.

Jean-Luc Bombardier, whose zest for adventure pushed the expedition to its best speeds over the ice, met a tragic end in 1972. The risk-taking personality that served him so well in the Arctic was his undoing in civilization. Although his obituary listed the cause of death as a heart attack, those closest to him knew it was due to an accidental overdose. His widow, Noelle, has never remarried; Jean-Luc was the one true love of her life.

Art Aufderheide returned from the Arctic to continue his practice as a pathologist. After his retirement he pursued his lifelong interest in anthropology, traveling to remote corners of the world to document ceremonial masks of vanishing native cultures. He still lives with his wife, Mary, in Duluth, Minnesota, not far from the restaurant where his North Pole joke with Ralph started everything.

Ralph Plaisted sold his insurance business in 1973 and bought some wilderness land on Russell Lake northern Saskatchewan. Working alone, he cleared the land and built a cabin that he later used as a summertime fishing resort. He acted as a fishing guide to supplement his retirement income even into his eighth decade. It was there in the summer of 2008 that he broke his femur, miles from medical assistance. A string of air ambulances brought him first to Winnipeg and then Minneapolis for grueling weeks of recovery. Ralph had always been an active outdoorsman, and weeks of forced inactivity were more than he could take. He died on September 8, 2008, at his home in Linwood, Minnesota, at the age of eighty. He had been given the first draft of this book just twelve days previously.